Old Master Drawings
from Chatsworth

Vandyke's Original Drawing, from which the Print by Van. Voerst was taken, in the Book of Vandyke's Heads. Given me by the Duke of Devonshire.

Burlington

167 Anthony Van Dyck: *Portrait of Inigo Jones*

Old Master Drawings
from Chatsworth

Michael Jaffé

Published for the British Museum
by British Museum Press

© 1993 The Trustees of the British Museum

Published by British Museum Press
A division of British Museum Publications Ltd
46 Bloomsbury Street
London WC1B 3QQ

British Library Cataloguing in Publication Data
A catalogue record for this book is available
from the British Library

Designed by James Shurmer

Set in Monotype Lasercomp Garamond
and printed in Great Britain by
BAS Printers Limited, Over Wallop, Hampshire

Contents

Foreword

In 1727 Pierre-Jean Mariette, the great French connoisseur of old master drawings, wrote to Arthur Pond in London: 'You are lucky to be within reach of the fine drawings in the collection of the Duke of Devonshire. I hear that he is acquiring new ones every day, but what is much more surprising, and which is highly satisfactory for those who have the honour of approaching him, is that he is himself such an expert and takes the greatest pleasure in showing them to others. It is especially in this that I consider you lucky; there are plenty of collectors, but almost no connoisseurs whose delight in their possessions is as much for others as for themselves.' The successors to the 2nd Duke have been no less generous in wishing to share their treasures, and the British Museum is very grateful to His Grace the 11th Duke, and the Trustees of the Chatsworth Settlement, for allowing us to mount what is the largest exhibition ever held of the drawings at Chatsworth. It includes no less than 220 works, dating from the fifteenth to the eighteenth centuries, and is the first to be seen in London since 1973–4, when 120 drawings were exhibited following a tour of the United States.

The historical links between the British Museum's Department of Prints and Drawings and the Chatsworth collection are strong, and can be traced to the days when it was still kept at Devonshire House in London. The Trustee and benefactor, Richard Payne Knight (1751–1824), and the Keeper from 1833 to 1836, William Young Ottley (1771–1836), were among the early 'amateurs' to study the Chatsworth drawings. Around 1870, George William Reid (1819–87), Keeper from 1866 to 1883, examined the collection and advised on its conservation, and since that time many of the drawings have been mounted or exhibited at the British Museum.

In more recent times, the scholarly efforts of staff of the British Museum – Campbell Dodgson, Philip Pouncey, J. A. Gere and especially A. E. Popham, who compiled the first exhibition catalogue devoted exclusively to the Chatsworth drawings for the Arts Council of Great Britain in 1949 – have contributed significantly to the study of the collection and to the steady growth in its renown. As a result of Government legislation on death duties, the Museum has possessed since 1956 two famous albums from Chatsworth, Claude Lorrain's *Liber Veritatis*, the book of drawings in which the artist recorded the compositions of his finished paintings (and to which a special exhibition was devoted here in 1977), and Anthony Van Dyck's *Italian Sketchbook*. The so-called 'Cavendish Album' was acquired privately by the Museum in 1952, and is a miscellaneous collection of drawings probably brought together by William, 2nd Duke of Devonshire, to encourage a taste for drawings in his younger son, Lord James Cavendish. The Museum also owns one of three fine studies by Raphael for his final masterpiece, the *Transfiguration*, which the third Duke presented to Sir Thomas Lawrence in June 1823 in return for a *Portrait of George IV* and endless promises of service from that painter. This was subsequently purchased by the Museum at the Woodburn sale in 1860.

The occasion of the exhibition is the publication of part one of the first complete catalogue of the Chatsworth collection under the title *The Devonshire Collection of Italian Drawings: a complete catalogue*. This has been compiled by Professor Michael Jaffé, and is being published by the Phaidon Press simultaneously with this exhibition catalogue. We are particularly grateful to Professor Jaffé for allowing us to use his text as the basis for the present catalogue; the revisions necessary for the purposes of the present exhibition have been made by Antony Griffiths (Italian school) and Martin Royalton-Kisch (Northern schools). We also thank his publishers, Phaidon Press, for their generous co-operation.

The selection of 220 works has been made by Professor Jaffé himself, and takes account of the particular strengths and range of the collection still at Chatsworth. It includes a number of drawings – though far from all – that have been freshly attributed by Professor Jaffé in the course of preparing the main catalogue, and these attributions are here presented for the first time. Otherwise respect has been paid to traditional attributions, except in those cases where they can be shown to be unlikely or impossible.

Professor Jaffé wishes to acknowledge the assistance he has been given by a number of persons. In the first place come two scholars who have died in recent years: James Byam Shaw and Philip Pouncey. Among others are David Ekserdjian, Michael Kitson, John Rowlands, Martin Royalton-Kisch, Stella Rudolph, Nicholas Turner and An Zwollo, as well as many who are individually acknowledged in particular entries. Peter Day, Keeper of the Devonshire Collections at Chatsworth, has given invaluable assistance at every stage. Professor Jaffé's full list of acknowledgements will be found in the Phaidon catalogue. The editor at the British Museum Press, Sarah Derry, has handled a tight production schedule with great efficiency.

Almost all the black and white photographs have been newly taken by Derek Witty; a few came from the Courtauld Institute of Art. The colour transparencies were kindly lent by the Phaidon Press.

Dr R. G. W. Anderson
Director

Introduction: The Devonshire Collection of Drawings

Thirty years ago the 11th Duke of Devonshire and the Trustees of the Chatsworth Settlement, with a liberality characteristic of the Cavendish family, allowed the Smithsonian Institution to exhibit, first at the National Gallery of Art in Washington, then at six other North American institutions, 114 drawings by European masters which had been selected from the Devonshire Collections.

For that tour, in 1962–3, the selection and cataloguing were undertaken by the scholar who had the best overall understanding of the famous hoard of drawings, A. E. Popham (1889–1970), then Keeper of the British Museum's Department of Prints and Drawings. In 1949 Popham had catalogued seventy-two *Old Master Drawings from Chatsworth*, an exhibition shown by the Arts Council of Great Britain at its galleries in London and afterwards in other British cities. In 1961 there was another, local exhibition under the same title, consisting of ninety-nine drawings lent from this mansion in Derbyshire to the Manchester City Art Gallery. The Manchester catalogue was based on the house records with some advice and extra information from Popham and from other scholars, but the catalogues of those exhibitions of 1949 and 1962–3, both under Popham's direct guidance, were effectively the first published probings of the collection.

Since S. Arthur Strong, who had become Librarian of the House of Lords as well as the 8th Duke of Devonshire's Librarian from 1896, the collection had been viewed as an entity, and he put out in facsimile seventy of the finer *Drawings by Old Masters in the Collection of the Duke of Devonshire at Chatsworth* (London, 1902) as a sequel to his choice of sixty *Facsimiles of Drawings by the Old Masters in the Collection of the Earl of Pembroke and Montgomery at Wilton House* (London, 1900–1902).

Strong was the first regular librarian at Chatsworth, although the 7th Duke had had some assistance in cataloguing the Library from Sir James Lacaita. Mrs Strong noted in 1909 that her husband, 'in order to satisfy certain conditions imposed upon him at the time, generally gave the popular and traditional attribution, but corrected this in his commentary', an observation of some historical significance. The Arundel Society publication in 1872, twenty-four years before Strong's appointment to Chatsworth, of those drawings traditionally accepted as by Raphael (four, still accepted, are exhibited here, cat. nos. 117–20), had been the prime attempt to disseminate knowledge of a particular miscellany, some superb treasures among them, but the scope had been limited to that one great master; and confidence was to be shaken by Giovanni Morelli's opinions published through Dr Habich in the *Kunstchronik* of 1891–2. In the words of Mrs Strong's *Report to the Duke* in 1909, 'the once celebrated collection of "Chatsworth Raffaelles" proudly numbered some sixty drawings, reduced however by the criticism of Morelli and his school to barely three or four, and even to them the name of Raphael was only dubiously and as it were grudgingly attached'. In this she, less respectful than her husband of Morelli's opinions, over-reacted. Not less than eighteen drawings kept at Chatsworth in her day could properly have been attributed to Raphael himself, most of them acquired from the collection of Sir Peter Lely, which was in the estimation of a fellow artist, Charles Beale, written on 14 June 1677, simply the 'best in Europe'.

The success in North America of the 1962–3 tour, which displayed no less than six of the drawings traditionally by Raphael (besides two justly attributed to him), led to the same selection being shown in 1969 in London, the city where during the late seventeenth and early eighteenth century the collection was formed, and where it had been housed until the early nineteenth century. It led also to the circulation by the International Exhibitions Foundation, during 1969–70, of an entirely fresh exhibition, selected and catalogued by the Englishman who after Popham had the greatest breadth of connaissance in this field of art, James Byam Shaw (1903–1992). The 120 drawings which Byam Shaw chose were shown first at the National Gallery of Art in Washington, and then at no less than eight other North American institutions. The standards of choice and scholarship, and the pleasure and interest which came with those, were again memorably high. London was glad to see such a Chatsworth exhibition back in England in 1973–4, and on the basis of the two important exhibitions across the Atlantic, loan exhibitions of diplomatic value were sent in September 1973 to Aarhus in Denmark, in January 1975 to Tokyo, and in April 1977 to Jerusalem.

Since then there has been a depletion by auction at Christie's of seventy drawings on 3 July 1984. Forty of those picked for sale had been included in either the 1962–3 or in the 1969–70 selections. Yet despite this much-advertised dispersal and some further sales in 1987, and despite whatever had slipped away in the previous century through the 6th Duke's generosity to his friends, and despite the transfer in 1957 to the national collections in London of the Holbein Cartoon, of Van Dyck's *Italian Sketchbook* and of Claude's *Liber Veritatis* in part settlement of capital taxes on the death of the 10th Duke, the assembly at Chatsworth remains richer than any private collection in Britain outside the royal collection at Windsor, and unrivalled in its quality and extent as a historic family collection.

A third major exhibition of Chatsworth drawings was taken by the International Exhibitions Foundation to five museums in the United States in 1987–8; and that was shown within months of its return to England at the Fitzwilliam Museum in Cambridge. The present British Museum display is, however, of larger scope than any previous exhibition of drawings from Chatsworth. They are selected across the whole collection and include sheets rediscovered or reattributed during the past decade as well as other masterpieces, more or less well known, which had been chosen for the three transatlantic tours.

The early history of the collection is difficult to reconstruct, but since at least the 6th Duke's day, William Cavendish, who became 2nd Duke of Devonshire on 18 August 1707, has been regarded as the hero of the collection. His passion would have been stimulated by his luck in obtaining after 1720 from Tart Hall, the inherited property of the widowed Lady Stafford, Arundel's daughter-in-law, a number of prints, only to discover, in the words of the younger Jonathan Richardson, 'behind them capital Draw(ings) of

Raph(ael), Poli(doro), Parmig(ianino), J.Rom(ano)'. He probably frequented London auctions, and he afforded himself drawings which had belonged to Arundel's agent, Nicholas Lanière, or to Sir Peter Lely, or to Lely's assistant for draperies, Prosper Henry Lankrink, or in some cases to more than one of these leading collectors. He may possibly have bought at the second Lely sale of 1688, aged twenty-two or twenty-three, and he could have been at the Lankrink sales in 1693 and 1694, as we may surmise from Lankrink's mark stamped next to his own on many important drawings.

In 1717, in his middle forties, he was interested by the sale in London of the large collection formed by John, Lord Somers, whose love for paintings and drawings had been fostered first by Simon Dubois and, after Dubois's death in 1708, by another portrait painter and collector, Jonathan Richardson senior. There he bought choice drawings from those collected and mounted in folio albums by the Oratorian Padre Sebastiano Resta (1635–1714).

In 1720, seven years after Carlo Maratti died in Rome, many of the painter's own drawings, which had been left in his studio, as well as those which he had collected from his fellow artists in the metropolis, were intended for sale by his daughter Faustina. The sale itself was aborted, but the 2nd Duke, in advance of the much larger haul of Maratti material acquired from Cardinal Alessandro Albani for the English royal collection, purchased a score of sheets drawn by Maratti himself. (Maratti's caricature of Padre Resta, here cat. no.95, was however amongst the Resta-Somers drawings at the 1717 sale in London.)

In 1724 the 2nd Duke bought for 12,000 florins at Rotterdam at least the 225 drawings at Chatsworth stamped with the mark of Nicolaes Anthonis Flinck (evidently nothing like all from that source were so stamped). Pierre Crozat, in his day the owner of the largest collection of drawings in Europe and who had himself had an eye towards this prize in Holland, wrote fulsomely on 10 February 1724, congratulating the purchaser on his acquisition from the collection of about five hundred available at Flinck's death in 1723: 'la plus belle collection et la mieux choisie que j'aye jamais vue'. Flinck, the son of Rembrandt's pupil, Govert Flinck, owned not only a matchless group of Rembrandt's views on the Amstel together with other distinguished northern drawings, including eight portraits taken from life by Van Dyck for his *Iconographie*, but also, almost certainly, all the Leonardo caricatures of heads which came to the Devonshire Collections. Furthermore, he owned a larger group of Italian drawings, collectively no less significant in the context of the 2nd Duke's purchase: fine examples by Raphael, Giulio Romano, Bandinelli, Rosso, Domenico Campagnola, Parmigianino, Pordenone, Romanino, Francesco Vanni, Testa, Domenichino, Reni and Schedoni. According to Arnold Houbraken (*De Groote Schouburgh der Nederlantsche Konstschilders en Schilderessen*, 1718–21, II, p.27 and III, p.394), Flinck's Italian drawings included 'de beste uit de beruchte [famous] Kabinetten van de Heeren van Bergesteyn, en Zuylichem'. The 2nd Duke had been forestalled by Somers for the Resta Albums, but he compensated himself magnificently at Flinck's death by prompt action, stealing a march upon the avid and immensely rich Crozat.

The 2nd Duke may be supposed to have continued to acquire drawings almost until his death on 4 June 1729. He bought Claude's *Liber Veritatis* in 1728; he bought individual sheets, privately as well as at auction, from his contemporary Nicolo Francesco Haym (*c*.1679–1729) and from Solomon Gautier and certainly also from other collectors and *marchands amateurs* such as A. C. Boulle and P.-J. Mariette. On 4 July 1727 Mariette wrote from Paris to Arthur Pond in London, the painter who is better known to us as a collector and dealer. The third paragraph of his letter (BL Add.Ms.45459), called to my attention by Antony Griffiths, is a particularly handsome tribute to the 2nd Duke's style of collecting, both to his connoisseurship and to his pleasure in communicating his interest to others:

Que vous etes heureux d'estre à porté de jouir des belles choses que possede Milord Duc de Devonshire, j'entends dire tous les jours qu'il en acquiert de nouvelles, mais ce qui est de bien plus surprenant, & ce qui est en même temps bien satisfaisant pour ceux qui ont l'honneur de l'approcher, c'est qu'il s'y connoiste si parfaitement, & qu'il se fasse son plus grand plaisir de les communiquer. C'est surtout en cela que je vous estime heureux, on trouve aisement des curieux, mais presque point de connoisseurs, & qui aime à posseder autant pour les autres que pour eux même. Je vous avoue que rien ne me flatteroit davantage que d'aller à Londres, & qu'au milieu de mille satisfactions que j'y aurois, celle de rendre mes devoirs à cet illustre seigneur, seroit peutetre celle qui me toucheroit davantage, par malheur pour moy, une suitte indispensable d'affaires, m'empeche même d'y penser.

The 2nd Duke indeed discriminated, not buying every good thing offered. In the British Museum is a pen and wash composition of *St Catherine Disputing*, and in supervising the mounting of this, Jonathan Richardson, senior, penned below it, on the face of the mount, not only the convincing attribution 'Mola' but also above it the word 'Devonre'. Nicholas Turner, in calling this sheet and its inscribed mount to my attention, suggested that Richardson may have kept it aside for the 2nd Duke and ended by keeping it for himself. It is possible that the Duke also had agents in Rome to acquire for him drawings from the vast collection of Benedetto Luti, as is suggested by the presence of his stamp on two drawings by Giuseppe Chiari (e.g. cat. no.49).

However, the 2nd Duke's father in his early forties had started the family collection by acquiring sometime between 1681 and 1689 from Benedetto Gennari, the Bolognese painter who served the Stuart Court in England from 1674 until the 'Glorious Revolution' of 1688, a set of fourteen landscapes drawn by Gennari's uncle Guercino (see cat. nos.77–8). These had been brought to Paris to be engraved by Jean Pesne. The 1st Duke may well also have acquired Polidoro da Caravaggio's drawing of *St. Albert of Trapani* at the Lely sale of 1688, since it does not bear the 2nd Duke's mark; but he seems later to have missed a greater prize, able like his heir to turn down a tempting offer. John Gere has passed to me a note from a MS account-book which he examined in around 1950, then in the possession of the Earl of Cardigan, a descendant of Robert Bruce, the second son of the 2nd Earl of Elgin. According to Richardson, Bruce owned a sheet of Raphael studies for a group in the *Disputà*. Among these accounts, kept by Bruce in Italy 1699–1701 and which record the formation of a large collection of drawings in Rome, is a draft copy of a letter to G. Gibbons (likely, as Gere suggests, to be Grinling Gibbons): 'If you have not parted with your School of Athens and continue still in the mind to do so at the price you offered it to the Duke of Devenshire [*sic*], I will give you that for it.' At this date the reference can only have been to the 1st Duke. Whether or not Bruce's offer was accepted, this drawing for the *School of Athens* has disappeared.

Of the eighty drawings in the Devonshire Collections which had belonged to Padre Resta, twenty-six of Resta-Somers provenance which do not bear the 2nd Duke's mark might have been acquired by the 3rd Duke at the Paris sale in 1741 of the Crozat collection, to which 112 Resta/Somers lots had gone at the 1717 sale in London. They may alternatively have come to the 4th Duke from Lord Burlington. However, since no drawing still in the Devonshire Collections this century bears a Crozat number penned boldly in the lower right-hand corner, Nicholas Turner reckons the former possibility most unlikely.

Moreover, in a margin of the London Library's proof copy of the elder Richardson's *Works*, annotated by the younger Richardson, there appears this reference to the drawings from Nicolas Lanière's collection, which William Gibson had left at his death to his widow:

This of ye Price was only to those which fell into the hands of Mr Gibson ye Painter & by him put there for the use of his widow, as she told us, and of which my F(ather) bought a large quantity of them but not until the D(uke) of Devon(shire) had taken what he chose. It was this Nobleman who had told my F(ather) of them when he sate to him for his Picture which of course faild not to go, & I with him that very night; & we bought home a large number wh(ich) ye D(uke) had left and wh(ich) were for ye most P(art) so Exc(ellent) & Capital as to have composed ye finest part of my F(ather's) collection.

Since it was the 3rd Duke soon after 1733, and not so far as is known the 2nd at any time, who sat to the elder Richardson, this anecdote points again to the 3rd Duke's enriching the 2nd Duke's collection. About a tenth of the Chatsworth drawings, not counting the Inigo Jones and other Burlington material acquired through the 4th Duke's marriage, might have been acquired before or after the 2nd Duke's day.

There is otherwise little known of the collection's history beyond what is to be found written or stamped either on the drawings themselves or on their mounts. Searches at Chatsworth and in London have not discovered other papers to chronicle acquisitions or attributions. We can only assume that aesthetic at least as much as historical considerations played their part in amassing and arranging the albums and portfolios.

We reckon that Arthur Strong, before his 1902 publication, brought in Bernard Berenson to advise at least on the drawings of the Florentine painters. Yet he only acknowledged 'for various assistance, Dr J. P. Richter; Dr Franz Wickhoff; Dr Ludwig; Dr Paul Kristeller; Signor Frizzoni and Mr Charles Loeser'. The notes left by Eugénie Strong, the classical archaeologist who succeeded her husband as Librarian at Chatsworth in 1904, remaining until she left to be Deputy Director of the British School at Rome in 1909, are confined to two volumes of typescript and manuscript prepared by her before leaving Derbyshire, a *Rough Catalogue of the/ Chatsworth Drawings/ vol.1/ compiled by E. Strong.* This was prefaced by her *Report on the collection of Drawings by the Old Masters at Chatsworth,* dated 7 September 1909, and completed by the *First Rough Draft/ for a / Catalogue of the Chatsworth Drawings/ by Old Masters/ vol. 11. The Sketch Gallery/ Aug.1909/ E.S.* (Eugénie

Strong). The latter deals with 703 drawings covering the sixteenth century 'Schools of Florence & Rome', from 'Raphael, Michelangelo and their contemporaries down to the Mannerists', as well as with the Holbein cartoon fragment of *Henry VII and Henry VIII*, now in the National Portrait Gallery – that is, with approximately one third of the collection. In 1925 Campbell Dodgson, Archibald Russell and, for the first time, A. E. Popham examined the collection at the request of the then Librarian, Mr F. W. Thompson. In 1928–29, Thompson, in addition to this triad of critical opinions, had use of Mrs Strong's notes in compiling what was intended as the first typescript *Catalogue of Drawings/in the collections of/The Duke of Devonshire*. Yet even Thompson's careful listing was incomplete.

It was, however, the basis of the Courtauld Institute 'List' of 1963, and was to be a limiting factor in the scope of photography then undertaken by the Institute. 'Mr. Strong and his successors were greatly hampered in their study of the more obscure Chatsworth drawings by the absence of any old catalogue', complained Mrs Strong in her *Report* in 1909 to the 8th Duke. Her complaint has had many echoes.

All the more precious, therefore, is the celebrated anecdote by Roger North, Sir Peter Lely's executor, of the sale in April 1688 of a 'Raphael' of *Constantine's allocutio to his Troops, startled by a Vision of the True Cross* (here cat. no.106), now generally accepted as a drawing by Raphael's pupil, Gian Francesco Penni:

I remember a lord, now a duke, said 'Damn me what care I whether the owner bids or not as long as I can tell whether I wish to buy and for what.' ... There was half a sheet that Raphael had drawn upon with amber and white, that we called washed and heightened; a tumult of Roman soldiery, and Caesar upon a suggestum with officers appeasing them. This was rallied at first, and some said 6d, knowing that it would come to; but then £10, £30, £50, and my quarrelsome lord bids £70, and Sonnius £100, and had it. The lord held up his eyes and hands to heaven, and prayed to God he might never eat bread cheaper. [Frederick Sonnius, an elderly member of Lely's studio, was the auctioneer's agent.]

The 'quarrelsome lord' was evidently that prime Whig, the 4th Earl of Devonshire (1640/1–1707), who had been fined £30,000 the previous year for striking Colonel Colepepper, a Tory, in Whitehall. He became the 1st Duke of Devonshire on 12 May 1694. His son William, 2nd Duke, was eventually to acquire the drawing in 1724 with so many others from Nicolaes Flinck. In 1722 the younger Richardson saw in Modena, as the work of Lodovico Carracci, Annibale's altarpiece of the *Assumption* (now in Dresden – see cat. no.34), and he noted that 'the D. of Devonshire has the Drawing', referring to the 2nd Duke; but there are few such pointers to the date by which any particular drawing came to Chatsworth. Passarotti's *Self-Portrait in Old Age* (cat. no.104) bears a tiny Boncompagni dragon in the ornamentation of its fine Italian mount, thereby signalling an appropriate provenance, but nothing indicates when, how, or where the 2nd Duke, whose mark is stamped on this impressive drawing, extra-mounted for him, actually acquired it. Another large drawing, here cat. no.105, signed and dated 1698 by Giuseppe Passeri in Rome, which until 1987 was described and exhibited as *Prelates under a Loggia*, is a finished version of a preliminary drawing for a *Tailpiece for Vol.XVI of Sebastiano Resta's Collection of Drawings*, drawn by the friend who had been Resta's travelling companion in 1690 on a tour of curiosity in Lombardy; and the Chatsworth drawing dated

25 April 1698 dates precisely for the first time this famous sale to the Bishop of Arezzo.

What the 2nd Duke achieved, supplemented by efforts made and chances taken by the 1st, 3rd and 4th Dukes, was imperilled by the bachelor 6th Duke's zest for rearrangements at Chatsworth. In Stephen Glover's *The Peak Guide*, published at Derby in 1839, which Peter Day, the present Keeper of the Devonshire Collections, kindly brought to my notice, we read (p.27) how, at Chatsworth, 'The Gallery leading to the Chapel contains nearly one thousand original sketches, by the most eminent Flemish, Venetian, Spanish and Italian masters: forming altogether an assemblage of drawings, which, for numbers and excellence, can hardly be surpassed in any part of the Kingdom'. The inclusion of Spanish was fanciful, as the one Spanish drawing in the collections, an unusual drawing by Ribera, was then by tradition attributed to Federico Zuccaro. The total number thus exposed was perhaps exaggerated. Then in the privately printed *Handbook*, in which the 6th Duke described for his sister, Lady Granville, his changes and additions to the house which the 1st Duke had built, he wrote (pp.134–6) of the galleries which in 1835 he had had reconstructed by Sir Jeffry Wyattville for an improved display of the drawings to the visiting public:

The Sketch Galleries

You now retrace your steps, and, beginning from the great staircase, you find arranged here the collection of drawings made entirely by the second Duke of Devonshire. I have classed them according to the several schools of painting; but I am sure that the arrangement must be very imperfect, and it is beyond me to make any description of the merits of this rich and valuable possession. Few things at Chatsworth are more admired. If I can obtain a good account of them, written to my mind, you shall have it – but I know not to whom to apply; amateurs would run into fanciful theory, artists would be prolix. Madame de Meyendorff should really come again to do it: she used to copy here at daybreak in the summer mornings, and her admiration of the sketches was without bounds.

They hardly ever saw the light in my Father's time, nor in mine often, till I rescued them from portfolios, and placed them framed in the South Gallery below.

Before that, a very few amateurs now and then got a peep at them in London – Lawrence, Mr Ottley, Mr Payne Knight, and so on. Sir Thomas, mad about his own collection of drawings, got from me three studies by Raffaelle for the Transfiguration: there were five of them, and I retained the two best. I resisted long; but he was so very anxious, and so full of promises of devoted service, of painting any thing for me, that I gave them at last. The way would have been to have given them for his life: he soon after died, and the sketches were sold with his collection.

M. Flinck's drawings were bought at Rotterdam in 1723 [old style]. Monsieur Crozat called them in his letters the finest and best collection he ever saw. They are all included here.

Prolonged exposure faded and stained many of the drawings which the 6th Duke 'rescued from portfolios' in Devonshire House and brought to Chatsworth, giving entire credit for the collection to the 2nd Duke. Some of the Claude drawings, as Marcel Röthlisberger has remarked, were conspicuous sufferers, only being removed for remounting at the British Museum in 1905. From about 1870 some deterioration was noted. George William Reid (1819–1887), Keeper of the British Museum Print Room (1866–1883), examined the collection and reported unfavourable conditions of light and atmosphere; moreover, according to Mrs Strong's *Report* of 1909, 'it was later discovered that the paste used in mounting had caused discolouration and other serious damage to many of the delicate drawings'. Pasting down was usual in early eighteenth-century collections. Thomas Pelletier, one of the Huguenot framemakers established in London, was paid in 1720 for 'pasting' sixty-eight drawings belonging to Lord Leicester.

Fortunately, a majority of the finest at Chatsworth escaped such well-meaning attention and they remain in pleasing condition on those early eighteenth-century mounts designed by the Richardsons. In 1906 the principal masterpieces were removed from display. Furthermore, the drawings from the 'Rembrandt-Rubens-Van Dyck Sketchbook', now on 1928 or later mounts, had been left unexposed and undisturbed.

Madame de Meyendorff's competence as a copyist or connoisseur is beyond assessment. Fortunately we can consult a publication made by the son of a fourth visitor whose connections and interest had given him first-hand knowledge of the Royal Collection and of other principal private collections in eighteenth-century England: Henry Reveley (d.1798). Under his name appeared the *Notices illustrative of the Drawings and Sketches of some of the most distinguished Masters* (London 1820). Not only is this book to be valued as a lively selection by an enthusiastic collector, but also it provides a valuable guide to the attributions accepted for the Devonshire drawings over the previous 75 years.

The attitude and ways of the 6th Duke at Chatsworth recall what little is known of those of the 2nd Duke at Devonshire House. A Monsieur Foucheroux, an amateur writing in 1728 from London his *Troisième Lettre*, one of a series apparently intended for publication (MS.L.1255–1912, V&A), described the collector as 'un des très gratieux Seigneurs qu'il y ait en Angleterre; il a beaucoup voyagé et reçoit fort bien les étrangers. C'est le Mécène: et le protecteur des arts qu'il aime infiniment et dans les quels il a beaucoup de Connaissance.' A French visitor previously unknown to London, M. Foucheroux was able to spend five or six mornings in the Duke's Library:

Les livres et les desseins de grand Maitres sont dans des armoires au bas des tablettes [then presumably mounted in albums]. Il y en a de toutes les mains, et la pluspart originaux, plusieurs de Raphael, entr'autres les douzes apostres [now generally agreed to be by Giulio Romano] des desseins du giorgion, du Parmesan, de Perrin del Vagua, du Correge, du Carrache, du guide, beaucoup du Guerchin et un livre entier de deux cent paysages de Claude Lorain [the first mention as Devonshire property of Claude's *Liber Veritatis*, now in the British Museum] que je regarde Comme un trésor. J'avois déja veu ce livre a Rome chez la Nièce de Claude Lorrain. Environ quarante desseins separez du meme.

According to *The Lives of the Earls and Dukes of Devonshire* (London, 1764), the 2nd Duke granted 'the easiest and readiest access to his collection' which, as J. Grove, the author, claims, 'facilitated studies of a kind previously possible only in Italy'. Writing in 1836 of his visit to Chatsworth, Passavant stated: 'The most valuable treasure this mansion can boast is the collection of drawings, by old masters, which adorn the south gallery. A written permission, kindly furnished me by the Duke, insured me ample time and convenience in their investigation, and enabled me leisurely to select those which were of most importance' (vol.11, p.23); and (pp.140–146) he offers a 'catalogue of some of the finest original drawings'. Waagen in his 'Letter XXX' records his frustration on his first visit to Chatsworth that 'alterations in the house' (evidently those by Wyattville) prevented his seeing the drawings. To examine these treasures was 'the chief motive for my visit to Chatsworth in 1850'.

In 1868, 271 'Drawings by the Old Masters' were selected by J. B. Waring for *The National Exhibition of Works of Art at Leeds*, 128 of them lent by the 7th Duke of Devonshire. Seventeen in the 1987–8 touring exhibition can be identified with loans listed by Waring, although he vouchsafed only the briefest descriptions and no dimensions. Yet he occasionally noted seventeenth-century ownerships and he kept to the attributions immemorially accepted. In 1894, two years before Arthur Strong became Librarian at Chatsworth, a loan was made to the New Gallery in Regent Street, London for the *Exhibition of Venetian Art*; initially of five Venetian drawings and, in the following year, of forty-five including sixteen by Domenico Campagnola, about half of the conspicuously rich holding of that draughtsman's work. Again, Waring's principle appears to have been followed, noticing provenance from Lely or from Flinck, but not hazarding fresh attributions. Berenson had left London before the second, major consignment had arrived.

In the nineteenth century the only opinions, other than traditional attributions held to in the list of the 1868 and 1894–5 exhibitions, or those implied by the Arundel Society's choice in 1872 of the *Chatsworth Raffaelles*, that were published since the observations of Passavant and Waagen (both of whom, like Waring and like writers in *The Athenaeum* for 1874 and 1883, were to be curiously neglected by twentieth-century writers on the Devonshire Collections) were extremely terse, and confined to a few score of the fifteenth- and sixteenth-century Italian drawings. Some had been made orally in 1886, on the evidence of the photographs taken by Braun & Co. of Dornach, by Giovanni Morelli, and taken down by Eduard Habich, and they appeared in the *Kunstchronik* for 21 July 1892. A few others had been published by Morelli himself in the second volume of his *Italian Painters. The Galleries of Munich and Dresden*.

'A good account' of the Chatsworth drawings, conformable to the 6th Duke's hope, was not to be realised either by Mrs Strong or by Mr Thompson. Hopes at Chatsworth during the subsequent Keepership of Mr T. S. Wragg to produce an illustrated *catalogue raisonné*, discussed in 1962 and for a few years after that with A. E. Popham, who had been approved as putative editor, failed, alas, for lack of a publisher to take the risks of so large an enterprise. It is only now that a full catalogue, involving over two thousand drawings, has been undertaken by the Phaidon Press with the agreement of the Trustees of the Chatsworth Settlement. The present exhibition catalogue and Introduction are based on the typescript that I have prepared for this. The catalogue entries for the drawings included here in general remain little changed, but the Introduction is considerably reduced.

MICHAEL JAFFÉ
King's College, Cambridge

April 1993

ITALIAN SCHOOL

(Nos 1–153)

1 Anonymous Sienese

early 15th century

Recto: The Betrayal of Christ

Verso: Christ before the High Priest

Pen and brown ink with brown wash over preliminaries in charcoal or black chalk, heightened with white bodycolour, 221 × 182mm. The lower right corner repaired.

Inscribed *verso*, lower left, in a 16th-century italic script, with pen and brown ink *di mo Simone Memmi da Siena.*

Chatsworth 716A

Literature: P. Pouncey, 'Two Simonesque Drawings', *Burl.Mag.*, LXXXVIII, 1946, p.168; Popham and Pouncey, 1950, no.269; L. Collobi Ragghianti, *Il Libro de' Disegni del Vasari*, Florence, 1974, p.32, figs.21, 22; Degenhart and Schmitt, I, 1969 no.108, pp.200–2, pls.158–9 (as 'Siena um 1390'); F. Ames-Lewis and J. Wright, *Drawing in the Italian Renaissance Workshop*, London 1983, no.48, pp.230–3 (as 'Sienese *c.*1410'); F. Ames-Lewis, 'Drawing for panel painting in trecento Italy: reflections on workshop practice', *Apollo*, June 1992, p.358

Exhibitions: Washington etc., 1962–3 and London, RA, 1969

(1)

1

A companion sheet of composition trials in the British Museum (1895–9–15–680) is similarly drawn on both sides with *Christ and the Woman of Samaria* and *Christ healing the Man born blind*. Quite possibly all four drawings are for a Sienese cycle of the Life of Christ, late in the fourteenth or early in the fifteenth century. The British Museum sheet was mounted by Vasari and bears his attribution to a certain Galante da Bologna of whom little but the name is known. The inscription on Chatsworth 716A is nearer the mark. The drawings must be by some follower of Simone Martini. Ames-Lewis and Wright suggested that these drawings may have been made to line up a series of designs for a predella of an altarpiece, or for a fresco cycle to be shown together to the artist's patron. In 1992 Ames-Lewis suggested that Lippo Vanni might be the author.

2 Niccolò dell'Abate

(Modena *c.*1509/12–1571 Fontainebleau)

Christ, surrounded by Apostles, healing the Lepers, after Parmigianino

Pen and brown ink with brown wash, heightened with white bodycolour, 300 × 445mm. Mounted in full for the 2nd Duke.

Chatsworth 334

Provenance: William, 2nd Duke of Devonshire (L.718)

Literature: Braun, 163; Copertini, 1949, pl.cxxxii (as by Parmigianino); Popham, 1971, under 690 (as after Parmigianino)

Exhibitions: London, RA, 1960 (586, as a copy of Parmigianino 'perhaps by Niccolò dell'Abate')

This is an old copy of a Parmigianino drawing (cat.3) by a skilful hand. It could well have been drawn by Niccolò dell'Abate (cf. Chatsworth 190, here cat. no.4). There are variations from the original, as D. Ekserdjian has pointed out: for example the 'colosseum' at the left is given two stories rather than one.

3 Girolamo Francesco Mazzuola, called il Parmigianino

(Parma 1503–1540 Casal Maggiore)

Christ healing the Lepers

Pen and brown ink with brown wash, heightened with white bodycolour on cream paper, 271 × 420mm. Fully mounted for the 2nd Duke.

Chatsworth 335

Provenance: Sir Peter Lely (L.2092); P.H. Lankrink (L.2090); William, 2nd Duke of Devonshire (L.718)

Literature: Popham, 1952, pp.20 and 57, pl.XX; Popham, 1971, p.690, pl.133; Quintavalle, 1971, pl.XXVIII; Anna Coliva,

2

3

'Disegni romani del Parmigianino' in *Aspetti dell'arte a Roma prima e dopo Raffaello*, Rome, Palazzo Venezia, 1984, pp.80–81, fig.30

Exhibitions: London, RA, 1960, p.224; Pittsburgh, 1987–8 (50)

This drawing was used by Nicoletto da Vicenza as the basis for a chiaroscuro woodcut (B.XII.39.15). It is a masterpiece demonstrating the youthful Parmigianino's powers of design in his years in Rome. It was evidently inspired by two of Raphael's tapestry cartoons: *The Consigning of the Keys* and *The Sacrifice at Lystra*. As Coliva points out, the palace in the background is appropriately Bramantesque. A not quite literal copy of this drawing, Chatsworth 334, was photographed by Braun (no.163) and illustrated by Copertini (pl.CXXXII) as the original (see no.2 above). It is proposed here that this could have been drawn by Niccolò dell'Abate. Another noteworthy copy is in the Schlossmuseum at Weimar (Inv.Nr. KK 7397).

4 Niccolò dell'Abate

(Modena *c*.1512–1571 Fontainebleau)

The Holy Family with St Elizabeth and the infant St John: the Angel appearing to the Shepherds in the Background

Pen and brown ink with brown wash over black chalk, heightened with white bodycolour on paper washed brown, 415 × 334mm.

Chatsworth 190

Provenance: Sir Peter Lely (L.2092); William, 2nd Duke of Devonshire (L.718)

Exhibitions: Manchester, 1965 (248); Washington etc., 1969–70 and London, V&A, 1973–4 (11); Tokyo, 1975 (37)

This beautiful drawing was formerly attributed at Chatsworth to Primaticcio; but, as A.E.Popham first suggested, it is by Niccolò. It shows him highly Parmigianinesque, but also close to Primaticcio at Fontainebleau.

5 Niccolò dell'Abate

(Modena *c*.1512–1571 Fontainebleau)

Two Putti, back to back, holding a Festoon hung with Fruits

Red chalk, heightened with white, on cream paper, 210 × 135mm. Mounted in full for the 2nd Duke.

Chatsworth 183

Provenance: N.A.Flinck (L.959); William, 2nd Duke of Devonshire (L.718) from 1723–4

Literature: S. Béguin, 'Dessins inédits de la période italienne de Niccolò dell'Abate', *Raccolta di saggi dedicati a Roberto Longhi in*

5

occasione del suo sessantesimo compleanno in *Arte antica e moderna*, XIII–XVI, 1961, p.229, fig.100b; M. di Giampaolo and S. Béguin, *Maestri Emiliani del Secondo Cinquecento*, Florence, 1979, p.25; W. Bergamini, 'Nicolo dell'Abate' in Fortunati, 1986, p.292, repr. p.338

Exhibitions: Bologna, 1969 (47); London, Courtauld Institute of Art, 1992 (2)

Formerly attributed in the Devonshire Collections to Primaticcio, this drawing was regarded by A.E.Popham (1962) as by one of the Campi, possibly Antonio. Clearly Emilian, with reflections of Correggio and of early Parmigianino at Fontenellata, it was identified by S.Béguin as a study for one of the groups of putti painted by Niccolò in the Sala con Storie di Camilla of the Palazzo Poggi, Bologna. Camilla served as the model of female virtue (see A.O.Cavina, *Palazzo Poggi*, Bologna, 1988, pp.101–7). It may be compared to a drawing previously attributed to Giulio Cesare Procaccini in the Albertina (Stix-Spitzmuller, VI, 1941, no.449), but attributed by Ober-

7

6

huber (1963, no.184) to Niccolò, likewise *c*.1550, in his Bolognese period.

There is a copy of this drawing in the Musée de Lille (P.L.629; pen and brown ink with white heightening), which was signalled to the 1969 exhibition in Bologna by Françoise Viatte.

6 Francesco Albani

(Bologna 1578–1660 Bologna)

Venus, reclining under a rustic Canopy, with Adonis fastening her Sandal

Pen and brown ink with brown wash, foxed, 192 × 165mm. Mounted in full for the 2nd Duke.

Chatsworth 507

Provenance: N. A. Flinck (L.959); William, 2nd Duke of Devonshire (L.718), from 1723–4

Literature: Reveley, 1820, p.75 (as Domenichino, 'Diana and her Nymphs, done slightly with pen and wash, of great beauty and grace.')

Attributed traditionally but implausibly in the Devonshire collection to Domenichino, this drawing shows

Venus having her sandal fitted. The treatment of the Venus theme, the morphology, and the landscape are all typical of Albani (cf. the Borghese roundels of *The Tribute of Venus* and *Mars jealous of Adonis*). The style and use of pen and wash is similar to *Venus discovers the dead Adonis gored by the Boar* in the British Museum (*ex* Spencer).

7 Francesco Albani

(Bologna 1578–1660 Bologna)

The Triumph of Galatea

Pen and brown ink, heightened with white bodycolour on a pink ground, 281 × 426mm. Mounted in full for the 2nd Duke.

Chatsworth 553

Provenance: William, 2nd Duke of Devonshire (L.718)

Exhibitions: Leeds, 1868 (2736, as 'Albano. Aphrodite')

Apparently always attributed to Albani in the Devonshire Collection. His elegant but frozen sense in decorative grouping has here the flavour of a centrepiece for a table. In style and character the design has many features in common with his *Sea Nymphs* for the carriage of the Cardinal de'Medici in the Medici Gallery (see the watercolour copy in the four volumes at Corsham Court lettered 'Albano dipse.... D. Gaglier del'). Nicolas Poussin, in his *Triumph of Neptune* painted in 1635–6 for Cardinal Richelieu (Philadelphia Museum of Art), may well have had in mind this drawing or some similar design by Albani. The ultimate inspiration, available to both Albani and Poussin in Rome, was Raphael's fresco in the Villa Farnesina.

8 Alessandro Algardi

(Bologna 1602–1654 Bologna)

Design for a Finial of a Coach

Pen and brown ink with brown wash, over preliminaries in graphite, 275 × 172mm (cut irregularly).

Inscribed on the verso in pen and brown ink, in a contemporary hand *algardi Delin*.

Chatsworth 1172

Literature: Hugh Macandrew, 'A drawing by Algardi' in *Festschrift to Erik Fischer*, Copenhagen, 1990, pp.157–66

The display of the eagle and the lily proclaim that this design for a baroque ornament is connected with the Este family. It is in fact for one of the four larger *vasi* at the corners of the roof of the town coach which Francesco I d'Este, duke of Modena, commissioned his brother in Rome, Cardinal Rinaldo d'Este (1610–1658), to procure for this carriage.

According to a letter from 14 March 1654 in the Archivo di Stato, Modena, these large *vasi* were to be

8

gilded. Algardi's name is mentioned once in the correspondence, and only in connection with the chioderia for the town coach (see Rinaldo's letter of 10 June 1654, in which he reports to his brother the sculptor's death). But there can be no doubt that all the ornaments for this luxurious and very expensive conveyance were designed by him. Algardi's so-called 'minor' works 'were the most entirely personal, the most inventive, and the most expressive of (his) true vision' (J. Montagu, *Alessandro Algardi*, New Haven/London, 1989, p.179).

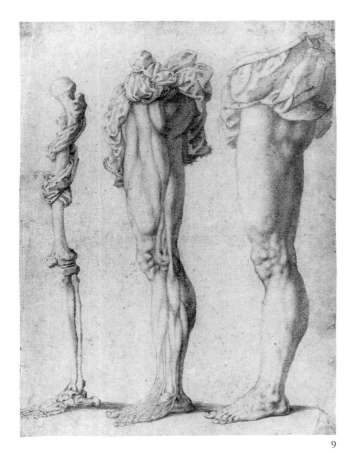

9

9 Alessandro di Cristofano di Lorenzo Allori

(Florence 1535–1609 Florence)

A Man's left Leg, progressively anatomised

Black chalk on discoloured white paper, 422 × 308mm.

Chatsworth 890

Exhibitions: London, NG, 1975 (103, as 'school of Michelangelo')

The traditional attribution in the Devonshire collection was to a 'follower of Michelangelo': but it is clearly by the same hand as the *Scheletro Animato* (Uffizi 6700F), traditionally attributed to Pontormo, but correctly reattributed by Forlani in 1963 (see R. Paolo Ciardi and L. Tongiorgi Tomasi, *Immagini anatomiche e naturalistiche nei disegni degli Uffizi, Secc. XVI e XVII*, Florence, 1984, no.22, fig.29). Allori was directed in his anatomical studies by a doctor, Alessandro Menchi, and he remained close to *Il primo (secondo) libro de' ragionamenti della regole di disegno*. His own manuscript on anatomy for artists is in the Biblioteca Nazionale of Florence, although the printed text is no longer to be found. Chatsworth 890 is likely to be of the mid-1560s. Four comparable drawings are in the Uffizi. Compare also the book represented in a painting by Allori, Christ between SS. Cosmas and Damian of 1589–90 in the Musées Royaux, Brussels (Ragghianti, 1972, fig.64 and pp.81–2, n.29).

10

10 Giovanni Baglione

(Rome *c.* 1573–1644 Sordo del Barezzo)

A young Ecclesiastic kneeling in adoration

Red chalk, heightened with white bodycolour on blue paper, 235 × 200mm. Mounted in full for Lord Somers.

Inscribed in pen and brown ink with the Resta-Somers mark, *n. 20*; and on the mount, in the hand of J. Richardson senior, *Cav: Gio. Baglione*, following Resta.

Chatsworth 390

Provenance: P. Sebastiano Resta; sold to Giovanni Matteo Marchetti (died 1704), Bishop of Arezzo, between 1698 and 1702; sold by his heir, the cavaliere Orazio Marchetti of Pistoia, to Lord Somers; Lord Somers from 1710 until 1716; his sale, London 1717; presumably William, 2nd Duke of Devonshire

Attributed correctly by Resta. This is the drapery study for the pose needed by Baglione for his painting of *Cardinal Sfondrato kneeling before S. Cecilia* in the Chiesa del Gesù, Rome (see Stephen Pepper, *Paragone* 211, Sept. 1967, p.70), and is more animated and more gracefully inclined than the definitive solution. Cardinal Paolo Emilio Sfondrato, nephew of Gregory XIV, was titular cardinal of S. Cecilia in Trastevere. On 20 October 1599 he recovered the saint's body. This event induced him to expand greatly the basilica in her honour. Baglione's painting, at present in the sacristy of the Gesù, was painted in 1603–5 during his intensive activity for the Cardinal, who is shown kneeling before St Cecilia in the company of other saints disinterred by him in the excavations of 1599. Behind him, represented from left to right, are Cecilia's husband Valerian, the centurion Maximus who was converted by Valerian, and Valerian's brother Tiburtius. Popes Lucian and Urban stand behind. Pepper, in publishing the Gesù painting, overlooked the relevance of Chatsworth 390.

11 Lazzaro Baldi, or Baldo

(Pistoia *c*.1623/4–1703 Rome)

St John in the Cauldron of boiling Oil

Pen and brown ink with brown wash, heightened with white bodycolour (oxydised), 401 × 257mm; squared in red and black chalks for enlargement. Mounted in full for Lord Somers.

11

Inscribed *h 156*; and on the mount in pen and brown ink, in the hand of J. Richardson senior, following Resta, *Lazaro Baldi*

Chatsworth 599

Provenance: P. Sebastiano Resta (as Lazzaro Baldi); Giovanni Matteo Marchetti (died 1704), Bishop of Arezzo, from 1698; sold by his heir, the cavaliere Orazio Marchetti of Pistoia; Lord Somers from 1710 until at least 1716; his sale, London 1717; presumably 2nd or 3rd Duke of Devonshire

Literature: Forcella, XI, no.303; Antonella Pampalone, *Disegni di Lazzaro Baldi nelle collezioni del Gabinetto Nazionale delle Stampe*, Rome 1979–80, p.16

Traditionally ascribed in the Devonshire collection to Lazzaro Baldi, this drawing, by one of the first generation of Pietro da Cortona's pupils, is a study for a fresco in the Tempietto of S. Giovanni in Oleo which was reconstructed in 1658 by Cardinal Francesco Paolucci to the design of Borromini. The five frescoes painted in 1658–61 show St. John being arrested; boiled in oil; drinking from a poisoned cup; dragged to martyrdom; and having his vision on Patmos. Martyrdom was for Baldi a favourite theme.

For his manner of hatching with greyish white, compare his *Annunciation to Joachim and Anna* (grey and white bodycolours and brown wash over black ink) and the *Birth of the Virgin* (see *Italian and other Drawings 1500–1800*, Courtauld Institute Galleries, 1979), and the *Annunciation* in the Marshall Collection. According to F. Titi (1674 edn., p.78) this cycle of frescoes by Baldi 'è delle meglio opere, che habbi fatto', but they are now in a sad state. The *Boiling in Oil* is illustrated by Pampalone as her fig.2. She refers to a drawing in Düsseldorf (inv.no.F.P.1022) on the verso of which are sketched the putti who hold up the crown of martyrdom.

12 Baccio Bandinelli

(Florence 1493–1560 Florence)

Two 'Mourners' seated on low Stools with open Books strewn on the Floor and on their Knees

Pen and brown ink with brown wash over preliminaries in red chalk and black chalk on white paper, 285 × 232mm. The edge, especially in the upper left corner has been repaired. Mounted in full for the 2nd Duke.

Chatsworth 32

A. E. Popham suggested that 'the wash, unusual in Bandinelli, might be an addition'. The addition, however, is likely to be by Bandinelli himself, for there would otherwise have been no drawing. It is perhaps a study for Bandinelli's *Allegory of Death* (engraved by Marco da Ravenna).

12

13 Baccio Bandinelli

(Florence 1493–1560 Florence)

The Massacre of the Innocents

Pen and brown ink with brown wash, over preliminaries in red chalk on cream paper, 388 × 566mm. Cut at the base, with a large repair, more or less central, along the lower edge. Fully mounted for the 2nd Duke.

Chatsworth 24

Provenance: N. A. Flinck (L.959); William, 2nd Duke of Devonshire, from 1723–4

Literature: Vasari, 1568, II p.418 ('intagliatori di stampe intagliere una storia disegnata da lui in una carta grandissima nella quale era l'uccisione de' fanciulli innocenti … la quale … gli reco per tutta Europa grande fama') and p.428 ('a Roma fece Marco da Ravenna et Agostino Veneziano'); Waagen, 1854, III, p.354; Strong, 1902, no.57; Bernice Davidson, *M. A. Raimondi: the Engravings of the Roman Period*, Harvard University Ph.D. dissertation, 1954, p.102

Exhibitions: Leeds, 1868 (2660); Manchester, 1961 (2); Providence, 1973 (1); Pittsburgh, 1987–8 (8)

The unfinished model for the famous engraving in the same sense by Marco Dente da Ravenna (B.XIV.24.21), which is lettered on the print itself, '*bacius florentinus*'. The

13

extraordinary vigour of Bandinelli's drawing, especially the shading, was refined and schematised by the engraver, who, as Davidson suggested, may in his hatching and schematisation have been imitating Marcantonio Raimondi. At this preparatory stage there are no agitated groups adumbrated behind the balustrade, of which the solid panels are capped by stone spheres. Preliminary use of red chalk is not only conspicuous in sketching the balustrade, in the heads of those two mothers which are silhouetted against the riser of the lowest step, and in the dead baby prostrate on that step at the right; it appears also in the group at the left, especially in developing the flare of the skirt of the mother climbing the steps at the left, clearly foretelling the definitive design of the print. In the print the loins of the youthful executioner at the left are bare, and the removal of drapery leaves room to insert a crouching figure with hand upraised.

This ideal *accademia*, designed in Rome, was the most important treatment of the theme since the publication of Marcantonio Raimondi's engraving of the *Massacre of the Innocents* after Raphael. The *terminus ante quem* is 1527, when Marco Dente died during the Sack. On stylistic grounds the date is likely to be nearer 1525 than 1520.

14 Federico Barocci

(Urbino 1535–1612 Urbino)

Recto: Study for the Virgin greeted by St Elizabeth

Black and white chalks, stumped, on paper prepared blue, 381 × 253mm. Squared for enlargement, and partly incised for transfer.

Verso: Study for the Virgin

Black chalk on unprepared buff paper.
Inscribed in black chalk (evidently by a northerner) on the recto *F Barotsius Urbino*, and on the verso in pencil *F Barocci portf. G.No.8* and *8*

Chatsworth 918A

Provenance: N. A. Flinck (L.959); William, 2nd Duke of Devonshire (L.718) from 1723–4

Literature: Schmarsow, 1914, p.40; Olsen, 1955, pp.140–1 and 1962, p.180, fig.63b; Emiliani, 1986, II, pp.217–29, figs.449 (verso) and 453 (recto)

Exhibitions: Washington etc., 1962, (17); Bologna, 1975 (154); Cleveland/Yale, 1978 (50)

Barocci was commissioned to paint *The Visitation* for the Pozzomiglio altar of the chapel in the Chiesa Nuova in Rome. The altarpiece commissioned by Francesco Pozzomiglio was painted between 1583 and 1586, and it became the favourite painting of the founder of the Oratory, San Filippo Neri.

On this sheet (recto and verso) are final drapery studies

14

before the completed design (National Galleries of Scotland). The squared lines assisted the transfer to the Edinburgh sheet. Comparable refinement of the Virgin's drapery on the verso, rehearsed on a lay figure, is to be found on Uffizi 11420F (repr. Emiliani, 1975, fig.157).

15 Federico Barocci

(Urbino 1525–1612 Urbino)

The Assumption of the Virgin

COLOUR PLATE I

Pen and brown ink with brown and grey washes over preliminaries in black chalk, heightened with white, on grey paper, with grey bodycolour on the apostle in the left foreground, squared in black chalk for enlargement, 522 × 367mm. Mounted in full for the 2nd Duke.

Chatsworth 364

Provenance: Sir Peter Lely (L.2092); P. H. Lankrink (L.2090); William, 2nd Duke of Devonshire (L.718)

Literature: Olsen, 1955, pp.59, 167 and 1962, pp.93, 212, pl.110;
Emiliani, 1986, p.405, fig.880

Exhibitions: London, RA, 1953 (106); Washington, 1969–70 and
London, V & A, 1973–4 (16); Cleveland/Yale, 1975 (70)

This is the *cartoncino* for the *Assumption* which was still
unfinished at Barocci's death. The foreground prone/
prostrate apostle is derived from the *Eucharist* in Santa
Maria Sopra Minerva. The altarpiece descended through
the Albani to the present owner, principe Cesare
Castelbarco Albani (Olsen, 1962, pls.104 and 111). Many
other studies for this painting have been identified, e.g.
Bologna, 1975, nos.281–6.

This beautiful drawing in chiaroscuro at Chatsworth,
in Pillsbury's words, 'shows not only all the elements of
the final design, including several cherubim in flight
around the Virgin which the artist failed to sketch on the
canvas, but also the lighting scheme ... To strengthen the
light effects – the abstract play of light, in fact, creates
the real drama in the scene – the artist added white and
grey gouaches. The grey, which is limited to the back of
the robe of the apostle kneeling in the foreground,
establishes the darkest spot in the composition, thereby
intensifying the contrast to the light-filled space above'.

16 Domenico Beccafumi

(Valdibiena, near Siena *c*.1486–1551 Siena)

Nude with the left Knee bent

Pen and brown ink over preliminaries in black chalk,
282 × 188mm. Fully mounted for the 2nd Duke.
Inscribed in pen and brown ink *mecarino* (scored through) *Di
mecarino* and *mecarino senese*

Chatsworth 5

Provenance: 2nd Duke of Devonshire (L.718)

Literature: Donato Sanminiatelli, "The Beginnings of
Domenico Beccafumi", *Burl. Mag.*, IC, 1957, pp.401–10

Mecarino was the nickname given to Beccafumi.
Chatsworth 6 (exhibited in Washington, 1962–3 (7)) is
similarly inscribed. A *Reclining Male Nude* drawn with
the same media and technique was in the exhibition of
*Sixteenth-Century Italian Drawings from the Collection of
Janos Scholz*, Washington/New York, 1973–4 (34).
K. Oberhuber and D. Walker did not notice in their catalogue entry that this drawing was mounted in characteristic fashion by Jonathan Richardson for an early
eighteenth-century collector in England, possibly the 2nd
Duke of Devonshire (it bears no collector's mark).

16

17

17 Domenico Beccafumi

(Valdibiena, near Siena c.1486–1551 Siena)

Two Nudes fighting, one with a Dagger in his left Hand

Pen and brown ink on dirty white paper, 204 × 181mm.
Mounted in full for the 2nd Duke.
Inscribed in pen and brown ink (now very faint) by an early
eighteenth-century hand *Perino del Vaga*

Chatsworth 160

Provenance: William, 2nd Duke of Devonshire (L.718)

A. E. Popham (1962) rejected the old attribution in the
Devonshire Collection to Perino without making any
other suggestion. The pen technique is very close to that
of Chatsworth 5 (here cat. no.16), and to that of the female
nudes mounted left and right of *Hercules* in the Louvre
(*Italian Renaissance Drawings from the Musée du Louvre*,
Metropolitan Museum, New York, 1974–5, no.9), dated
1520–5, soon after Beccafumi's trip to Rome, by
D. Sanminiatelli (*Burl. Mag.* July 1975). Compare also the
copy from the pavement of the Duomo in Siena: Moses
strikes the water (Exodus 17.6), and St Joseph (?) under
a tree (exhibited Siena, 1990 (90)).

18 Girolamo Francesco Maria Bedoli, called Girolamo Mazzola-Bedoli

(Viadana 1500–1569 Parma)

Design for a Funerary Monument: Apollo standing in a Niche flanked by sorrowing Muses

Red chalk, 171 × 180mm, under 86 × 102mm. Mounted in full
for the 2nd Duke.

Chatsworth 808

Provenance: William, 2nd Duke of Devonshire (L.718)

Literature: Copertini, 1949, p.15, fig.16 (as Parmigianino)

Exhibitions: Viadana, 1971 (63)

The drawing, traditionally attributed in the Devonshire
collection to Girolamo Francesco Mazzola, was attributed by A. E. Popham (1971, Appendix III) to Girolamo
Francesco Maria Bedoli. It is a rare example of an architectural design by him, and is presumably for a poet's tomb.
From April 1547 to some date in 1567, he was working
the Steccata almost constantly cf. *Canefora* (pen and brown
ink with brown wash over black chalk, on buff paper,
262 × 147mm: exhibited Torgiano (Umbria), Museo del
Vino, 'Dal Disegno all'Opera Compiuta', 1987, no.4).

18

19 Gentile Bellini

(Venice 1429–1507 Venice)

A Venetian Procession moving from a Scuola to a flanking Church

Pen and brown ink over preliminaries in red chalk on cream
paper, 145 × 211mm (trimmed irregularly and the upper right
corner missing). Mounted in full for Lord Somers.
Inscribed in pen and brown ink *g. 32*; and on the mount in
J. Richardson the elder's hand *Gio: Bellini*

Chatsworth 738

Provenance: P. Sebastiano Resta (as Giovanni Bellini, for the *Pro-
cession of Alessandro III* in the Sala del Gran Consiglio, Palazzo
Ducale, Venice); Giovanni Matteo Marchetti (died 1704),
Bishop of Arezzo, from 1698; sold by his heir, the cavaliere
Orazio Marchetti of Pistoia; Lord Somers from 1710 and at least
until 1716; his sale in London 1717; William, 2nd Duke of
Devonshire (L.718)

Literature: D. von Hadeln, *Venezianische Zeichnungen des Quattrocento*, Berlin, 1925, pp.44–5, pl.8; A. Venturi, *L'Arte*, xxix, 1926,
p.2; Popham, 1931, I, p.244 (no.169, as Carpaccio); Tietzes,
1944, no.263

19

Exhibitions: London, RA, 1930 (604); Nottingham/London, 1983 (57)

Traditionally in the Devonshire Collections by Giovanni Bellini: no writer has followed Venturi in his suggestion of Lazzaro Bastiani. A typical narrative scene of the Venetian scuola type. The building in the centre is in the Lombard style of the late *quattrocento*. Frizzoni and conte Gamba referred to the drawing as 'tecnicamente nella maniera di Carpaccio'. A. G. B. Russell attributed it to Carpaccio, and von Hadeln to Bellini. A related drawing of *The Procession of the Relic of the Holy Cross, Piazza di S. Marco* was sold at Sotheby's, 2 August 1933 (58), as Gentile Bellini; when in the Resta/Somers and J. Richardson collections it was called Giovanni Bellini. It is now in the British Museum (1933-8-3-12, Popham & Pouncey, 1950, no.34) as Vittore Carpaccio.

For this type of outdoor procession in a piazza, see also the painting of a *Procession in the Piazza San Marco* now in the Accademia in Venice. As Deborah Howard has pointed out to me, the domed canopy at the right was either invented for pictorial purposes or for a piece of festive scenery for a passing event; and the reference might be to the Scuola di San Marco or to the Scuola di San Rocco (earlier buildings than those we know today), the latter being more probable. However, the scene might well be completely imaginary.

20 Jacopo Zanguidi, called Bertoia

(Parma 1544–1574 ?Parma)

Venus and Adonis, with Cupid

Pen and brown ink, over preliminaries in black chalk on white paper, 180 × 120mm, the upper corners chamfered. Mounted in full for the 2nd Duke.

Chatsworth 368

Provenance: Sir Peter Lely (L.2092); William, 2nd Duke of Devonshire (L.718)

Literature: A. G. Quintavalle, *Il Bertoja*, Milan, 1963, pp.39, 47n, 52, 70, fig.68; Popham, 1967, p.133 (under no.233); de Grazia Bohlin, 1972, p.128, cat.no.4, pl.212; de Grazia, 1991, D4, fig.118

A. E. Popham made the attribution to Bertoia in 1952, which was passed to Quintavalle by P. M. R. Pouncey. The drawing had passed in the Courtauld Institute List of 1963 as by Giulio Cesare Amidano (1566–1630). The elegant elongation of limbs is typical of Bertoia. Compare Louvre inv.no.285, in the same technique, of an epicene youth (?Ganymede) and a fancy vase (reproduced *MD*, VIII, 1970, p.47b), a drawing attributed to Bertoia by Vasari. De Grazia dates Chatsworth 368 *c*.1570–2. She calls it *Venus, Mars and Cupid*: but the only martial accoutrement to be descried could as well indicate a hunting spear. We retain the title adopted in the Courtauld Institute List of 1963.

21 Andrea Boscoli

(Florence *c*.1560–1607 ?Florence)

The Deposition

Pen and brown ink with brown wash over preliminaries in black chalk, heightened with white bodycolour on blue paper, 256 × 190mm. Mounted in full for the 2nd Duke.

Chatsworth 492

Provenance: William, 2nd Duke of Devonshire (L.718)

21

As N. Turner and P. M. R. Pouncey concluded independently (1988), this drawing is surely a very fine and typical Boscoli, hitherto misattributed in the Devonshire Collections to G. A. Sirani. The elongated limbs and curious attitudes of Christ and His Mother are particularly relevant.

22 Luca Cambiaso

(Moneglia 1527–1585 El Escorial)

Venus playing with Cupid under a Tree

Pen and brown ink with brown wash, 270 × 215mm. Mounted in full for the 2nd Duke.
Inscribed on verso, in pen and brown ink, *Cambiaso*.

Chatsworth 386

Provenance: N. A. Flinck (L.959); presumably 2nd Duke of Devonshire from 1723–4

Literature: Reveley, p.53

Exhibitions: Manchester, 1961 (12)

Traditionally in the Devonshire Collections as Cambiaso. A superb drawing, probably of the mid 1560s, for which no development in his painting is known.

20

22

23 Domenico Campagnola

(?Padua 1484–1564 Padua)

Landscape with a winding River

Pen and brown ink, 272 × 420mm. The lower right corner has been eaten away. Mounted in full for Lord Somers.

Inscribed in pen and brown ink in the hand of J. Richardson the elder, following Resta, *i. 124* on the drawing; and on the mount *Mutiano*

Chatsworth 229

Provenance: P. Sebastiano Resta; Giovanni Matteo Marchetti (died 1704), Bishop of Arezzo, from 1698; sold by his heir, the cavaliere Orazio Marchetti of Pistoia; Lord Somers from 1710 until at least 1716; his sale, London 1717; William, 2nd Duke of Devonshire (L.718).

Sent to Resta unconvincingly attributed to Girolamo Muziano (he himself thought rather of Titian), this drawing shows so strongly the influence of Domenico Campagnola that it is hard to believe it is not by his hand. It is to be regarded as one of seventeen such drawings in the Devonshire collection; compare especially Chatsworth 260, 265 and 269.

23

24

25

24 Domenico Campagnola

(?Padua 1484–1564 Padua)

Virgin and Child in glory: Cherubim with musical Instruments, a Wreath etc.

Pen and brown ink, 220 × 193mm. Mounted in full for the 2nd Duke.

Inscribed with pen and brown ink, lower left, in a late seventeenth-century hand, possibly that of Lanière, *Campagnola*

Chatsworth 255

Provenance: N. Lanière (L.2886); Sir Peter Lely (L.2092); N. A. Flinck (L.959); William, 2nd Duke of Devonshire (L.718)
Exhibitions: London, New Gallery, 1894–5 (841)

The traditional attribution to the first artist who made pen drawing his profession is undoubtedly correct; a copy is in the British Museum (Payne Knight bequest, pp.2–112). Compare the *Virgin and Child in the Clouds* in the Uffizi (called Agostino Carracci), and the *Madonna and Child with St Anne*, appearing cloudborne above two pairs of saints and musical angels, in Berlin (KdZ433).

25 Domenico Campagnola

(?Padua 1484–1564 Padua)

The Holy Family

Pen and brown ink, 157 × 175mm. Mounted in full for the 2nd Duke.

Chatsworth 648

Provenance: P. H. Lankrink (L.2092); presumably the 2nd Duke of Devonshire

Attributed at Chatsworth, at least since 1929, implausibly to Guercino, this appears to be by the same author as Chatsworth 255 (here cat. no.24) and the Uffizi *Madonna and Child in the Clouds* (called Agostino Carracci): Domenico Campagnola. The hands and the shading are especially characteristic. The morphology generally reflects Campagnola's attraction to the *maniere* of Parmigianino and Francesco Salviati.

26 Simone Cantarini, called il Pesarese

(Pesaro 1612–1648 Verona)

Diana and Actaeon

Red chalk, 273 × 209mm. Mounted in full for the 2nd Duke.
Chatsworth 496
Provenance: William, 2nd Duke of Devonshire
Literature: Catherine Johnston, 1970, p.87, pl. XXXIV

26

28

Exhibitions: Washington etc., 1969–70 and London V & A, 1973–4 (21)

The splintery and only slightly plastic treatment of the female figures and the hound in the foreground, also the background of Actaeon transmogrified into a stag and gored by his own hunting pack, are entirely typical of Cantarini, to whom Chatsworth 496 has traditionally been attributed, along with other red chalk studies for the Diana story in Windsor (Kurz, 1955, nos.41 and 42) and in the Brera.

27 Vittore Carpaccio

(active Venice 1486–*c*.1525)

Cardinal Bessarion presenting to three Representatives of the Scuola della Carità in Venice the Reliquary with a Fragment of the True Cross, 1472

Pen and brown ink over preliminaries in red chalk on cream paper, 166 × 197mm. There are holes and tears along the irregular top margin. Mounted in full for Lord Somers.

Inscribed in pen and brown ink, on the mount, in the hand of J. Richardson the elder, following Resta, *Gio Bellini*

Provenance: P. Sebastiano Resta (as Giovanni Bellini); Lord Somers from 1710 until at least 1716 (Resta-Somers g.29); his sale in London 1717; 2nd or 3rd Duke of Devonshire

Literature: Strong, 1905, p.120; Lauts, 1962, p.266 (7)

Exhibitions: London, Arts Council, 1949 (3); Washington etc., 1962–3 and London, RA, 1969–70 (10)

Lauts's suggestion for the identification of the subject is most plausible; and the current attribution can hardly be doubted. Strong's assertion that the ecclesiastical dignitary is Lorenzo Giustiniani is to be set aside; and there is no sure foundation for the suggestion, which Strong says he received from Dr Ludwig, 'that in this drawing we have a relic of an important work carried out by Carpaccio, toward the close of his life, in the Palace of the Patriarch at Venice'.

28 Agostino Carracci

(Bologna 1557–1602 Parma)

Madonna and Child with St John, all asleep

Pen and brown ink and brown wash, 176 × 145mm. Mounted in the early 19th century.

Chatsworth 407

Provenance: William, 2nd Duke of Devonshire (L.718)

Traditionally in the Devonshire collection as by Ludovico Carracci. However his cousin Agostino was more interested in this kind of pose; like his etching of *A Satyr and*

27

Sleeping Nymph (B.XVIII.101.112) this drawing is strangely poetical. The deep shading, the hatching and the cross-hatching, fit well enough with Agostino, although still reminiscent of Passerotti, e.g. the drawing of *A seated Woman asleep*, formerly in the collection of Sir Robert Mond (Michel Gand sale, Sotheby's Monaco, 20 June 1987 (34)). For Agostino compare with the grouping in *Latona with Infants Apollo and Diana* (Christie's, 9 December 1980 (23)).

29 Agostino Carracci

(Bologna 1557–1602 Parma)

Head of a young Woman looking down over her right Shoulder

Red chalk, 243 × 184mm; the corners nicked and repaired. Mounted in full for the 2nd Duke.

Chatsworth 451

Provenance: William, 2nd Duke of Devonshire (L.718)

Exhibitions: Leeds, 1868, (2673 or 2684, as 'Annibale Carracci. Female Head. Red Chalk')

Manifestly not a seicento portrait, as had been supposed. 'A late school drawing' according to Bodmer. It was perhaps developed after the antique. Comparison can be made with Agostino's *Head of the West Wind*, (ex-Duke

29

of Devonshire) now in the Fogg Museum, Cambridge, Mass. (Mongan and Oberhuber, 1988, no. 50) which bears on the verso in pen and brown ink an inscription, *Augustin Caraza*. There is a similar hatched background, similar shadowed eyes, a comparable modelling of surface by crosshatching, and a comparably unusual inclination of the head.

30 Agostino Carracci

(Bologna 1557–1602 Parma)

Recto : Landscape with the Riposo

Pen and brown ink on cream paper, 197 × 278mm. Mounted presumably for the 2nd Duke.

Chatsworth 816A

Verso : Draped female Figure

Inscribed in pen and brown ink, *di Agostino Carazo bolognese* (the remains of the inscription cut off at the base)

30 *recto*

30 *verso*

Chatsworth 816B

Provenance: Sir Peter Lely (L.2092); presumably 1st or 2nd Duke of Devonshire

Both recto and verso were classed by S. A. Strong as 'style of Francesco Grimaldi Bolognese or else French'. On the verso is a particularly attractive and characteristic drawing by Agostino of a standing figure; the loose pen strokes wander, here and there concentrating into plastic form. The recto, also an excellent original drawing, can surely be taken to be by the same hand. Therefore it can be treated, like Chatsworth 923 (cat.31), as a paradigm of Agostino's landscape drawing. Chatsworth 923 is considerably the larger sheet, and more loosely handled, while 816A is the smaller and more finished drawing.

31 Agostino Carracci

(Bologna 1557–1602 Parma)

Recto: A rocky Landscape with Figures

Pen and brown ink, 276 × 433mm.

Verso: Studies of a Man's left Leg, a left Hand and a Man's Head in profile

Red chalk reinforced with pen and brown ink, on cream wire-laid paper. A thin vertical strip added on the right has now (1986) been detached.

37

Inscribed on the verso in pen and brown ink, in a late 16th- or early 17th-century hand *A. Carrazzio*

Chatsworth 923

Provenance: Sir Peter Lely (L.2092); William, 2nd Duke of Devonshire (L.718)

Exhibitions: Pittsburgh etc., 1977–8 (13)

Sidney Colvin (in a manuscript note at Chatsworth) attributed the verso (see illustration) to Bartolomeo Passerotti (*c*.1525–92), leaving the *recto* indistinctly attributed to the 'Bolognese School'. Yet both sides appear to have been drawn by the same hand, that of Passerotti's pupil Agostino Carracci. The *verso* may be compared with various drawings at Windsor (2129 *verso* and *recto*; 1848 *recto*; 1836: Wittkower, 1952, nos.134, 137 and 152). The studies of the profile head, the hand, the feet and the legs are similar to those engraved after Agostino by Odoardo Fialetti in *Il vero modo et ordine per dissegnar tutte le parti et membra del corpo humano*, Venice, 1608, nos.8, 17, 23. The *recto* may be compared with the earliest frieze frescoed by the Carracci in Palazzo Fava, Bologna, in particular with the first scene of Jupiter disguised as a bull approached by Europa. As Malvasia remarked, 'Quindi è che tante volte si equivoca frà loro disegni, massime di semplici nudi; prendendosi bene spesso quei di Bartolomeo per

di Agostino e que' di Agostino per di Bartolomeo' (1678, I, p.235). An amusing insight into the naturalistic habit of the young Carracci brothers as draughtsmen in Bologna is the witty profile of a cat's head, which is almost absorbed in the middleground of the extensive landscape.

32 Agostino Carracci

(Bologna 1557–1602 Parma)

Five winged Amorini playing with a Goat

Pen and brown ink, 124 × 226mm. Trimmed on the left and right

Chatsworth 333

This frieze *all'antica* was evidently designed for a *quadro riportato* panel to decorate a palace ceiling, as the shaped ends indicate. Although A.E.Popham (1962) found it 'quite unlike any drawing by Girolamo Carpi known to me', the attribution to that artist, apparently traditional in the Devonshire collection, was accepted in the Courtauld Institute List of 1963. It is surely a witticism by Agostino Carracci, connected with his frescoes on the vault of the Palazzo del Giardino, Parma, his last work after his quarrel with Annibale, and datable between 1600

31 *recto*

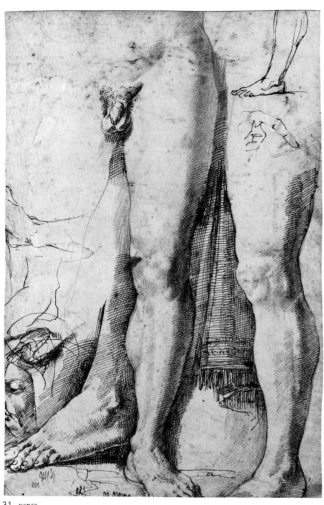

31 *verso*

and 1602, the year of his death. Compare the study, with important differences, for *Three Amors in the Garden of Venus*, sold with the Ellesmere Collection of drawings, Sotheby's, 11 July 1972, 34 verso. That drawing was acquired by the Metropolitan Museum, New York.

33 Annibale Carracci

(Bologna 1560–1609 Rome)

The Battle between the Romans and the Sabines

Pen and brown ink, with brown wash, heightened with white bodycolour on paper washed brown, 362 × 473mm. Mounted in full for the 2nd Duke.

Chatsworth 661A

Provenance: William, 2nd Duke of Devonshire (L.718)

Hitherto classified in the Devonshire collection as 'Italian school, late 16th century', this masterly drawing in the chiaroscuro technique developed by the Carracci, clearly relates to the ninth of the stories of Romulus in the frieze frescoed by them in Palazzo Magnani, Bologna: *The Battle between the Romans and Sabines*, and at an advanced stage of composition. Between the Chatsworth drawing and the frescoed scene there are numerous telling differences, ranging from rearrangement of the weapons strewn in the foreground, to the angling of the horses' heads, to the description of the distant mountains, and to the removal of the mother and child at the right from the definitive version. The drawing is certainly preparatory to, not a copy of that.

32

33

The best discussion of the fresco, made without knowledge of this drawing, is to be found in A. Emiliani, *Le storie di Romolo e Remo di Ludovico, Agostino e Annibale Carracci in Palazzo Magnani a Bologna*, Bologna, 1989, especially pp.163 and 182–3, and pls. XI and XVIII. Emiliani follows Malvasia in attributing the ninth scene, *The Battle between the Romans and Sabines*, to Agostino, a view supported by Bodmer (1933). Cavalli (1956) and Volpe (1972) give a share in the work to Annibale. As N. Turner has pointed out to me (1989), Annibale is most convincingly the draughtsman of so vigorous a preparatory model.

34 Annibale Carracci

(Bologna 1560–1609 Rome)

The Assumption of the Virgin

COLOUR PLATE II

Pen and brown ink with brown wash, over indications in black chalk, heightened with white bodycolour, and squared for enlargement in black chalk, 541 × 355mm. Fully mounted; although lifted in 1986, the 18th-century mount is preserved.

Chatsworth 420

Provenance: Sir Peter Lely (L.2092); William, 2nd Duke of Devonshire (L.718)

Literature: Richardson, 1722, p.343; Waagen, 1854, III, p.358 (as by Annibale); Posner, 1971, II, p.19 (under cat.no.40, as 'by a Carracci follower … a variant copy of the Dresden picture'); A.W.A.Boschloo, *Annibale Carracci in Bologna*, The Hague, 1974, I, p.14, pl.17

Exhibitions: Pittsburgh etc., 1987–8 (17); London, Courtauld Institute of Art, 1992 (14).

A brilliant modello, *pace* Posner, for the altarpiece which Annibale painted in 1587 for the Confraternity of San Rocco, Reggio Emilia (Scannelli, 1657, p.339; Bellori, 1672, p.28). The painting was transferred in 1661 to the Ducal Collection in Modena. There it was seen as 'Lodovico Carracci' by the younger Richardson, who noted 'In another Room ... On another side is the Assumption, of which the D. of Devonshire has the Drawing'. The painting went in 1746 to Dresden. Thus the drawing must have been at Chatsworth by the spring of 1722 when the younger Richardson set out for his few months' continental tour. Waagen described it justly: 'Drawing for the picture of the *Assumption of the Virgin* in the Dresden Gallery. Of exaggerated dramatic action, but of great effect. Admirably drawn with pen, bistre and white'.

35 Annibale Carracci

(Bologna 1560–1609 Rome)

St Gregory attended by Angels praying for Souls in Purgatory

Pen and brown ink with brown wash, heightened with white, 393 × 263mm.

Inscribed in pen and brown ink, *f.77*; and on the mount for Lord Somers in pen and brown ink, in the hand of J. Richardson the elder, following Resta, *Annibale Caracci*

35

Chatsworth 435

Provenance: P. Sebastiano Resta; Lord Somers from 1710 until at least 1716; his sale in London 1717; William, 2nd Duke of Devonshire, by 1722 and presumably from 1717

Literature: Richardson, 1722, p.190; Posner, 1971, p.57, and no.130, pl.130b

Exhibitions: London, RA, 1938 (391); Bologna, 1956 (120); Newcastle, 1961 (153); Washington etc., 1962–3 and London, RA, 1969 (13)

A study for the altarpiece, with an arched top (the decorative framework only indicated fully in part), commissioned for S. Gregorio Magno, Rome by Cardinal Antonio Maria Salviati, which Annibale finished in 1603. (Formerly in Bridgewater House, London, it was destroyed in the Second World War.) In 1722 the younger Richardson saw Annibale's altarpiece in 'The Church of St Gregorio. The Bishop at Prayers (St Gregory). The Duke of Devonshire has the Drawing'. H. Tietze's proposal that Chatsworth 435 is by Albani and O. Benesch's proposal that the drawing was reworked by Rubens ('Neue Beiträge zum Werk des Rubens' in *Walter Friedlaender zum 90. Geburtstag*, Berlin, 1965, p.45) can both be set aside. A composition study for this altarpiece at a slightly earlier stage is at Windsor (Wittkower, 1952, no.351).

36 Annibale Carracci

(Bologna 1560–1609 Rome)

A Woman seated in a Room

Pen and brown ink over preliminaries in black chalk, 220 × 170mm. Mounted in full for the 2nd Duke.

Chatsworth 436

Provenance: Sir Peter Lely (L.2092); P. H. Lankrink (L.2090); William, 2nd Duke of Devonshire (L.718)

Literature: Martin, 1965, p.25, no.51, with other literature

Exhibitions: Newcastle, 1961 (81); Washington etc., 1969–70 and London, V & A, 1973–4 (25)

Martin suggested that this may be an early idea for the treatment of the end walls of the Galleria Farnese. The present writer (*Burl.Mag.* CIV, 1962, p.29) had proposed (and remains convinced of) a date 1604–5, after the frescoing of the Gallery was finished, when the artist, having been miserably requited by Cardinal Odoardo Farnese, was in a mood of deep depression. It is manifestly drawn as a private expression of feeling, and, as Byam Shaw wrote in the 1969 Washington exhibition catalogue, 'surely in Annibale's latest style'.

37 Annibale Carracci

(Bologna 1560–1609 Rome)

A hunchback Boy, half-length

Red chalk, with red wash, 264 × 225mm. Mounted in full for the 2nd Duke.

Inscribed in pen and brown ink, upper left, in a 17th-century hand, *disegno di Messer An: Carrazzi* (below this, hardly legible, in pen and brown ink, *Paulo de Verona*); also inscribed on the right by Annibale himself, *Non so se Dio m'aiuta* (I do not know if God helps me)

Chatsworth 443

Provenance: William, 2nd Duke of Devonshire (L.718).

Exhibitions: Newcastle, 1961 (89); Washington etc., 1969–70 and London, V & A, 1973–4 (27); Jerusalem, 1977 (19)

This early and very moving drawing, traditionally attributed in the Devonshire collection to Annibale, was generally disregarded by scholars until Ralph Holland included it in his 1961 exhibition.

38 Annibale Carracci

(Bologna 1560–1609 Rome)

Trees, a Town, and a more distant Mountain

Pen and brown ink, 253 × 185mm. Mounted in full for the 2nd Duke.

Chatsworth 467

Provenance: Sir Peter Lely (L.2092); William, 2nd Duke of Devonshire (L.718)

Literature: Harris, 1989, p.76 (as by Pietro Paolo Bonzi)

Exhibitions: Leeds, 1868 (2680, as by Annibale Carracci); Pittsburgh etc., 1987–8 (18)

A drawing probably of the 1590s such as this shows the attraction which Annibale's penwork in landscape was to hold for seicento artists as diverse as Poussin and Rembrandt. It shows his superbly controlled response to the stimuli of nature and atmosphere. At the same time it shows his decorative sense for landscape painting. Without being the study for any particular picture, it recalls that combination of motifs for the curved closure at the left, and the extension toward distant buildings and more distant mountains, which is crucial to the prospect in the oval landscape of *c.* 1590 in the Bayerische Staatsgemäldesammlungen, Munich (Clovis Whitfield, 'Early Landscapes by Annibale Carracci', *Pantheon*, XXXVIII, 1980, p.50, colour plate 1). Disregarding the attribution which goes back to the early eighteenth century, and presumably to the late seventeenth century, Dr Sutherland Harris attributed this drawing with confidence to Bonzi.

36

38

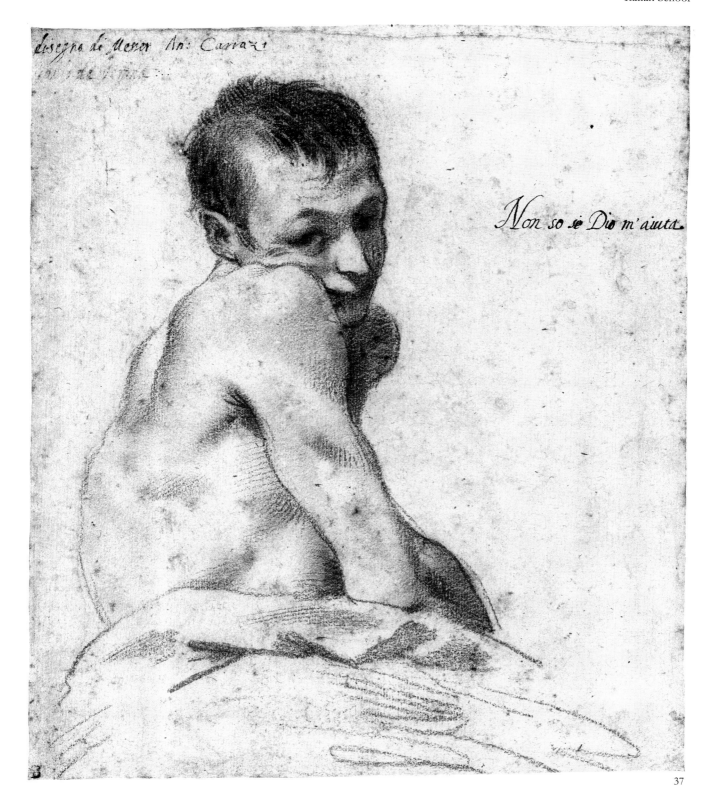

disegno di Messer An: Carrazi

Non so se Dio m'aiuta

39 Lodovico Carracci

(Bologna 1555–1619 Bologna)

Man pulling on a Rope, his left Leg rehearsed a second time

Black chalk, 350 × 260mm. Mounted in full for the 2nd Duke.

Inscribed in pen and brown ink, in a 17th-century hand (? Venetian), *di lodovico Carazo*

Chatsworth 410

Provenance: Sir Peter Lely (L.2092); William, 2nd Duke of Devonshire (L.718)

Literature: Bodmer, 1939, pp.74, 148, no.10; Wittkower, 1952, p.101, under no.13; Denis Mahon, *Mostra dei Carracci: catalogo antico dei disegni* (2nd edn.), Bologna, 1963, no.14; D. Mahon, *Apollo*, LXXXII, 1965, p.390, n.7; Paris, Petit Palais, *Le XVIe siècle européen*, 1965/66, p.56, under no.69 (entry by P. Rosenberg); Bohn, 1984, p.174, no.26; F. Arcangeli, *Natura ed espressione in arte bolognese-emiliana*, Bologna, 1972 (?), p.204, no.56; *Seicento: le siècle de Caravage dans les collections françaises*, Paris/Milan, 1988–9, p.159 under no.37; Renato Roli in *The Age of Correggio and the Carracci*, Washington/New York/Bologna 1986–7, under no.107; Paris, Grand Palais/Milan, Palazzo Reale, *Seicento, le siècle de Caravage dans les Collections françaises*, 1988, p.159

Exhibitions: Leeds, 1868 (2686); London, RA, 1953 (153); Bologna, 1956 (14); Manchester, 1961 (22); Newcastle, 1961 (3); Washington 1962–3 and London, RA, 1969 (17); Sheffield, 1966 (11); London, Courtauld Institute of Art, 1992 (15)

Bodmer connected this to the somewhat similar figure of a monk drawing water in one of Lodovico's frescoes in San Michele in Bosco. Never doubted as the work of Lodovico, this is a study for an executioner in the *Flagellation of Christ* (acquired 1964 for Douai, Musée de la Chartreuse), a painting of *c*.1587–8, initially regarded as the work of Annibale with the assistance of Lodovico: but both P. Rosenberg and D. Mahon (1965) attributed it firmly and correctly to Lodovico.

40 Lodovico Carracci

(Bologna 1555–1619 Bologna)

Apparition of 'Cristo Portacroce' ('Christ carrying the Cross') to Monks of the Charterhouse, Bologna

Pen and brown ink, with brown wash, on cream paper, 362 × 250mm. Mounted in full for the 2nd Duke.

Chatsworth 497

Provenance: William, 2nd Duke of Devonshire (L.718)

Literature: J.M. Stock, *Catalogue of The Ellesmere Collection of drawings by the Carracci and other Bolognese Masters collected by Sir Thomas Lawrence*, Part I, sale Sotheby's 11 July 1972, p.23 (mentions Lenore Street's attribution under lot 4, and her dating *c*.1589); L. Street, 'La vendita Ellesmere di disegni dei Carracci', *Arte Illustrata*, no.50, September 1972, p.356, fig.12 (redating the drawing 1592)

Exhibitions: Pittsburgh etc., 1987–8 (20); London, Courtauld Institute of Art, 1992 (17)

L. Street (1971) assigned the correct authorship to this beautiful drawing, which had been attributed unaccountably during the first half of the twentieth century to Lionello Spada (1576–1622). Miss Street had for secure comparison another version of the composition drawn for the same fresco in S. Gerolamo, Bologna, dated by her at the sale *c*.1589, but revised to 1592, remembering the Venetian influence on Lodovico (see Titian's *Christ and Joseph of Aramathea on the Road to Calvary* in the Prado). For the second drawing see H. Bodmer, *Lodovico Carracci*, Burg bei Magdeburg 1939, pp.46, 122, 150, figs.59, 114 as *c*.1593–5, a sheet formerly in the Ellesmere collection (pen and wash, correctly inscribed 'L. Caratio'). The fresco survives only as a damaged fragment. Both drawings differ from the fresco in that there the Carthusians carry their own crosses. The two towers of Bologna can be seen in the distance at the left. As the Sotheby catalogue entry states, this mystical subject lodged in the Carthusian tradition at least from the time of Ambrogio Bergognone's work for the Certosa di Pavia (B. Berenson, *Central Italian and North Italian Schools*, London, 1968, III, pl.1474).

39

40

41

41 Lodovico Carracci

(Bologna 1555–1619 Bologna)

The Rest on the Flight, with Cherubim bearing Fruit

Pen and brown ink with brown wash, over preliminaries in black chalk, 393 × 281mm. Much damaged, and the lower left corner is missing. Mounted in full for Lord Somers.

Inscribed in pen and brown ink, *d. 61*; the mount inscribed in Richardson's hand, following Padre Resta, *Annibale Carracci*

Provenance: given to Padre Resta by Giuseppe Magnavacca, 1706; P. Sebastiano Resta; Lord Somers until at least 1716; his sale in London 1717; 2nd or 3rd Duke of Devonshire

The traditional attribution from Resta, and possibly from the Bolognese collector, Magnavacca, was to Annibale. However the flattening of the figure composition in the foreplane and the weird treatment of landscape speak rather for Ludovico in his final decade.

42 Alessandro di Agostino della Torre, called Casolani

(Siena 1552–1606 ?Siena)

A bearded Pope enthroned under a Canopy, attended by Cardinals and the Swiss Guard, receives a Deputation

Pen and brown ink with point of brush and brown wash over preliminaries in black chalk, extensively heightened with white bodycolour, 310 × 244mm. Trimmed left and right. Mounted in full for the 2nd Duke.

Chatsworth 280

Provenance: GHO (L.1158), almost effaced; presumably William, 2nd Duke of Devonshire

P. M. R. Pouncey (1989) suggested an attribution to Casolani or to Muziano, in place of the implausible classification 'attributed to Paolo Veronese' which had been accepted at Chatsworth. Casolani appears correct by comparison with a black chalk drawing, squared for enlargement, in Turin (Biblioteca Reale 15733) depicting the *Handing over the keys of the Castel Sant' Angelo to the Pope Urban VI on the Advice of Santa Catarina*, a preparation, omitting St. Catherine of Siena, for the painting in the Casa di Santa Caterina in Siena (Venturi, *Storia*, IX. vii, fig.629). The Turin drawing, traditionally attributed to Beccafumi, was reattributed by C. Brandi to Pomarancio,

42

43

who was the master and subsequently the collaborator of Casolani. The Chatsworth drawing has so many compositional elements in common as to make it likely a preparation for the same commission, although the offering of the keys is not visible.

43 Giovanni Battista Castello, called il Bergamasco

(Bergamo 1509–1569 Madrid)

The Road to Calvary

Pen and brown ink with brown wash, touched with white bodycolour, 431 × 573mm. The lower left corner is missing. Mounted in full for the 2nd Duke.

Inscribed in pen and brown ink, on the banner, by the draughtsman *S P Q R*

Chatsworth 189

Provenance: P. H. Lankrink (L.2080); William, 2nd Duke of Devonshire

This splendid drawing was kept in the Devonshire collection as 'style of Primaticcio?' (Polidoro da Caravaggio had also been suggested). A. E. Popham (1962) thought that it might be by Giuseppe Porta; and some comparison may be made with *The Story of the Seven Kings* for the unexecuted fresco in the Vatican (Chatsworth 16); see also *Apollo*, October 1974 and Tietzes, no.1376; also J. Scholz collection, exhibition Fondazione Giorgio Cini 1957, cat.no.24. P. M. R. Pouncey (1989) suggested a Veronese mannerist (?del Moro), thinking of a distant connection with the painting in San Polo, Venice. J. Byam Shaw (1990) was the first to suggest a Genoese draughtsman, one close to Bernardo Castello, comparing Mary Newcome Schleier, *Genoese Baroque Drawings*, exhibition Binghampton/Worcester 1962, cat.15 and E. Bora, *I Disegni italiani, Lombardi e Genovesi del Seicento*, 1980, cat.102; cf. also *Erminia and the Shepherds*, Bernardo Castello's preliminary drawing in pen and wash for his ceiling fresco in the atrium of palazzo Centurione at Sampierdarena (*Le dessin à Genes du XVI au XVIII siècle*, Louvre 1985, cat.26), and

45

Popham and Wilde, 1949, cat. 205. But it is more likely in my view to have been drawn by Giovanni Battista Castello, il Bergamasco.

44 Giovanni Benedetto Castiglione, called il Grechetto

(Genoa 1609–1664 Mantua)

The Plague at Ashdod (I Samuel 5 : 1–7)

COLOUR PLATE III

Point of brush and brown ink, with brown wash, heightened with bodycolours of cream and grey blue, on cream paper, 412 × 283mm. Mounted in full for the 2nd Duke.

Chatsworth 621

Provenance: P. H. Lankrink (L.2090); William, 2nd Duke of Devonshire (L.718)

Literature: Ezia Gavazza, Federica Lamera, Lauro Magnani, *La Pittura in Liguria. Il Secondo Seicento*, Cassa di Risparmio di Genova e Imperia, Genoa, 1990, fig.500

Exhibitions: Manchester, 1961 (23, as 'Figures mourning before a tomb'); Philadelphia, 1971 (13, as 'The Plague at Ashdod'); Pittsburgh etc., 1987–8 (22)

Seraphim either end of the object raised in front of the triangular pediment identify it as the Ark of the Covenant. Castiglione, to whom this drawing is traditionally attributed, has adopted the hovering poses of cherubim from Poussin's 1630–1 *Plague at Ashdod*. He could have been attracted also during his second 1647–51 stay in Rome to Poussin's architectural landscapes of the late 1640s. He was then principally concerned to evolve as a draughtsman a fluent, richly baroque manner.

45 Giovanni Benedetto Castiglione, called il Grechetto

(Genoa 1609–1664 Mantua)

'Et in Arcadia Ego'

Pen and brown ink with brown wash over black chalk, 207 × 290mm. Mounted in full for the 2nd Duke.

Chatsworth 858

46

Literature: Reveley, p.55 (as Barocci); Schmarsow, 1914, IIIB, p.40; Olsen, 1955, p.221

Exhibitions: Manchester, 1961 (24, as Barocci)

The traditional attribution in the Devonshire collection to Barocci was accepted by Schmarsow, but rejected by Olsen. The current and convincing attribution of this fine drawing was made by A.E. Popham (1962). Cavedone entered the Carracci Academy in 1591, studying with Annibale until Annibale's departure for Rome in 1595; he continued in Bologna, becoming one of Lodovico's principal assistants. He visited Rome in 1609 and Venice in 1612–13. The painterly richness of Chatsworth 362 is in terms of his Venetian experience. The deaths of his wife and children by the plague of 1630 seem to have ended his artistic career prematurely. Little is known of his production during his remaining thirty years.

47 Giuseppe Cesari, called il cavaliere d'Arpino

(Rome 1568–1640 Rome)

A naked Youth astride a filled Sack, working Bellows

Red chalk, 226 × 180mm. Mounted in full for the 2nd Duke.

Inscribed lower right (almost effaced) in pen and brown ink *Cavalliere Giusepe*

Chatsworth 220

Provenance: N. A. Flinck (L.959); William, 2nd Duke of Devonshire (L.718), from 1723–4

Exhibitions: Washington etc., 1969–70 and London, V & A, 1973–4 (30)

Formerly attributed to Nicholas Poussin, but surely by Castiglione, it relates only in subject to Poussin's celebrated paintings in the Louvre and in the Devonshire collection (Chatsworth 501).

46 Giacomo Cavedone

(Sassuolo, Modena 1577–*c*.1660 Bologna)

St Francis in prayer (?receiving stigmata)

Black chalk and oiled charcoal, touched with white, on faded blue paper, squared for enlargement in black chalk, 291 × 195mm. Mounted in full for the 2nd Duke.

Chatsworth 362

Provenance: N. A. Flinck (L.959); William, 2nd Duke of Devonshire, from 1723–4

47

49

Provenance: N. A. Flinck (L.959); William, 2nd Duke of Devonshire (L.718) from 1723–4

The style of drawing in chalk from the nude is close to that of a *Male Nude, Resting*, the pose of which bears a remarkable resemblance to that of the Barberini Faun (Munich), in the Kunstmuseum, Basel, signed and dated by Arpino 1600 (see Tilman Falk, 'An unknown collection of drawings in the eighteenth century' in *Drawing. Masters & Methods: Raphael to Redon*, London, 1992, p.183, fig.6). Chatsworth 220 may be dated *c*.1600. A. E. Popham observed that it was engraved by Jan de Bisschop. The inspiration of the artificially heroic pose of this youth is an allusion to the ignudo designed by Michelangelo to sit to the right of the Cumaean Sibyl on the Sistine Chapel vault. Cesari's range of interest as a draughtsman extended from classical Antiquity to the High Renaissance.

48 Giuseppe Cesari, called il cavaliere d'Arpino

(Rome 1568–1640)

Andromeda chained to the Rock

COLOUR PLATE IV

Red chalk on cream paper, 270 × 197mm. Mounted in full for the 2nd Duke.

Chatsworth 218

Provenance: William, 2nd Duke of Devonshire (L.718)

Literature: Reveley, p.81; Campbell Dodgson, OMD, December 1926, pp.37–8, fig.42

Exhibitions: Leeds, 1868 (2717); Rome, 1973 (106); Pittsburgh etc., 1987–8 (23)

This delectable study, traditionally at Chatsworth by Cesari, is for his *Perseus rescuing Andromeda* (Kunsthistorisches Museum, Vienna), signed and dated 1602, and highly characteristic of the artist's mature draughtsmanship from the late 1590s. It may be compared to a study for Eve in an *Expulsion from Eden* in the British Museum (Pouncey and Gere, no.25), which uses the same style of drawing and seemingly the same model. A black chalk drawing of closely similar character and date for *Perseus flying to rescue the Princess* is Chatsworth 217, which was also exhibited at Rome, 1973 (105); but no Cesari painting known shows Perseus without his horse.

49 Giuseppe Bartolomeo Chiari

(Rome 1654–1727 Rome)

Bacchus visiting Ariadne on Naxos

Black chalk, 287 × 390mm. Mounted in full for the 2nd Duke.

Chatsworth 586

Provenance: William, 2nd Duke of Devonshire (L.718)

Literature: Kerber, 1968, p.79, no.37, fig.9 (still mistakenly titled *Bacchus and Venus*)

The subject was traditionally misinterpreted in the Devonshire collection as Bacchus and Venus. The youthful Bacchus holding a *thyrsis* approaches the seated nymph, who is attended by a nymph and by two satyrs offering grapes while another male figure (possibly a third satyr) pours from a wineskin into the bowl held up by a second, seated nymph. The ship on which Bacchus has arrived is partly visible behind the drapery which is spread in the tree behind Ariadne. The Poussinesque figure of the god, as F. Zeri observed, seems to have been modelled on Andrea Sacchi's *Apollo crowning Marc Antonio Pasqualini*. The subsidiary group on the right recalls Annibale Carracci's work for Cardinal Odoardo Farnese. The composition is connected with the *Metamorphoses* series which Chiari painted in 1708 for Cardinal Fabricio Spada Veralli. The painting which develops the composition of the drawing, is in the Galleria Spada in Rome (Kerber, fig.10). The art of Chiari, alive in Rome during the 2nd Duke's collecting period, suited his early eighteenth-century taste.

50 Antonio Allegri, called Correggio

(? Correggio 1489?–1534 Correggio)

Two Putti supporting a Medallion on which the cloudborne Christ is represented

Red chalk on pinkish surface, partly heightened with white, squared in red chalk, 191 × 140mm. Mounted in full on an early 18th-century mount

Chatsworth 763

Literature: Vasari Society (1905–35) 1920, no.18; A. Venturi, *Correggio*, Rome 1926, p.420; C. Ricci, *Correggio*, London/New York 1930, p.184 ('maniera di Cignani'); Popham, 1957, pp.58, 66, 158, no.45; A. G. Quintavalle, *Gli Affreschi del Correggio a*

50

S. Giovanni Evangelista a Parma, Milan 1962, p.32; C. Gould, 1976, *The paintings of Correggio*, London 1976, pp.80, 258

Exhibitions: London, Arts Council, 1949 (4); Washington, etc., 1962–3 and London, RA, 1969 (20); Tokyo, 1975 (31); Washington/Parma, 1984 (17)

A study for the decoration of the underside of the same arch as in two other drawings at Chatsworth (762 and 764). On the arch the Virgin does not appear. As D. Ekserdjian pointed out, Correggio exchanged from left to right the putti in painting the underside of the archway. The attribution and date of the fresco on the *sottarco* of the Del Bono chapel of S. Giovanni Evangelista in Parma is a matter of controversy, but the preparatory drawings are certainly by Correggio.

51 Antonio Allegri, called Correggio

(?Correggio 1489?–1534 Correggio)

Three Putti

Red chalk on cream paper, 188 × 109mm. Torn upper left. Mounted in full for the 2nd Duke.

Chatsworth 766

51

Provenance: William, 2nd Duke of Devonshire (L.718)

Literature: Passavant II, 1836, p.146 (as Parmigianino); Waagen, 1854, III, p.347 (as Correggio); Popham, 1971 (as Parmigianino)

Although traditionally in the Devonshire collection as Correggio, this tradition lapsed in the twentieth century. A.E.Popham (1962) suggested that it was drawn by Antonio Campi (Cremona 1524–87); and the standing putto more or less corresponds with one frescoed on a decorative strip in S. Sigismondo, Cremona (Aurelia Perotti, *I Campi*, Milan, *c*.1932, fig.31); such playful putti appear also in the altarpiece of the *Mystic Marriage and Saints*, in S. Pietro, Cremona (Venturi, ix.6, no.541). Popham later proposed Parmigianino (1971). Cirillo and Godi (1978) proposed Anselmi in relation to his (lost) decoration of the Duomo. Anselmi indeed used the draw-

ing, supplied by Parmigianino, of *Charity* (Chatsworth 785) at S. Giovanni Evangelista, Parma; and Parmigianino could have provided him also with drawings for the Duomo, to the decoration of which this drawing (as the Seilern sheet; Popham 1971, no.821) has no ascertainable connection. However, the character of so very lively and witty a drawing is truly Correggesque. N. Turner has argued plausibly that it is indeed by Correggio himself. A date close to Chatsworth 413 in the mid 1520s may be presumed.

52 Pietro Berettini, called Pietro da Cortona

(Cortona 1595–1669 Rome)

St Bibiana lies martyred before the Prefect Apronianus

Black chalk with red ink outlines in pen and reddish brown wash, 236 × 185mm. Mounted in full for the 2nd Duke.

Chatsworth 611

Provenance: William, 2nd Duke of Devonshire (L.718)

Literature: Merz, 1991, p.130, fig.164 (as a copy after a lost drawing by Pietro da Cortona)

Formerly classed in the Devonshire collection as *A Female Saint martyred in the presence of a Roman Emperor* by Ciro Ferri (1634–89), there should be no doubt that this is by

52

Pietro da Cortona

the young Pietro Cortona, a preparatory drawing at an advanced stage for one of his frescoes on the left wall of the nave in S. Bibiana. This commission was put in his way by marchese Marcello Sacchetti, his first important patron in Rome. A Florentine canon, Domenico Fedini, in his *Vita di Santa Bibiana Vergine e Martire*, Rome, November 1627, dedicated to Urban VIII, records that under the high altar were found the bodies of three martyrs, S. Dafrosa, wife of S. Flavian, and her daughters SS. Demetria and Bibiana; and he attributes, 'Tutta questa facciata è opera di Pietro Berettini da Cortona, ingegno osservantissimo dell'antichità'. In 1624 Bernini had been commissioned by the Pope to restore the ancient Christian basilica. Paintings were entrusted to Agostino Ciampelli, since 1623 principe of the Accademia di S. Luca, and to his junior Pietro da Cortona. Pietro was paid on account on 5 December 1624, and his work was finished by 1626. Chatsworth 611 may be presumed to be of 1624 or 1625.

This drawing, a brilliant original, shows a much more advanced stage in Pietro's thinking than his drawing for *S. Bibiana refusing to adore the idols* (G. Briganti, *Pietro da Cortona*, Florence, 1962, pp.168–9, figs.37–40). The creative energy and numerous *pentimenti* exclude the possibility of its being a copy from another drawing. The wall frescoed by Pietro shows many differences: Apronianus is sandalled; the lictor has no beard and does not wear an animal skin on his head; the pavement is squared; saints are haloed and St Demetria's left hand is confined to her side of the pillar; the left hand helmet is plumed; the lancer's hand lacks a tassel, and he no longer stares at St Bibiana; and so on.

The figure of St Bibiana is clearly inspired by Stefano Maderno's *St Susanna*. The variety of styles in preparatory drawings made by Pietro in his late twenties and early thirties is evident. Closest to this Chatsworth drawing is the Haarlem drawing for *St Bibiana and St Demetria before the Prefect of Rome* (*Master Drawings from the the Teyler Museum*, Pierpont Morgan Library, New York 1989, cat.35).

53 Pietro Berettini, called Pietro da Cortona

(Cortona 1595–1669 Rome)

Urban VIII carried down the Nave of St Peter's

Pen and brown ink with brown wash, heightened with white bodycolour on paper washed brown, 505 × 458mm. The sheet has been cut irregularly, both vertically and horizontally and repaired. Mounted in full on an early 18th-century mount.

Inscribed with pen, lower right (implausibly) *1636*; and, lower centre, in an early 18th-century script, *Pietro da Cortona*

Chatsworth 591

Provenance: N. A. Flinck (L.959); presumably 2nd Duke of Devonshire, from 1723–4

Literature: Walter Vitzthum, *Burl. Mag.*, 1963, p.215 (reviewing Giuliano Briganti, *Pietro da Cortona*, Florence, 1963); Walter Vitzthum, 1971, p.87, fig.1; Anne Sutherland Harris, MD, XXVII, 1989, pp.76–7; Merz, 1991, pp.158, 161–3, fig.301

Exhibitions: Leeds, 1868 (2723, as by Pietro da Cortona); Sheffield, 1966 (31, as by Pietro da Cortona); Pittsburgh, 1987–8 (25, as by Pietro da Cortona)

Always recognised in the Devonshire collection as by Pietro, this is his preparation for a painting of unknown date, inventoried in 1666 in the Galeria del Cierzo of the Madrid Alcazar, as *The Ceremony of the Presentation of the Chinea in Sign of the annual Tribute due from the Kingdom of Naples to the Pope* together with its pendant, *The Pope and the Curia receiving the Ambassador of Spain in a Saloon of the Vatican*. Both paintings, now lost, were seen by Antonio Ponz at the end of the eighteenth century in the Palaçio de Buen Retiro (A. E. Pérez Sanchez, *Pintura Italiana del Siglo XVII en España*, Madrid, 1965, p.266). Vitzthum, disregarding the date written on this Chatsworth drawing, dated it after 1626 but before 1631, since Pietro shows Bernini's *baldacchino* according to the project of 1624 and before the radical change in its superstructure. Dr Sutherland Harris takes the view that '1636' may have been inscribed by the same hand as 'Pietro da Cortona' and is not to be trusted as by Pietro himself.

The Chatsworth composition appears as a fully finished baroque parallel to Giulio Romano's composition (now divided between the Louvre and the Nationalmuseum, Stockholm) which Pietro may well have known intact: *The Emperor Constantine kneeling before Pope Sylvester I borne on the sede gestatoria* (Hartt, 1958, p.45, cat.nos.32, 33, fig.85).

54 Giovanni Antonio Creccolini

(Rome 1675–1736 Rome)

The Virgin in Glory appearing to a kneeling Saint

Pen and brown ink with brown wash, heightened with white bodycolour on paper washed brown, 285 × 195mm. Mounted in full for the 2nd Duke.

Inscribed in pen and brown ink, upper left, *36*

Chatsworth 654

Attributed in the Devonshire collection to Creccolini. The saint's bell and candles lie in the foreground. He could be St Dominic, St Hyacinth or St Stanislas Kostka. Creccolini was alive in Rome during the 2nd Duke's collecting period. Another drawing attributable to this follower of Maratti is Chatsworth 578, formerly attributed in the collection to Maratti himself.

54

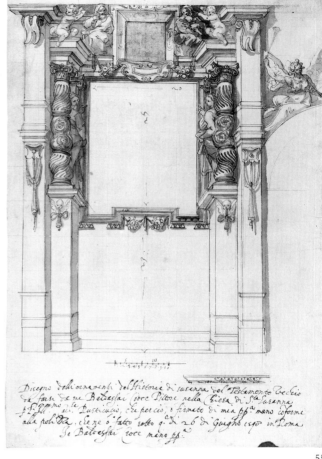

55

55 Baldassare Croce

(Bologna 1558–1628 Rome)

Design for an Enframement in S. Susanna, Rome, 1598

Pen and brown ink, with rose-red and blue watercolours, 358 × 245mm. Mounted in full on a 20th-century mount.

Inscribed in pen and brown ink by the draughtsman *Disegno delli ornamenti del Historie di susanna del Testamento Vechio/ da farsi da me Baldassar Croce Pittore nella Chiesa di Sta. Susanna/ per l'Illmo Cardle Rusticucio, che percio, o firmato di mia propria mano conforme/ alla polizza che ne o fatto sotto questo di 26 Giugno 1598 in Roma/ Io Baldessar Croce mano propria* and with measurements in *piedi*

Chatsworth 1063

Provenance: John Talman; Richard, 3rd Earl of Burlington; William, 4th Duke of Devonshire

In 1595 the basilica of S. Susanna was reduced to a single nave by Cardinal Girolamo Rusticucci, who commissioned from Croce the four large frescoes to be painted in imitation of tapestries with stories from the life of Santa Susanna and from Susanna in the Old Testament. Croce is best known for these murals. The Devonshire drawing is of special interest for the holograph inscription below the design for the feigned architectural enframements of one of the histories. The use of the word *polizza* implies that the drawing was in fulfilment of the contract.

56 Fra Diamante

(Terranova, Val d'Arno *c.*1430–after 1498)

Studies of male Figures, nude and draped, including two in monkish Garb; lower right a Composition of the Virgin and St Elizabeth with the Infants Christ and St John; upper left part of a Deposition from the Cross; lower centre, a portrait Head

Pen and brown ink with brown wash, 286 × 212mm. Mounted in full, presumably for the 2nd Duke.

Inscribed in pen and brown ink, once lower left, in a late 15th-century hand, *Leonardo diamante anz(iché) per pagam(ento)/pagolo di giov/per di PP*, and again lower right, in a 17th-century hand, *Leonardo Da Vinci*

Chatsworth 894

56

Provenance: presumably William, 2nd Duke of Devonshire

The attribution of this evidently late fifteenth-century Florentine sheet on the basis of the seventeenth-century inscription is surely incorrect. Some hopeful seventeenth-century owner presumably derived it from the easily legible 'Leonardo' of the original inscription (the remainder being then undeciphered) and from the character of the composition lower right, sophisticated by acquaintance with the style of Leonardo da Vinci. The second word of the original inscription is unmistakably 'Diamante', viz. Fra Diamante who entered the Carmelite Order young (the monkish figures appear to be Carmelites). A payment of 29 May 1452 names him as an assistant of Fra Filippo Lippi in painting the choir of the Cathedral of Prato; and the middle-aged man in a hat drawn low down on the sheet is Lippesque. Fra Diamante left Vallombrosa. By 1466 he had joined the Monastery of S. Margherita in Prato, transferring in 1472 to the Compagnia di S. Luca in Florence. There, we may presume, he became aware of the style associated with Leonardo da Vinci and Fra Bartolomeo in the 1480s. In 1493, after papal service in Rome, he became Prior of S. Pietro di Gallo in the Spengel of Volterra.

The significance of the quattrocento inscription, of which the reading of the third word was suggested to me by dottoressa Cinzia Sicca, appear to be that a certain Paolo (Pagolo) di Giovanni gave a receipt on behalf of the Fathers (or the Father Prior) for this sheet of drawings offered by the draughtsman instead of payment. The Prior may have been Diamante himself.

57 Carlo Dolci

(Florence 1616–1686 Florence)

The Artist's Shoemaker

Red and black chalks, 328 × 240mm; some staining. Mounted in full for Lord Somers.

Inscribed in pen and brown ink, *d.110*; and on the mount, in pen and black ink in the hand of J. Richardson the elder, *Carlino del Dolce*

Chatsworth 1053

Provenance: P. Sebastiano Resta; Lord Somers, after 1710, until at least 1716; his sale, London 1717; 2nd or 3rd Duke of Devonshire

Exhibitions: Manchester, 1961 (26); Washington etc., 1969–70 and London, V & A, 1973–4 (32)

Jonathan Richardson transcribed Resta's note for this drawing as follows: 'Ecco un altro modo di Carlin del Dolce questo Ritratto era del suo Calzolaio. fu discipolo del Vignoli. Carlino era nato nel 1616: mori nel 1686' (British Library, Lansdowne Ms.802, reference d.110).

58 Domenico Zampieri, called Domenichino

(Bologna 1581–1641 Naples)

Tavern Brawl at Night

Pen and brown ink with brown wash, 202 × 269mm. Repaired with a large inset along the right margin. Mounted in full for Lord Somers.

Inscribed in pen and brown ink *k. 117*

Chatsworth 508

Provenance: P. Sebastiano Resta; Giovanni Matteo Marchetti (died 1704), Bishop of Arezzo, from 1698; sold by his heir, the cavaliere Orazio Marchetti of Pistoia; Lord Somers, from 1710 until at least 1716; his sale in London 1717; William, 2nd Duke of Devonshire (L.718)

The caricature element is pungent of Domenichino's upbringing in Bologna. The attribution has been consistent since Resta. G. Warwick (1991) has made the suggestion to me that the repair could have been done by him: the work may as well have been done by J. Richardson the elder at the time of his mounting the drawing for Lord Somers.

57

58

59 Domenico Zampieri, called Domenichino

(Bologna 1581–1641 Naples)

Landscape with a Cascade, at the foot, two Men, one mounted

Pen and brown ink (considerably faded), 360 × 245mm (irregular left edge). Mounted in full for the 2nd Duke

Chatsworth 506

Provenance: William, 2nd Duke of Devonshire (L.718)

Literature: Catherine Johnston, 1970, p.90, fig.17

Exhibitions: Washington etc., 1962–3 and London, RA, 1969 (23); Tokyo, 1975 (55)

This superb drawing, one of Domenichino's finest studies of landscape, is a reminiscence of the falls at Terni.

60 Domenico Zampieri, called Domenichino

(Bologna 1581–1641 Naples)

The Calling of Peter and Andrew

Pen and brown ink with brown wash, 190 × 202mm. Mounted in full for Lord Somers by J.Richardson the elder.

Inscribed in pen and brown ink by Domenichino *p.10, 33 1/2, 36 1/2* (being measurements in palmi); and by J.Richardson the elder *e.91*

Chatsworth 502

Provenance: P. Sebastiano Resta (L.2992), as Domenichino; Giovanni Matteo Marchetti (died 1704), Bishop of Arezzo, from 1698; sold by his heir, the cavaliere Orazio Marchetti of Pistoia; Lord Somers (L.2981) from 1710 until 1716; his sale, London 1717; William, 2nd Duke of Devonshire (L.718)

Literature: Bellori, 1672, pp.325; Spear, 1982, p.251, pl.287

Exhibitions: Pittsburgh, 1987–8 (28)

Effectively, as Bellori states, the first model for the central scene on the conch of the apse vault which was to be

59

60

frescoed by Domenichino in the choir of S. Andrea della Valle, Rome. The landscape background is evidently developed from the style of Annibale Carracci. Other drawings for this *quadro riportato* are at Besançon, Florence, Rome, Venice and Windsor. The decoration of the choir was completed by 15 November 1628.

61 Pietro Faccini

(Bologna 1560/62–1602 Bologna)

Family Group in an Interior

Pen and brown ink with brown wash, 298 × 204mm. The gall in the ink has consumed the paper in four places (unfortunately including the child's eye). Mounted in full for the 2nd Duke.

Chatsworth 524

Provenance: N. A. Flinck (L.959); presumably William, 2nd Duke of Devonshire from 1723–4

61

61 Comparative illustration

A very Bolognese huddle, but not very close to Guercino to whom it was traditionally attributed in the Devonshire collection. The influence of Passarotti is evident both in the choice of subject and in the technique of draughtsmanship (cf. *Bolognese Drawings*, Uffizi, 1973 as Bartolommeo Passarotti, no.27, fig.18: *Due donne sedute e bambino* no.12227F; the old inscription on the verso reads 'del Passerotto vechio' and 'del Passerotto'). However the tilt and turn of the heads, and the deep shading of faces, as well as the peculiar hatching and washing, indicate Faccini working more broadly than in Chatsworth 817 in which we see the rear view of a Bolognese huntsman as St Christopher, with the Christ Child seated on his shoulder looking backwards (see comparative illustration).

Faccini began his artistic career relatively late. He was about twenty-eight when he joined the Carracci Academy: but his progress is said to have excited the jealousy of Annibale, and in the early 1590s he opened his own school in competition with his former teachers. However his developed, idiosyncratic style found few obvious followers.

62 Pietro Faccini

(Bologna 1560/62–1602 Bologna)

Christ appearing to Mary Magdalene outside the Sepulchre ('Noli me tangere')

COLOUR PLATE V

Pen and brown ink with brown wash, heightened with white bodycolour, squared in charcoal, 314 × 426mm. The top and bottom edges have been repaired, e.g. the toes of Christ's left foot. Mounted in full for the 2nd Duke.

Chatsworth 323

Provenance: Sir Peter Lely (L.2092); William, 2nd Duke of Devonshire (L.718)

Attributed at Chatsworth formerly to Correggio, this drawing was described by A.G.B. Russell as 'not like, or even in the manner of Correggio'; by A.E. Popham (1962) as 'more like Cavedone'; and by J.A. Gere convincingly as Faccini. The squaring indicates an intention to execute a painting on a larger scale, but none such is known to us.

63 Paolo Farinati

(Verona 1522–1606)

Jupiter and Faunus

Pen and dark brown ink with brown wash, heightened with white and rose bodycolours on paper washed brown, 325 × 257mm. Squared in black for enlargement; some abra-

63

sions in the foliage and clouds. Mounted in full for the 2nd Duke.

Inscribed in pen and brown ink, on the verso (visible through recto) *No.13*

Chatsworth 308

Provenance: William, 2nd Duke of Devonshire (L.718)

Exhibitions: London, New Gallery, 1894–5 (870, as Paolo Farinati)

Faunus, son of Picus, reigned in Italy *c.*1300 BC. He raised a temple in honour of Pan, on whose pipes he is shown playing to his flocks. He was worshipped after death as a country god, exciting the jealous wrath of Jupiter. The strength of chiaroscuro is impressive in Farinati's rendering of this mythology.

64 Ciro Ferri

(Rome 1634–1689 Rome)

Jacob and Rachel at the Well

Pen and brown and grey inks, over preliminaries in red chalk, with brown and red washes heightened with white bodycolour, 230 × 282mm. Squared in black chalk. Mounted in full for the 2nd Duke.

Chatsworth 610

64

Provenance: Unidentified ?English collector of the first half of the 18th century (L.1160); William, 2nd Duke of Devonshire (L.718)

Traditionally attributed in the Devonshire collection to Ciro Ferri, and perhaps a study for the painting in the Galleria Nazionale at Palazzo Corsini, Rome (no.934).

65 Lavinia Fontana

(Bologna 1552–1614 Rome)

The Virgin and Child enthroned, adored by Sts Louis of Toulouse and Francis of Assisi

Pen and brown ink, heightened with white bodycolour, on brown paper, 430 × 305 mm. Mounted in full for the 2nd Duke.

Chatsworth 124

Provenance: William, 2nd Duke of Devonshire (L.718)

The previous classification at Chatsworth of this elegant drawing as 'School of Giulio Romano' calls attention to the Giuliesque character of the bishop saint, of the tense contrapposto of the seated Virgin and of such details as the flying putti with the cloth and the straggly hair of the Child; and the *Virgin and Child enthroned between SS. Roch and Sebastian* (formerly Ellesmere Collection) comes to mind. Comparison with the *Annunciation*, a drawing which was likewise conceived *en camaieu*, but in yellow bodycolour on a brown ground (*ex*-Earl of Pembroke, in the Morin sale at De Vries, Amsterdam, 10–11 May 1927 (196)), and which is inscribed at the foot 'Livinia Fontana' by an old hand, manifests that both drawings were the work of one artist during approximately the same period.

Sotheby's (4 March, 1970, lot 63) sold as 'Munari' a

painting of the same composition as Chatsworth 124, only with different saints. On the Virgin's right is St Anthony of Padua instead of St Louis, from whom the child accepts a lily; and Santa Scolastica instead of St Francis at her right. There are other minor changes; the scalloping of the niche in the drawing is omitted, a tasselled and embroidered fringe is added to the *baldacchino*, and the lowest step of the Virgin's throne is serpentine shaped. Whether the painting in question or a replica was engraved in 1818 as no.6 in the Stafford House collection ('Pellegrino da Modena, *Madonna & Child & Saints*'), the invention appears to be by Lavinia Fontana, strongly influenced by the work of Giulio's final period in Mantua, and surely neither by Pellegrino Munari (1460–1523) nor by Cesare Munari degli Aretusi (*c.*1540–1612). I am grateful to Aidan Weston-Lewis for calling my attention to the Stafford House engraving.

65

66 Lavinia Fontana

(Bologna 1552–1614 Rome)

An Allegory of Music: Fame at the virginals, two young Lutenists seated, and a bearded Elder teaches a Boy to follow a Score

Pen and brown ink with brown wash, heightened with white bodycolour over preliminaries in black chalk, 302 × 282mm. Squared in black chalk. Mounted in full.

Chatsworth 206

Formerly attributed at Chatsworth to Frederico Zuccaro, this drawing was tentatively ascribed by P. M. R. Pouncey to Lavinia Fontana. It is in every way characteristic of her work in the last quarter of the sixteenth century; and the attribution is strengthened by stylistic comparison, particularly in the folding of draperies and the extensive work with white bodycolour, with Chatsworth 124 (here cat. no.65).

67 Giovanni Battista Franco, il Semolei

(Venice 1510–1561 Venice)

Woman carrying a Warming-pan filled with Charcoal

Pen and brown ink, 131 × 100mm. The upper corners are chamfered. Mounted in full for the 2nd Duke.

Chatsworth 753A

Provenance: William, 2nd Duke of Devonshire (L.718)

Unattributed in the Devonshire collection. 'Style of Battista Franco' was suggested by S. A. Strong. A. E. Popham (1962) changed the traditional attribution from Battista Franco to Palma Giovane; and so it appeared in the Courtauld Institute List of 1963. While it has no resemblance to any drawing known to be by Palma Giovane, it appears typical of Battista Franco; and in penwork it corresponds closely to the drawing engraved in Richard Cosway's collection of a *Seated Woman draped* (engraved in C. M. Metz, *Imitations of Drawings*, 1798).

68 Pier Leone Ghezzi

(Rome 1674–1755 Rome)

Recto: A Jesuit Procession caricatured, with a Crucifer, and five others following; an additional Man's Profile wearing Spectacles left; and right a vertical line of script

Verso: Four lines of script, visible, but undecipherable through the mounted paper

Pen and brown ink, 135 × 116mm. Mounted in full.

Chatsworth 642A

66

Provenance: presumably William, 2nd Duke of Devonshire

Exhibitions: Sheffield, 1966 (15)

Kept traditionally in the Devonshire collection as by Ghezzi, whom the 2nd Duke probably knew through Arthur Pond (see Chatsworth 639 and 640), this drawing shows the characteristic vertical or slightly slanting hatching and the profiles beloved of this draughtsman (in contrast to the more slanting hatching used by Agostino Carracci e.g. Kurz, 1955, cat.176, fig.22). In a *Collection of Prints in Imitation of Drawings*, London, 1778, with the text by Charles Rogers, there is reproduced opposite p.173 a *Self-portrait* of the young Ghezzi in which the draughtsman points to a drawing closely resembling the subject and composition of Chatsworth 642A, but providing the figures with a background of ecclesiastical buildings and landscape. The print was engraved by W.W.Ryland in 1762. The drawing used for it was in Rogers's own collection.

69 Domenico Bigordi, called Ghirlandaio

(Florence 1449–1494 Florence)

Recto: Head of a Woman, wearing a Coif

Verso: Whole-length of a Woman (drawn on top of a faint black chalk drawing of a youth's head turned three-quarters right)

Black chalk, the outlines of the recto pricked for transfer, 346 × 221mm.

Chatsworth 885

Literature: George W.Reid, 'Drawings found at Chatsworth', *Athenaeum*, 1883; Strong, 1902, XXII; Strong, 1905, p.111; Berenson, 1938 (866, fig.283); J.A.Gere, *Burl. Mag.* XCI, 1949, p.169; Vasari Society 2nd Series, VI. 5; Ames-Lewis, 1981, p.159, fig.160 (recto); Knab, Mitsch, Oberhuber, 1983, p.40, pl.48 (recto), always as Domenico Ghirlandaio

Exhibitions: London, RA, 1930 (37); London, Arts Council, 1949 (5); London, RA, 1953 (23); Manchester, 1961 (29); Washington etc., 1962–3 and London, RA, 1969 (24); Tokyo, 1975 (12); Richmond etc., Va., 1979–80 and London, RA, 1980–1 (53); Nottingham/London, 1983 (71); Florence, Uffizi, 1992 (4.6, and under 4.7)

The *recto* is a study for the head of a woman standing by the staircase at left in the fresco of *The Birth of the Virgin* in the Tornabuoni Chapel of S.Maria Novella, Florence. This is the most important cartoon to survive from late quattrocento Florence. On the *verso* is a study for a spectator in the same fresco for Giovanni Tornabuoni (whose sister Lucrezia was the mother of Lorenzo de' Medici, il Magnifico). As B.Berenson noted, Ghirlandaio here uses chalk 'almost as a pen'. The commission for the extensive series of frescoes in this church was given in 1485 to

67

68

69 recto

69 verso

Domenico and Davide Ghirlandaio, and completed in 1490.

As Strong pointed out, the pricking and pouncing is evidence that, *pace* Crowe and Cavalcaselle (*History of Painting in Italy*, ii, p.479), Ghirlandaio did not 'confine himself to the method of tracing over the cartoon with a stylus'. He also called attention to the tradition that Chatsworth 885 is 'a preliminary sketch for the portrait of Ginevra de'Benci, which the master introduced into the fresco of the *Salutation of the Virgin* in the same series'.

70 Giulio Pippi, called Giulio Romano

(Rome 1499–1546 Mantua)

Head of Pope Leo X

Black chalk, elaborately heightened with white chalk, 337 × 268mm. The outlines are indented, the upper part is irregularly torn and cut and backed on another rectangular sheet, 480 × 299mm. Mounted in full on an early 18th-century mount.

Inscribed in pen and brown ink by J.Richardson the elder *Ritratto de Leon oxo*. On the mount *Michelangelo Buonaroti*; and on the backing sheet *KK39*

Provenance; J.Richardson the elder; William, 2nd Duke of Devonshire (L.718)

Chatsworth 38

Literature: Passavant, 1836, ii, p.145 ; Strong, 1902 (40); O.Fischel, 1935, pp.484–6; Berenson, 1938, 2477 (as Raphael); J.Hess, GBA, XXXII (1947), p.84 (29); J.A.Gere, *Burl. Mag.*, XCI, 1949, pp.169–73; Hartt, 1958, I, pp.51, 289 (39) (as Giulio); J.Shearman, 1972, p.61 and no.88 on p.60 (as Raphael); Oberhuber-Fischel, 1972, 482 (as Giulio); Knab, Mitsch, Oberhuber 1983, p.142, fig.148; Joannides, 1983, p.27 and no.455; D.Rosand, 'Raphael drawings revisited', MD, XXVI, 1988, pp.359–360, fig.2 (as Raphael?); K.Oberhuber et al., *Giulio Romano*, Milan, 1989, p.258 (as Giulio; entry by Sylvia Ferino)

Exhibitions: London, Arts Council, 1949 (6); Washington etc., 1962–3 and London, RA, 1969 (69, as attributed to Sebastiano del Piombo); London, BM, 1983–4 (183); New York, 1987 (42, as Raphael?); Mantua-Vienna, 1989–90, p.258 (as Giulio)

Richardson's attribution is unacceptable, and was thus remarked by Passavant. The inscription identifies the sitter who died in 1521. This over-life-size fragment of a cartoon was used for Pope Clement I, painted in oils in the Sala di Costantino of the Vatican, where, after the death of Raphael, Sebastiano, with the backing of Michelangelo, had sought to obtain the commission for decorating the walls. Wickhoff (1899) attributed Chatsworth 38 to Sebastiano del Piombo, although Vasari had named Giulio Romano as the painter of the series of the Popes depicted in this room. No other portrait drawing by Giulio is of comparable potency. However, its style and strained expression have not been matched among the known drawings of Raphael, although J.Shearman suggested that it was originally intended for the colossal statue of Leo X commissioned by the Conservatori (now in S.Maria in Aracoeli), and called it 'the most intensely realised (and the last) of all Raphael's portraits of Leo'. It is of almost grotesque strength of surface articulation, externalised rather than filled with inner life: by Giulio, not Raphael.

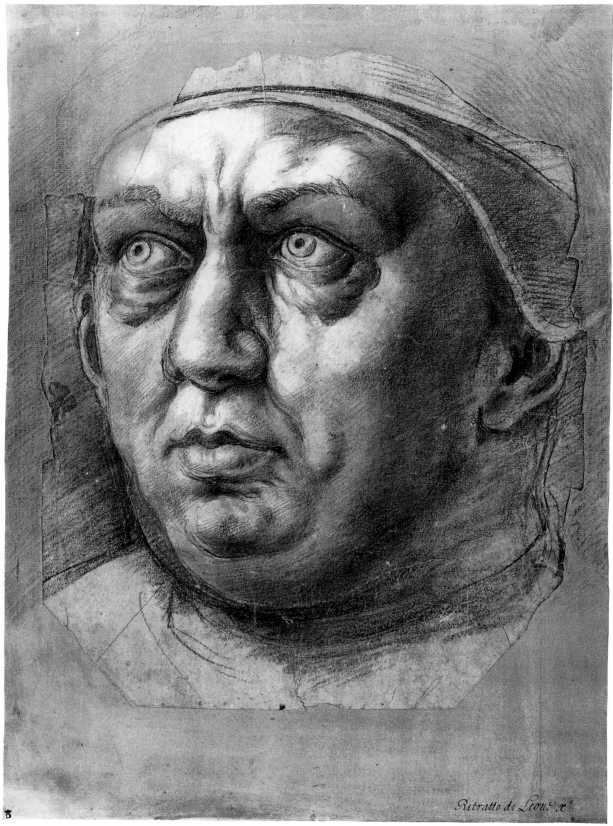

Ritratto di Leon.x°

71

71 Giulio Pippi, called Giulio Romano

(Rome 1499–1546 Mantua)

The Holy Family and St Anne with the Child about to be taught to walk

Pen and brush with brown ink over preliminaries in black chalk, 206 × 288mm. The corners are chamfered. Mounted in full for the 2nd Duke.

Chatsworth 90

Provenance: Sir Peter Lely (L.2092 twice); William, 2nd Duke of Devonshire (L.718)

Literature: Ruland, 1876, p.100, x,1; Fischel, 1898, no.408 (as a copy after Catena's painting of the subject in Dresden); Giles Robertson, *Vincenzo Catena*, Edinburgh, 1954, p.57f, pl.26a (as 'studio of Raphael'); P. Joannides, *Paragone*, 425, 1985, p.44 n.32; K. Oberhuber et al., *Giulio Romano*, Milan, 1989, p.252

Exhibitions: London, RA, 1953 (67); Washington etc., 1962–3 and London, RA, 1969 (63, as 'school of Raphael'); Mantua-Vienna, 1989–90, p.252

Traditionally in the Devonshire collection as Raphael. Of the possible authors of this highly Raphaelesque drawing named by A. E. Popham, including Perino del Vaga and G. F. Penni, Giulio Romano *c*.1517–18 seems the most convincing. S. A. Strong, *Wilton House Drawings*, London, 1900, 11 (19) illustrated a copy in the Pembroke collection as 'Roman School'. Vincenzo Catena repeated this group in a painting (now at Dresden: Robertson, p.27), which led Fischel to dismiss Chatsworth 90 as a copy after this Venetian contemporary of Raphael. Later, in a letter to G. Robertson, he stated that it was a product of Raphael's studio not earlier than 1518.

The drawing was engraved by Elisha Kirkall (1682?-1742?) in his combination of chiaroscuro woodblock and mezzotint, 1724 (as Raphael) with a dedication, 'E Collectione Nobilissimi Ducis Devoniae' (Le Blanc 6). I owe the reference to the Kirkall print to T. P. P. Clifford.

72

73

72 Giulio Pippi, called Giulio Romano

(Rome 1499–1546 Mantua)

The musical Contest between Apollo and Pan

Pen and brown ink with brown wash, 205 × 207mm. The corners are chamfered. Mounted in full for the 2nd Duke.

Chatsworth 86

Provenance: N. A. Flinck (L.959); William, 2nd Duke of Devonshire (L.718), from 1723–4

Literature: M.S. in the exhibition catalogue 'de verzameling van mr. Carel Vosman (1826–1888)', Rijksmuseum, Amsterdam, 1989, p.79 (under no.33)

Exhibitions: Amsterdam, 'het Rembrandthuis', 1992–3 (57)

An excellent example of Giulio's draughtsmanship in Mantua, which was copied, presumably in Amsterdam and perhaps already in the collection of N. A. Flinck (1646–1723), by Jan de Bisschop (1628–1671). Of this copy a print appeared in the posthumous publication of Bisschop's *Paradigmata*.

73 Giulio Pippi, called Giulio Romano

(Rome 1499–1546)

The Vestal Tuccia with the Sieve

Pen and brown ink with brown wash on greenish-brown (faded blue) paper, heightened with white bodycolour and squared in black chalk, 208 × 356mm. Mounted in full for the 2nd Duke.

Chatsworth 110

Provenance: N. A. Flinck (L.959); William, 2nd Duke of Devonshire (L.718)

Literature: Hartt, 1958, VI, 14 (no.229, fig.366); K. Oberhuber et al., *Giulio Romano*, Milan, 1989, p.404

Exhibitions: Leeds, 1868 (no.2657, as Giulio Romano); Mantua-Vienna, 1989–90, p.404 (as Giulio Romano)

A modello for the Camera dei Cesari ceiling fresco (the preliminary pen sketch is listed by Hartt as in the Alte Pinakothek, Munich). The fresco's precarious state allows only hypothetical interpretation of its precise meaning: but elements common to this drawing and to the two others discussed by Hartt, together involving winds, thunder, pouring of liquid and sieving of grain, suggest the elements of earth, air, fire and water. Bette Talvacchia (1989) called attention to the broken chain fastened to the upper arm of the wind at the right, implying the freeing of a celestial force.

74 Giulio Pippi, called Giulio Romano

(Rome 1499–1546 Mantua)

Design for a sweetmeat Box

Pen and brown ink with brown wash, 176 × 308mm.

Inscribed in pen and brown ink by the artist *Questo feci alo Sr. do(n) ferrante gonzaga*

Chatsworth 117

Provenance: William, 2nd Duke of Devonshire (L.718)

Literature: Hartt, 1958, vol.ii, III.13, fig.139; John Pope-Hennessy, *Cellini*, London, 1985, p.27, fig.4

Exhibitions: London, V & A, 1981 (189)

A metalwork fancy for the table developed from a sarcophagus with a strigilated front, lion masks and lion monopodia. As the inscription indicates, this box was made for Ferrante Gonzaga (1507–57), brother of Duke Federico. In 1531, when Don Ferrante was made a Knight of the Golden Fleece, Giulio designed his collar, *pace* Hartt, who dates the box 1524–6 (when the teenager Ferrante was with Castiglione at the Spanish Court). The first likely time that he might have ordered such an object was after his marriage in 1530 to Isabella of Capua, soon after which he could afford to buy the Principality of Guastalla with her dowry, as J. T. Martineau points out in her 1981 catalogue entry. The description of silver designs that Ferrante ordered from Giulio in the 1540s does not coincide with this box (P. Pungileone, *Lettere Sopra Marcello Donati*, Parma 1818, pp.53–8). The putto skirted with acanthus leaves and holding a water pitcher presumably refers to Ferrante's astrological sign: born on 28 January, he was an Aquarian. The inspiration for this finial derives from relief panels on the bases of antique Roman candelabra such as appear on red chalk drawings by Hendrik Goltzius in the Teylersmuseum, Haarlem. (Peter Fuhring, 'Jacob Matham's Verscheijden cierage' in *Simiolus*, 21, 1992, p.64, fig.11, discusses two of these drawings in another connection).

75 Giovanni Francesco Barbieri, called il Guercino

(Cento 1591–1666 Bologna)

The Riposo

Pen and black ink with brown wash, 200 × 270mm. Mounted in full for the 2nd Duke.

Chatsworth 518

Provenance: Sir Peter Lely (L.2092); William, 2nd Duke of Devonshire (L.718)

The Holy Family and their pack mule are seen behind an ashlar wall – evidently a surface for the play of light. As

74

75

often with Guercino, there is no painting known to connect with this composition, which appears to have been drawn shortly after he returned to Bologna from Rome.

76 Giovanni Francesco Barbieri, called il Guercino

(Cento 1591–1666 Bologna)

The 'Madonna del Rosario', with Saints Dominic and Catherine of Siena

COLOUR PLATE VI

Red chalk, 334 × 215mm. Fully mounted for the 2nd Duke.

Chatsworth 515

Provenance: Casa Gennari; William, 2nd Duke of Devonshire (L.718)

Literature: Bologna (Disegni), 1968, under no.145 (as 'un disegno di un seguace, eseguito nella bottega del maestro'); Luigi Salerno, *I Dipinti del Guercino*, Rome, 1988, under no.202; Mahon and Turner, 1989, pp.57–8 under cat.98 (Guercino) and p.188 under cat.643

Exhibitions: Pittsburgh, etc., 1987–8 (41); London, BM, 1991 (129); Bologna, 1991 (110)

A showpiece modello for Guercino's altarpiece, executed in 1641–3 for S.Marco at Osimo (the pala reproduced by Pietro Zampetti, *Note sparse sul '600*, 1907, fig.38). Guercino's *libro dei conti* records a payment on account for it on 10 August 1641 and a settlement on 27 April 1643: the drawing is therefore presumably of 1641. A pen study for the composition at an earlier stage was in the 1991 London exhibition, cat.128. Sir Denis Mahon has come to share my view of Guercino's authorship of Chatsworth 515, a rarity in Guercino's known oeuvre as a model brought to such exquisite finish. In the altarpiece the two saints occur in more or less corresponding positions, but the Virgin and Child are seated left, looking right. A facsimile copy is in the British Museum, 1874–8–8–109, drawn by Hugh Howard, a talented draughtsman who enjoyed the patronage of the 2nd Duke (London, 1991, Appendix 109).

77 Giovanni Francesco Barbieri, called il Guercino

(Cento 1591–1666 Bologna)

A River in Flood, and Peasants with Axes and other Tools

Pen and brown ink, over preliminaries in black chalk (visible chiefly in the left background and clouds), 263 × 424mm. Mounted in full for the 2nd Duke.

Chatsworth 544

Provenance: Casa Gennari; sold by Benedetto Gennari in London to William Cavendish, later 1st Duke of Devonshire, before 1689

Literature: Renato Roli, *G.F.Barbieri, Guercino*, Milan, 1972, pl.52; Bagni, 1985, no.116 (reviewed by Nicholas Penny, *Burl.Mag.* CXXIX, 1987, pp.542–4); G.Bora, *I disegni della Collezione Morelli*, Bergamo, 1988, under no.58; Mahon and Turner, 1989, under no.246

Exhibitions: Washington, etc., 1962–3 and London, RA, 1969 (30); Bologna, 1968 (196); Tokyo, 1975 (59); London, BM, 1991 (166)

An early drawing, before Guercino's visit to Rome, showing his excellence in combining genre with landscape. The river Reno, which flows near Cento, on several occasions in Guercino's life flooded its banks. The black chalk (left background) is included in an engraving (in reverse) after the drawing by J.Pesne, which is one of a set of fourteen executed in Paris for Guercino's heirs. The original drawings were then taken by Benedetto Gennari for sale in England.

78 Giovanni Francesco Barbieri, called il Guercino

(Cento 1591–1666 Bologna)

Landscape with a broken Column, a Castello and numerous Figures right

Pen and brown ink, 250 × 415mm. Mounted in full for the 2nd Duke.

Chatsworth 533

Provenance: Casa Gennari; sold by Benedetto Gennari to William Cavendish, later 1st Duke of Devonshire before 1689

Literature: Bagni, 1985, no.121; Mahon and Turner, 1989, under cat.246

Exhibitions: Washington, etc., 1962–3 and London, RA, 1969 (29); Bologna, 1968 (208); Tokyo, 1975 (60); London, BM, 1991 (167)

Engraved by J.Pesne (no.12, in reverse).

79 Leonardo da Vinci

(Vinci 1452–1519 Amboise)

Leda and the Swan

Pen and brown ink with brown wash over black chalk, 160 × 137mm. Mounted in full on an early 18th-century mount.

Inscribed in pen and brown ink, lower right, in an old (?18th-century) hand, *Leonardo da Vinci*

Chatsworth 717

Literature: Strong, 1902 (35); Berenson, 1938 (1013A); Clark, 1959, pp.116–17; Clark and Pedretti, 1968, p.33 (under Windsor no.12337).

77

78

Exhibitions: Milan, 1939 (78); London, Arts Council, 1949 (7); London, RA, 1952 (135); Washington, etc., 1962–3 and London, RA, 1969 (32); Richmond, Va., 1979–80 (54); Nottingham/London, 1983 (45); Cambridge, 1988 (1); London, Hayward Gallery, 1989 (75)

Called Sodoma on the Chatsworth mount following Morelli's attribution, but clearly, as Oscar Fischel (1928) was the first to see, a study by Leonardo about 1503/4, one of his earliest designs for a composition of Leda the Aetolian princess and Jupiter in the guise of a swan with Castor and Pollux and Helen and Clytemnestra being hatched from the eggs resulting from this union. K. Clark (op.cit.) discussed the development of the idea in very sim-

ilar studies in the Koenigs Collection in the Museum Boymans-van Beuningen (Berenson, 1020A) and at Windsor, in which Leda also kneels. But in the painting she was represented upright (Leningrad, Hermitage). The attitude of Leda, as F. Ames-Lewis and J. Wright pointed out in their catalogue (1983) is inspired by antique sculpture, for example the Crouching Venus of Doidalsas and the Venus Anadyomene. The vegetation in which her babes are hatched derives directly from Leonardo's studies of nature.

In 1625, when Cassiano dal Pozzo saw Leonardo's picture, the panel was already in a bad state. The most Leonardesque copy is by Cesare da Sesto at Wilton House.

79

80(a)   80(b)   80(c)   80(d)

80 Leonardo da Vinci

(Vinci 1452–1519 Amboise)

Four small drawings of grotesque Heads

Pen and brown ink, respectively 49 × 33mm; 50 × 35mm; 50 × 40mm; 49 × 41mm. All mounted in full for the 2nd Duke.

Chatsworth 819A–D

Provenance: Thomas Howard, 2nd Earl of Arundel; his daughter-in-law, Viscountess Stafford?; N. A. Flinck (L.949 only on Chatsworth 824B, but presumably all from this same collection); presumably William, 2nd Duke of Devonshire

Literature: Strong, 1905, p.114; Comm. Vinc., fasc.v, pls.212–16; Clark & Pedretti, 1968, I, p.59 (under Windsor no.12398)

Clark and Pedretti suggest a date for the whole series of grotesques of 1505–10, following Heydenreich. Clark writes of 'an unattractive spontaneity as in some of the grotesques, especially those in the Devonshire Collection at Chatsworth'; and (p.xliv), 'Unlike the profiles which Leonardo drew throughout his life, the grotesques seem almost all to date from the Sforza period ... to his years of full employment as a Court artist, and the minute finish of many of the drawings supports the supposition that they were done in response to some craze or fashion, similar to that for riddles and trials of wit which also occupied him at that time. On the other hand there is no doubt that they grew out of the interest in bizarre heads and freaks which was part of Leonardo's character'.

81 Piro Ligorio

(Naples *c*.1500–1583 Ferrara)

Holy Family with the Child St John the Baptist

Pen and brown ink with brown wash, heightened with white bodycolour, on blue paper, 304 × 270mm. A tear upper left has removed part of the Greek inscription. Mounted in full for the 2nd Duke.

Inscribed with pen and brown ink on the wall *ΟΣ ΑΙ|ΠΟΙΕΙ* and signed on the throne, *ΠΥΡΡΟΣ|ΛΙΓΟΡΙΟΣ*

Chatsworth 127

Provenance: William, 2nd Duke of Devonshire (L.718)

Literature: F. Antal, AB, 1948, pp.97ff.; Gere, 1971, pl.xiii; Gere and Pouncey, 1983, pp.97–8 (under no.155) and p.115, under no.198

The traditional attribution of this signed drawing is correct, although F. Antal, in drawing attention to the pseudo-antique flavour of the composition, regarded it as a copy. A. E. Popham noted a copy on the recto of a sheet of studies by Girolamo da Carpi in the British Museum; see Gere and Pouncey, 1983, 155 *recto* and pl.144. Popham also recognized (1944) on a sheet of studies in the British

81

82

Museum of a *Virgin and Child* by Piro (not, as hitherto had been thought, by Peruzzi) a study, in the centre of the upper register, of the *Child offering Flowers to the Baptist* (Gere and & Pouncey, 1983, no.198, pl.190), which is prepared directly for the Chatsworth drawing.

82 Piro Ligorio

(Naples *c.*1500–1583 Ferrara)

The young St John the Baptist taking leave of his Parents

Pen and brown ink with brown wash, with fine white heightening in bodycolour, on paper washed brown, 399 × 511mm. The upper corners are chamfered (otherwise apparently complete). Mounted in full for the 2nd Duke.

Chatsworth 46

Provenance: N.F. Haym (L.1972); Sir Peter Lely (L.2092); William, 2nd Duke of Devonshire (L.718)

Literature: Gere, 1981, pp.246–7, n.40, pl.24; David Jaffé, 'Daniele da Volterra and his followers', *Burl.Mag.*, CXXVIII, 1986, p.184, n.8

A. E. Popham (1962) recognised Piro's authorship of this drawing, formerly attributed to Baldassare Peruzzi. Gere suggested a possible connection with the scenes from the life of the Baptist frescoed in the Oratory of S. Giovanni Decollato in Rome. In 1938 Francesco Salviati's *Visitation* and Jacopino del Conte's *Baptist Preaching* were there complete. A space was unfilled in 1540. Piro was in Rome from about 1534. The space was filled in 1551 by a second Salviati painting, *The Birth of the Baptist*. In any case this Chatsworth drawing is singular in Piro's oeuvre as his only known modello for an ecclesiastical commission. Its proportions, higher and narrower than the painted *Birth*, are, as Gere points out, close to the *Annunciation to Zacharias*, the counterpart at the other extreme of the same side wall of the Oratory. The claim of Chatsworth 46 to

connect with this Florentine place is strengthened, as D. Jaffé points out (loc.cit.), by the antiquarian inclusion of the rearing horse on a column, if that be taken as a reference to the equestrian statue on the Arno, the so-called Mars, which was there until the early fourteenth century.

83 Jacopo Ligozzi

(Verona 1547–1627 Florence)

The Entombment

Pen and brown ink with brown wash, heightened with pink and white bodycolours on blue paper, 505 × 362mm. Mounted in full for the 2nd Duke.

Chatsworth 198

Provenance: William, 2nd Duke of Devonshire (L.718)

The traditional and unlikely attribution in the Devonshire collection was to Taddeo Zuccaro. A.E. Popham (1962), stating that it was not drawn by either of the Zuccari, classed it simply as 'North Italian'. The claustrophobic treatment of the scene, emphasized by the strength of chiaroscuro and the attention to still life, as well as the intense gloom of expression (all suited to the theme) ally it to the Frits Lugt drawing of *Isaac blessing Jacob* (Byam Shaw, 1983, no.36: 'a very handsome example of Ligozzi's elaborate technique, probably of the early part of the artist's Florentine period'). The curiously inert folds, arranged ornamentally, and the oversize, flattened hands and feet are characteristics which the Chatsworth drawing exaggerates. The background figures in this reflect Ligozzi's Veronese training; and it is likely to have been drawn well before Ligozzi moved to Florence in 1578. The closest parallel however in style, technique and presumably date is with *The Presentation of the Infant Christ in the Temple* from the Gelosi, Hampden and Esdaile collections, sold Sotheby's, London, 23 March 1971, lot 48. The treatment of hair, clothing, still life, and even the display of Christ with bent knees and prominent toes, all crowded in a claustrophobic space show remarkable similarities. N. Turner (1989) however regards the Chatsworth drawing as nearer in technique to Camillo Procaccini.

84

84 Jacopo Ligozzi

(Verona 1547–1627 Florence)

The Martyrdom of St Paul, after Taddeo Zuccaro

Pen and brown ink with brown wash, heightened with white bodycolour on faded blue paper, 404 × 288mm. The top is curved, and the spandrels have been pieced out. Mounted in full for the 2nd Duke.

Chatsworth 201

Provenance: N. A. Flinck (L.959); William, 2nd Duke of Devonshire (L.718), from 1723–4

Literature: de Grazia, 1991, D5, fig.94 (as Bertoia, c.1569)

Traditionally in the Devonshire collection as Federico Zuccaro, this is a copy of the fresco of c.1558–66 by Taddeo on the vault of the Frangipane Chapel of S. Marcello al Corso, Rome (Gere, 1969, pl.83). A. E. Popham (1962) had noted a study of the executioner in the British Museum, and a feeble copy of the whole composition. An original drawing by Taddeo is in the Lehman Collection at the Metropolitan Museum, New York (Gere, 1969, no.147, pl.82). Federico finished his brother's work in the chapel.

85

The technique of chiaroscuro, using fine pen silhouettes in combination with wash and fine strokes of white bodycolour, the morphology of hands with spiky fingers and sharpened noses, the fold style, and the taste for a foreground overcrowded with figures, point to Ligozzi. De Grazia has found the use of white heightening to emphasize the drama of light and shade reminiscent of Bertoia's drawings for the Sala d'Ercole of 1569 in Caprarola (op.cit. figs.80, 83). One of these in the Louvre drawing comes fairly close in technique but not in style of folds or morphology of limbs.

85 Jacopo Ligozzi

(Verona 1547–1627 Florence)

Frieze of Cupids, Satyrs and Monsters with acanthus Tendrils

Pen and brown ink with brown wash, heightened with white bodycolour on faded blue paper (on three pieces conjoined, with a vertical fold), 150 × 531mm. The right corners are missing. Mounted in full for the 2nd Duke.

Inscribed in pen and brown ink (not in the Resta/Somers hand) *h 463*.

Chatsworth 147

Provenance: Sir Peter Lely (L.2092); presumably 1st or 2nd Duke of Devonshire

The traditional attribution in the Devonshire collection was to Polidoro da Caravaggio. At Chatsworth it was called 'Italian early 16th century' by A. E. Popham (1962), who regarded it as an interesting, important decorative drawing earlier than Polidoro. T. P. P. Clifford suggested Baldasarre Peruzzi, by comparison with a drawing in the Whitworth Art Gallery, Manchester (D/240/1960; there as Perino del Vaga). P. M. R. Pouncey suggested Giulio Campi. However in tonality, technique and morphology it appears to be by the same hand as *The Entombment* (Chatsworth 198), attributed here to Ligozzi, and the case for a portable altar at Oberlin College, Ohio, already

attributed to Ligozzi. The latter may especially be compared in the formal decoration by acanthus and the forms of the putti heads. Both the Oberlin and the Chatsworth designs simulate a tense, refined metallic grille.

86 Filippino Lippi

(Prato 1457–1504 Florence)

Head of an elderly Man, wearing a Cap

Metalpoint on bluish grey prepared paper, heightened with white bodycolour, 190 × 140mm (cut to an oval). Fully mounted for the 2nd Duke.

Chatsworth 705

Provenance: Giorgio Vasari; N. A. Flinck (L.959); presumably William, 2nd Duke of Devonshire, from 1723–4

Literature: Vasari, 1568, III, 57 ('Il ritratto di Mino è nel nostro libro de'disegni non so di cui mano, perchè a me fu dato con alcuni disegni fatti col piombo dallo stesso Mino, che sono assai belli'); Morelli, I, 1892, p.90 (as portrait of Mino da Fiesole by Lorenzo di Credi); Strong, 1902 (XXIX, as Lorenzo di Credi); O. Kurz, OMD, V, 1937, p.12; Berenson, 1938 (1274B); B. Berenson, *Disegni dei Pittori fiorentini*, (3rd ed.), Milan, 1961, II, p.249, no.1274B; L. Ragghianti-Collobi, *Il Libro de' Disegni del Vasari*, Florence, 1974, pp.69, 86

Exhibitions: London, RA, 1930 (58; cf. A. E. Popham, *Italian Drawings exhibited at the Royal Academy*, 1930, as Lorenzo di Credi, pl. XLVII); Paris, 1935 (585); London, Arts Council, 1949 (9); Washington, etc., 1962–3 and London, RA, 1969 (35); Nottingham/London, 1983 (66); Florence, Uffizi, 1992 (4.10)

Vasari used this drawing in the second edition of his *Vite* for the woodcut portrait of the sculptor Mino da Fiesole (1429–1484). Berenson, in his *Drawings of the Florentine Painters* (2nd edn.) corrected to Filippino his previous attribution to Lorenzo di Credi, which he had taken over from Morelli. Morelli had already changed the traditional attribution to Daniele da Volterra. It is surprising that Vasari himself did not recognise the hand of Filippino. The portrait belongs to the time of fresco additions to the Cappella Brancacci (1484–5).

86

The original mounting by Vasari of Chatsworth 705, now alas shorn, may well have been of elegantly figural character such as we find in the mounting of another metalpoint portrait drawing which he also shaped as an oval, Domenico Ghirlandaio's study of the *Old Man with a deformed Nose* (Stockholm, Nationalmuseum, inv.1863/1) which Domenico used for his famous double portrait in the Louvre of the *Old Man with the young Boy*.

87 Workshop of Filippino Lippi

(Prato 1457–1504 Florence)

Recto: Two drawings: (a) *Nude Man seated, and* (b) *Two male Nudes*

Silver point, heightened with white bodycolour, on mauve prepared paper. 199 × 285mm and 198 × 283mm respectively. At the head is a woodcut of Alesso Baldovinetti from (Vasari's *Vite*).

Verso: (c) *Architectural frame* (from which the drawing has been removed) (*'Antonello da Messina Pitt.'?*)

198 × 283mm.

Chatsworth 961A–C

ALESSO BALDOVINETTO
PITTORE FIOR.

87

88

Provenance: Giorgio Vasari; Niccolò Gaddi (d.1591); Thomas, 2nd Earl of Arundel; presumably William, 2nd Duke of Devonshire

Literature: Strong, 1902 (12, as Signorelli); Kurz, 1937, p.11; Berenson, 1938, no.772G (as Davide Ghirlandaio); Ragghianti and Delli Regoli, 1975, under Gruppo B, pp.58, 87, 103, 106, 113 (as by Filippino Lippi or a collaborator), nos.86, 87, figs.120, 119

Exhibitions: London, RA, 1930 (50); Arezzo, 1981/2 (VIII.4, p.248, fig.190); Washington, etc., 1969/70 and London, V&A, 1973 (34)

Attributed in the Devonshire collection to Luca Signorelli: although on Vasari's mount, and for him by 'Alesso Baldovinetto pittore Fior'. For B. Berenson (772G; incorrectly as *recto* and *verso*), Davide Ghirlandaio; and surely by the same hand as most of his grouping of drawings. Popham and Pouncey, 1950, were to include several as of the workshop of Filippino. The attribution of Chatsworth 961 to Baldovinetti, as Ragghianti and Delli Regoli point out, was traditionally given also to their no.36, fig.31, and to comparable drawings in Liverpool, the Hornby Library, and in the Albertina, Vienna. They compare 961A to Uffizi 304E for analogous standardization of the bodily parts, and suggest that the left study on 961B might be for a *Preaching of the Baptist*. They make no particular suggestion of intention for the right study (?for a flagellator), but note both studies as developments of Uffizi 225E (their no.93, fig.118). The drawings on Chatsworth 961 are generally in Filippino's style, but too weak to be by the master's own hand.

The portrait used by Vasari for 'Baldovinetto', as was pointed out in the Arezzo catalogue, corresponds to the 'figure d'un vecchio raso con un cappuccio rosso in testa' in the fresco of *Joachim despatched from the Temple* by Domenico Ghirlandaio in the Cappella Tornabuoni, S. Maria Novella, taken by Vasari to be of Baldovinetti (but in fact of Tommaso, father of Domenico Ghirlandaio).

89

88 Benedetto Luti

(Florence 1666–1724 Rome)

Adonis takes his leave of Venus

Pen and brown ink, with brown and grey washes, heightened with white bodycolour, over preliminaries in black chalk, 184 × 233mm. Mounted in full for the 2nd Duke.

Chatsworth 629

Provenance: presumably William, 2nd Duke of Devonshire

Always in the Devonshire collection as Luti, this drawing does indeed appear to be by this contemporary of the second Duke who was also one of the best known collectors and dealers in Rome. Luti was a Florentine pupil of Gabbiani, himself a pupil of Cortona. Kent, who designed the interiors at Chiswick and Devonshire House in London, trained in Rome under Luti, who was in the city during the second Duke's collecting period. Luti's 194 portfolios of drawings were brought to England after his

death by a 'Mister Kent' and sold in 1762, during the reign of the fifth Duke.

89 Alessandro Maganza

(Vianza 1556–1631 Vianza)

Flight from a burning City

Pen and brown ink with brown wash over preliminaries in black chalk, heightened with white bodycolour (partly oxydised), 329 × 424mm. Mounted in full for the 2nd Duke.

Chatsworth 276

Provenance: William, 2nd Duke of Devonshire (L.718)

Exhibitions: Leeds, 1868 (2725, as by Tintoretto); Manchester, 1961 (59, as by Jacopo Tintoretto); Tokyo, 1975 (38, as by Jacopo Tintoretto)

Although an original drawing, if unlikely to be by Tintoretto, it was not to be listed as a Venetian drawing either

90

by Hadeln or the Tietzes. However it reflects an interest in the drama of Tintoretto; and it has close affinities with the style in pen and wash of Maganza, who was influenced by Veronese and Tintoretto. Both the fluttering draperies and the exaggerated transitions from swelling calves to narrow ankles are typical of Maganza's manner. Comparisons may be made with *The Denial of St Peter* (New London, Lyman Allyn Museum) and *The Adoration of the Shepherds* (Munich), both drawn in the same technique (see *Pantheon*, VI, 1962, figs.10 and 11). A dome, a tower and an obelisk appear in the background (there are pentimenti in the buildings): but what is the story? If it were Aeneas and Anchises who formed the central group, where is Ascanius to be descried?

90 Giannicola di Paolo Manni

(Perugia *c.*1460–1544 Perugia)

The Eucharist

Pen and brown ink, diameter 241mm. Mounted in full for the 2nd Duke.

Inscribed in pen and brown ink on the label above central columns ACCIPITE ET CO/MEDITE HOC EST/ENIM CORPUS ME/UM (take this and eat for this is my body); and above the exergue IOANNES BERNARDINUS BALLEONUS (Giovanni Bernardino Baglioni)

Chatsworth 391

This pupil of Perugino, influenced also by Pinturicchio, was active in Perugia from 1484 (see G. N. Crispotti, *Perugia Augusta*, 1648, pp.65, 140, 150; also O. Fischel, *Die Zeichnungen der Umbrer*, 1917, p.232). Francis Russell recognized this drawing as reminiscent of the St John scenes in the Chapel of the Cambio (ceiling 1513–18;

91

92

altarpiece 1516 and walls 1526–8), rejecting the absurd attribution to Giovanni Baglione already rejected by A. E. Popham (1925), but kept in the Courtauld List of 1963 (accepted presumably from misunderstanding of the lower inscription). Comparison may also be made with the *Feast of Herod* frescoed in the Collegio in 1526. The tondo form suggests a roundel of stained glass to commemorate Giovanni Bernardino Baglioni, son of Francesco (mentioned in 1483 and 1501; cf. Comte L. de Baglion, *Histoire de la Maison de Baglion*, Poitiers, 1907, p.480). The armorials, strictly interpreted as drawn, viz. a purple band on an argent field (unknown to Vittorio Spreti, *Encyclopedia storico – nobiliare, italiano*, Milan, 1935–43) were surely intended to be those of Baglioni (azure with a band of gold: Spreti, *Appendice*, Parte I, p.261). On stylistic grounds the dating is *c*.1525.

91 Carlo Maratti

(Camerano 1625–1713 Rome)

The School of Design (Accademia della Pittura)

Pen and brown ink with brown wash, heightened with white bodycolour, over preliminaries in black chalk, and indented with a stylus, 402 × 310mm. Mounted in full for the 2nd Duke.

Inscribed by the draughtsman, in brown ink and pen, *SENZA DI NOI OGNI FATICA E VANA/ MAI A BASTANZA/ TANTO CHE BASTI* (repeated three times)

Chatsworth 646

Provenance: presumably William, 2nd Duke of Devonshire

Literature: Bellori (ed. E. Borea, Turin, 1976), pp.629–31 (with a detailed description, including the changes in the inscription); Reveley, 1820, pp.103–4 ('the most capital one in England is a large emblematic representation of Painting, with many figures, in the possession of the Duke of Devonshire'); Vitzthum, 1971, pp.89–90, fig.21; Rudolph, 1978, p.201, no.39; M. Winner, 'Una certa idea: Maratta zitiert einen Brief Raffaels in einer Zeichnung', in *Acts of the International Colloquium 'Der Kun-*

stler über sich selbst in seinem Werk', Rome, Biblioteca Hertziana, 1989, published Weinheim, 1992.

Traditionally and correctly in the Devonshire collection as Maratti, this famous drawing is his *modello* for an etching (in reverse) made by Nicolas Dorigny in 1728, as P.M.R. Pouncey was the first to observe. An earlier version of the composition is in the Wadsworth Atheneum (A. Golohany, in Philadelphia, 1981). The print is a pair to *The Triumph of Ignorance*, also etched by Dorigny.

Annibale Carracci is shown raising up the figure of Pittura. The students are to learn geometry, optics (especially perspective) and anatomy, this last from Leonardo da Vinci. The three Raphaelesque Graces are cloudborne, upper left. They point to the paradigms of beauty and strength in antique sculpture: Apollo, Venus and Hercules. O. Kutschera-Woborsky in *Mitteilungen der Gesellschaft für vervielfältigende Kunst*, 1919, pp.9–28, points out the allusion to the Farnesina loggia.

Bellori records that Maratti drew this for the marchese del Carpio during the time that he was Spanish ambassador in Rome (1677–1683). S. Rudolph (1992) kindly informs me that she has established the exact year as 1682. Maratti's other programmatic engraving for the marchese del Carpio was used much later, in reverse, for the frontispiece of Bellori's edition of engraved illustrations of the Galleria Farnese.

92 Carlo Maratti

(Camerano 1625–1713 Rome)

Tuscany in her car: Modello for the 'Piatto di San Giovanni' of 1681

Pen and brown ink with brown wash, over preliminaries in red and black chalks, 563 × 474mm. Mounted in full for the 2nd Duke.

Chatsworth 291

Provenance: presumably intended to be sold (with Chatsworth 288, 289 and 290) by Maratti's daughter in Rome on 27 March 1720, and available after the aborted auction for purchase by the 2nd Duke of Devonshire

Literature: Arnold Nesselrath, MD, 1979, pp.417–26, pls.34–9 (reproduces the plaster casts made in 1746, now in Florence, Museo degli Argenti, for all four designs at Chatsworth)

By his fourth and final will Cardinal Lazzaro Pallavicini specified that his heirs should present each year on the feast day of S. Giovanni a silver dish to the value of *c*.300 Roman scudi to Cosimo III of Tuscany. He died too soon before the festa of 1680 for a special design to be commissioned and executed; that first year a piece of silver plate (?Genoese) may have been presented. Chatsworth 288–291 are therefore the first four designs known; and the

designs of the finished plates are preserved in the plaster casts (the plates having been melted by the French *c*.1800): see K. Aschengreen–Piacenti in *Kunst des Barock in Toskana*, Munich, 1976, pp.188–207. Maratti's part is certified by the inventory (fol.446) drawn at the death of his wife Francesca, 'Molti disegni del Med.o Sig.r Cav.r Maratti tra quali vi sono … e non so quanti pezzi di disegni per li bacili serviti per li Sig.ri Rospigliosi p.donare a Sua Altezza di Toscana'. The traditional attribution in the Devonshire collection to Battista Franco was accepted by A.E. Popham, since he believed that these drawings had to do with maiolica dishes, of which Franco designed several. All four were designed to flatter the Medici dynasty.

The silversmith made few noteworthy changes in the design. Only the *imprese* in the cartouches, the fleur-de-lys, the Medici balls and the central medallion were not filled in by Maratti. Maratti had made clear through his designs for two programmatic engravings (see 91) that Raphael and Annibale Carracci were the heroes of painting. Tuscany's car and pose reflect the central field in the Galleria Farnese, of which Maratti had earlier copied the cartoon.

93

94

93 Carlo Maratti

(Camerano 1625–1713 Rome)

Hagar and Ishmael in the Wilderness, comforted by the Angel

Red chalk, 485 × 336mm.

Inscribed in pen and brown ink *h. 154* and *7*; and in pencil *56 e 57 110*. The mount for Lord Somers is inscribed in pen and brown ink, by the hand of J. Richardson the elder, following Resta, *Carlo Maratti*

Chatsworth 571

Provenance: P. Sebastiano Resta; Giovanni Marchetti (died 1704), Bishop of Arezzo, from 1698; sold by his heir, the cavaliere Orazio Marchetti of Pistoia; Lord Somers from 1710 to at least 1716; his sale, London 1717; William, 2nd Duke of Devonshire (L.718)

Literature: Blunt and Cooke, 1960, under cat.nos.269 and 270; Rudolph, 1978, p.202

A painting of the subject, probably a schoolwork, from the Duke of Westminster's collection was sold at Christie's on 4 July 1924 (16). It was later with Brunner, Paris, and resold at Christie's, together with its pendant of Bathsheba, 9 April 1991 (66A), as S. Rudolph informs me (1992). For preparatory drawings at Windsor and Düsseldorf towards this model at Chatsworth, see Schaar, 1967, nos.437, 438 on p.150. The drawing was engraved by Robert van Audenaerd (Le Blanc, 1, p.67, no.2).

94 Carlo Maratti

(Camerano 1625–1713 Rome)

Summer and Autumn

Pen and brown ink on paper that was white, some heightening with white bodycolour, 286 × 452mm. The ink gall has consumed the paper in places and it is also foxed. Mounted in full for the 2nd Duke.

Chatsworth 582

Provenance: William, 2nd Duke of Devonshire (L.718)

Literature: Bellori (ed. E. Borea, Turin, 1976) pp.609–11; F. H. Dowley, 'A few drawings by Carlo Maratti', MD, IV 1966, pp.422–34.

A preliminary sketch for one of the paintings (in which the positions of Summer and Autumn are reversed), commissioned *c.*1678 from Maratti for Cardinal Porto Carrero as a present for Charles II of Spain. This was itself preceded by a sketch in the Uffizi (Dowley, pl.396), the pendant to Winter and Spring. Confusingly the same pair of subjects was later to be commissioned by Don Livio Odescalchi. Snakes draw Summer's car, as in the drawing by Guercino in the Fitzwilliam Museum.

The pair to this, an *Allegory of Winter and Spring*, was engraved by R. van Audenaerd (Le Blanc, 1, p.68, no.78).

95

95 Carlo Maratti

(Camerano 1625–1713 Rome)

Padre Sebastiano Resta examining a Folio of Drawings

Red chalk, 257 × 198mm.

Inscribed below the margin line, in Maratti's hand, in pen and brown ink *Ritratto dell. Me Reverendo Padre Sebastiano Resta della congregatione del. Oratorio di San felippo Neri in Roma, che mostra all Sig Carlo Maratti il presente Libro con le accutissime sue eruditioni – l'ultimo di Marzo = 689 = ;* in black chalk, in Resta's hand *furto e Dono dell Autore*; and in pen and brown ink *k303* (Resta/Somers)

Chatsworth 584

Provenance: P. Sebastiano Resta by 1689; Giovanni Matteo Marchetti (died 1704), Bishop of Arezzo, from 1698; sold by his heir, the cavaliere Orazio Marchetti of Pistoia; Lord Somers from 1710 until at least 1716; his sale London, 1717; William, 2nd Duke of Devonshire (L.718)

Literature: J. Meder, *Die Handzeichnung*, Vienna, 1919, p.654, fig.319; A. E. Popham, OMD, XI, 1936, p.5; Vitzthum, 1971, p.89, fig.16

Exhibitions: Washington, 1969–70 and London, V&A, 1973–4 (43)

The second inscription implies that Maratti filched the drawing from one of the volumes of Resta's collection, and later returned it as a 'gift'. The sitter in Maratti's portrait is the celebrated antiquary (1635–1714) who assembled and annotated, in more than thirteen folios which he sold to the Bishop of Arezzo, a very large collection of drawings by the old masters. Another portrait of Resta in profile, in old age, was drawn by P. L. Ghezzi in Rome and etched by Arthur Pond in 1738 when in the possession of William Kent.

96

97

96 Pier Francesco Mola

(Coldrerio 1612–1666 Rome)

The Forge of Vulcan

Pen and wash with brown ink, heightened with white body-colour, on blue paper, 260 × 405mm. Mounted in full for the 2nd Duke.

Chatsworth 555

Provenance: William, 2nd Duke of Devonshire (L.718)

Literature: R. Cocke, 'Mola's designs for the Stanza dell'Aria at Valmontone', *Burl. Mag.*, CX, 1968, pp.558ff

Exhibitions: Pittsburgh, etc., 1987–8 (48); Lugano-Rome, 1989–90 (III.36)

A sketch, typical of Mola's hasty calligraphy, for one of the four frescoed compartments of the coved cross-vault of the Sala d'Aria in Palazzo Pamphilj at Valmontone, near Rome, which he began to paint in July 1658, but left incomplete in December. These four principal compartments are shown in Mola's early project: Jupiter presiding over the four elements (see N. Turner in Lugano, 1989 no.III.30). In 1661 they were destroyed to make room for the work of Mattia Preti. The Chatsworth drawing, as Turner points out, is dependent for a part of its inspiration on Mola's knowledge of the analogous scene in Pietro da Cortona's fresco in Palazzo Barberini in Rome. Mola was to substitute for the present subject *Iris sent by Juno to Turnus* (Aeneid, IX, 2–4), for which Chatsworth 556 is a preliminary sketch. That drawing and this, both acquired by the 2nd Duke, presumably have always been kept together.

98

97 Pier Francesco Mola

(Coldrerio 1612–1666 Rome)

Recto: St Jerome reading in the Wilderness, after Titian

Verso: Mathematical Calculations (perhaps Accounts)

Reed pen and brown ink with brown wash on cream laid paper, 387 × 295mm. Mounted in full for the 2nd Duke.

Inscribed by a collector in pen and brown ink *titianus invenit* (and an illegible word due to a tear)

Chatsworth 909

Literature: Vasari (1568), ed. Milanesi, VII, p.440; Gaye, 1840 III, p.242, no.218 (Lampsonius's letter); Morelli, 1893, p.293 (as Titian); Strong, 1905, p.127 (as Titian, the last period); D. von Hadeln, *Titian's Drawings*, 1924, p.17 ('only a copy of an engraving by Cornelis Cort, engraved on Titian's order'); Palluchini, 1969, p.339 (in relation to San Fantin); Chiari, 1982, pp.48–9, no.4; Wethey, 1987, x–31, fig.167

Exhibitions: London, New Gallery, 1894–5 (844, as Titian)

This composition was engraved by Cornelis Cort in 1565, and published with a privilege taken out by Titian himself (Bierens de Haan, 1948, pp.8, 141, no.134). It is presumably a record of Titian's lost painting of St Jerome in the Scuola di San Fantin at Venice, which was praised by Vasari with the lament that it was destroyed by fire in 1566. Domenico Lampsonius, in an enthusiastic letter to

99

Titian (13 March 1567) from Liège, praised Cort's engravings after the master, which he had recently acquired; among them he mentions with special eloquence the St Jerome.

The vigour and assurance of this copy points to a masterly draughtsman of the second half of the seventeenth century in Italy, almost certainly P.F. Mola. Comparison may be made with his drawings in a similar technique, such as the Louvre drawing of *The Prodigal Son* (Cocke, 1972, cat.53, pl.77) and the V&A drawing of Venus and Adonis (N. Turner in Lugano, 1989, no.111,37). A possibly later copy drawn by Mola after Titian's *Three Ages of Man* was drawn from memory. It was on the London art market in 1972 (Cocke, 1972, p.44, pl.124).

Wickhoff, according to Strong, recognised in Chatsworth 909 'the style of Marco Ricci'. Strong himself, following Morelli, wrote: 'His (Titian's) intention is as firm as ever; but there is a wandering and faltering in the motion of the hand'.

98 Girolamo Muziano, called 'il Giovane dei paesi'

(Aquafredda, Brescia 1528–1592 Rome)

Landscape with St Jerome

Fine pen and brown ink, 538 × 395mm. The upper border is irregularly demarcated. Mounted in full for the 2nd Duke.

Chatsworth 228

Literature: Waagen, 1854, III, p.358; Ugo da Como, *Girolamo Muziano*, Bergamo 1930 (mentioned in Appendix XI, p.211)

Traditionally in the Devonshire collection as Muziano. W. Friedländer (1928) called this drawing 'a very fine and genuine Muziano, of great interest as one of the earliest landscape drawings'. It convinces as a highly finished original. Others of the series of penitent saints in the wilderness inspired by Muziano's master, Titian, are in Paris; two in the Frits Lugt collection (no.131, St Onophrius and no.132, the Penitent Magdalene); also one in the Ecole des Beaux-Arts. That the draughtsman has demarcated by a line his area for drawing suggests that he had in mind from the outset to have the subject engraved, presumably by Cornelis Cort (1533–1578), who engraved a suite of seven such scenes in 1573–1575.

99 Lelio Orsi

(Novellara 1511–1587 Reggio Emilia)

Study for the Decoration of a Ceiling

Pen and brown ink with grey brown wash, 213 × 213mm. Mounted in full for Lord Somers by J. Richardson the elder.

Inscribed in pencil, lower right, *c.23*; and on the mount, in pen and brown ink in the hand of the elder Richardson, following Resta, *Lelio di Novellara*

Chatsworth unnumbered

Provenance: P. Sebastiano Resta; Giovanni Matteo Marchetti (died 1704), Bishop of Arezzo, from 1698; sold by his heir, the cavaliere Orazio Marchetti of Pistoia; Lord Somers from 1710 until at least 1716; his sale, London 1717; 2nd or 3rd Duke of Devonshire

Literature: Vittoria Romani, *Lelio Orsi*, Modena, 1984, pp.61–4, fig.40

Exhibitions: Pittsburgh, 1987–8 (49)

A display of elegant *quadratura*, using at each corner the Gonzaga eagle so as to decorate an octagonal perspective. The pairs of tortile columns are linked by balustrades. Dawn clasping flowers, her putto in attendance bearing a torch and a jar of dew, descends in clouds through the opening in the simulated sky. They are seen in sharp *sotto-in-sù*. Orsi in the early 1560s used lessons which he had assimilated from Correggio at Parma with others from Mantegna and Giulio Romano at Mantua and from Pellegrino Tibaldi in the Ulysses Rooms of Palazzo Poggi at Bologna.

100 Jacopo Negretti, called Palma il Giovane

(Venice *c.*1548–1628 Venice)

St Jerome seated on a Rock, writing

Pen and brown ink with brown wash, 132 × 103mm. Mounted in full.

Inscribed in pen and brown ink by the artist *Giacomo Palma Fecit*

Chatsworth 617

Provenance: N. Lanière (L.2886); presumably 1st or 2nd Duke of Devonshire

A favourite subject of Palma. For the treatment of it compare on a study in Berlin (KdZ Nr. 18049), the pen sketch lower left; compare also *St Jerome in the Desert*, engraved in 1596 by Hendrik Goltzius (1558–1617) after a comparable composition (B.266).

100

101 Girolamo Francesco Mazzuola, called il Parmigianino

(Parma 1503–1540 Casal Maggiore)

Recto: *Virgin and Child standing in a round-headed Niche*

Verso: *Crouching female Figure, her arms clasping an Infant (?)* (visible from the *recto*)

Pen and brown ink with brown wash, the borders of the design indicated in pen; 192 × 94mm.

Chatsworth 1076

Literature: Popham, 1971, no.741

Probably a study for the Virgin and Child in the National Gallery *Vision of St Jerome* (cf. the drawing for the whole altarpiece in the British Museum: Popham, 1971, no.181, pl.95). She is also represented in an arched niche (ibid., no.54, pl.97) in the Chantilly drawing for the altarpiece, although there seated.

101

102 Girolamo Francesco Mazzuola, called il Parmigianino

(Parma 1503–1540 Casal Maggiore)

Bearded Figure, sleeping

Red chalk, 191 × 273mm. Mounted in full for the 2nd Duke.

Chatsworth 806

Provenance: Sir Peter Lely (L.2092); William, 2nd Duke of Devonshire (L.718)

Literature: Popham, 1971, no.734

Exhibitions: Washington, etc., 1962–3 and London, RA, 1969 (46)

A superb drawing, dating from the Bolognese period. It is doubtless a study either for a disciple asleep during the *Agony in the Garden* or in *The Transfiguration*, or for a composition of *Christ rising from the Tomb*. It is possibly connected with Parmigianino's own etching (B.XVI.9.6). D. Ekserdjian (1989) has pointed out that the legs especially relate in pose to the figure of the saint in the *Conversion of Saul*.

103 Girolamo Francesco Mazzuola, called il Parmigianino

(Parma 1503–1540 Casal Maggiore)

Recto: Self-Portrait, imposed on preliminary studies for two Canephori of the Steccata

Verso: Three Studies of a standing St Jerome, reading

Pen and brown ink, 107 × 75mm, the lower corners chamfered (a small tear upper right). Mounted in full.

Chatsworth 790

Provenance: Thomas Howard, 2nd Earl of Arundel (Inv.no.790); his daughter-in-law, Viscountess Stafford; bought from her by William, 2nd Duke of Devonshire (L.718)

Literature: Freedberg, 1950, pp.255–6 (as a copy of a lost drawing by Parmigianino); Popham, 1952, pp.20, 53; M. Fagiolo dell'Arco, *Il Parmigianino*, Rome, 1970, pp.276–7 (as by Parmigianino); Popham, 1971, no.719 (as by Parmigianino); Quintavalle, 1971, LXXVII (as by Parmigianino)

Exhibitions: Manchester, 1965 (352); Pittsburgh, etc., 1987–8 (52)

The self-portrait, aged about 30, on the recto may reflect either Dürer's *Self-Portrait* at about the same age (Munich, Alte Pinakothek), known perhaps to Parmigianino through a copy, or even the missing *Self-Portrait* which Dürer sent to Raphael. The head of Parmigianino only was engraved in reverse by Hendrik van den Borcht for the title-page of the *Libreto di diverse figurine dissegnate da franc. Parmensis et conservata nella Colettne Arondleyna* (in the British Museum, 1851-3-8-901). The canephori, which

102

differ considerably from those of the Steccata vault, were probably included, as Popham pointed out (1971), to show the work on which Parmigianino was engaged or which he was about to undertake.

The studies on the verso for the St Jerome in the background of Parmigianino's *Madonna dal Collo Lungo* indicate that this sheet was drawn about the end of 1534, the date of his commission for that painting. The younger Richardson records the good fortune of the 2nd Duke who purchased a series of framed prints formerly in Arundel's collection from Arundel's daughter-in-law, Lady Stafford, only to discover 'behind them capital Draw(in)gs of Raph(ael), Poli(doro), Parmeg(ianino), J. Rom(ano)'.

104 Bartolommeo Passarotti

(Bologna, 1529–1592 Modena)

Self-Portrait in old Age, with simulated Enframement

Pen and brown ink, on cream paper, 319 × 248mm (oval, expanded by its late 16th-century mount to 455 × 380mm). Mounted in full for the 2nd Duke.

Inscribed in pen and brown ink, at the base of the original mount, on a scroll, *BARTOLOMEO PASSEROTTI PITT./BOLOGNESE*

Chatsworth 393

Provenance: Boncompagni; William, 2nd Duke of Devonshire (L.718)

Literature: Babette Bohn, 'Bartolommeo Passarotti and Reproduction Etching in seventeenth-century Italy' in *Print Quarterly*, v, 1988, p.117, fig.59 (accepting it as Passarotti's *Self-Portrait*); Höper, 1988, Kat.z.40 (as *Self-Portrait*)

Exhibitions: Leeds, 1868 (2730, as Passarotti *Portrait of Scaliger*); Pittsburgh, etc., 1987–8 (54, as Passarotti *Self-Portrait*)

The attribution of this impressive portrait appears never to have been doubted. The elderly man's appearance is

103 recto

103 verso

consonant with that of Passarotti, which is known only from his prime by the engraving after the Uffizi portrait (see G.D.Ferretti, *Museo Fiorentino: Serie di Ritratti*, Florence, 1752–62). In 1678 Malvasia recorded of this earlier citizen of Bologna: 'La sua penna ... fu delle più brave che mai si vedesse, e tanto nè vennero stimati i suoi profili ed i suoi tratti, che non era personaggio grande, no virtuose primario, che di qualche disegno del Passerotti, non andasse vago e curioso, e ne suoi studii di far vedere fra l'altre più belle cose non ambisse' (1841 edition, I, p.90).

The winged dragon, at the head of the fine sixteenth-century Italian mount, signifies Boncompagni ownership; if not of Gregory XIII (Pope 1572–85), since the drawing is unlikely, on grounds of the subject's age and appearance, to be earlier than 1590, then that of another member of this leading family of Bologna; possibly Gregorio Boncompagni, duca di Sora.

105 Giuseppe Passeri

(Rome 1654–1714 Rome)

Tailpiece for Volume XVI of Sebastiano Resta's Collection of Drawings

COLOUR PLATE VII

Pen and brown ink with brown wash over preliminaries in black chalk on a paper washed brown over faint squaring in black chalk, heightened with white bodycolour, 698 × 435mm. There is an overlay added by the draughtsman in brown ink on a separate sheet of paper, to cover the vault of the left arcade with a fresh head. Mounted in full for Lord Somers by J.Richardson the elder.

Inscribed by Passeri on the right hand page of the open volume *FINIS Tom.III*. Signed and dated lower right *1698 Joseph Passarus Rom. 25 Aplis*

Chatsworth 634

Provenance: P.Sebastiano Resta; Giovanni Matteo Marchetti (died 1704), Bishop of Arezzo, from 1698; sold by the cavaliere Marchetti of Pistoia, his heir; Lord Somers from 1710 until 1716; his sale, London 1717; 2nd or 3rd Duke of Devonshire

Literature: Popham, 1936, p.6 (edited J.Talman's letter, see below: but did not connect the description of Passeri's drawing with this sheet at Chatsworth); G.Fusconi and S.Prosperi Valenti Rodino, 'Un'aggiunta a Sebastiano Resta collezionista: il *Piccolo Preliminare al Grande Anfiteatre Pittorico*', in *Prospettiva*, 33–6, 1984, p.238, no.21 (the date imperfectly transcribed)

Exhibitions: London, RA, 1938, no.424 (as 'Prelates under a Loggia'); Pittsburgh, etc., 1987–8 (53, as Tailpiece for vol.XVI of Sebastiano Resta's Collection of drawings)

John Talman, writing from Florence to Dean Aldrich of Christ Church, Oxford, on 2 March 1709/10, about the offer of sale of the drawings which the cavaliere Orazio

BARTOLOMEO. PASSEROTTI PIT.
BOLOGNESE.

104

Marchetti of Pistoia had inherited in 1704 from his uncle Giovanni Matteo Marchetti, sixteen volumes assembled and mounted by Padre Sebastiano Resta (Milan 1635–1714 Rome), described the sixteenth volume:

'This volume contains a variety of designs of all the great masters, as of Correggio, his disciples and imitators, &c. In the title page is an emblem, with this motto, 'Nostri quondam libamen amoris'. Pages 65, drawings 219. Of the principal masters, Del Sarto, 4. Procacino, 3. Baroci, 4. Bernin, 2. Correggio, 35. Lod. Caracci, 12. Anab. Caraci [sic], 12. Polidoro, 4. Parmegianino, 19. Cortona, 3. Raphael Urbin, 10. A. Sacchi, 2. Titian, 4. Zuccari, 5. The last drawing but one is a lofty and noble portico, called the Academical; in which are represented Father Resta, and several other figures, bringing this collection to the bishop, who is sitting in a chair with the Cavalier Marchetti, his nephew, standing by him; to whom the bishop, by laying his hand on his heart, shows the great satisfaction he has in being the possessor of so noble a collection, which consists of 2111 drawings. This great drawing is of Passeri and finely coloured.'

This 'great drawing' evidently celebrates the Bishop's acquisition and documents that precisely to 25 April 1698. Resta bearded, spectacled and, as an Oratorian, wearing a biretta, is recognisable, his right hand on the open album in-folio, his left pointing towards it. The middle-aged prelate seated at the round table is evidently the Bishop of Arezzo: and the fashionably dressed young man with whom he is conversing is his nephew, the cavaliere Marchetti of Pistoia. The cleric (?Oratorian) standing beside Resta, perhaps his friend the Abbate Alessandro Piccolomini, summons a servant to bring the next album from a pile of three, presumably nos. IV, V and VI. Vol. III, shown by Resta to the Bishop, is shown open at the last pages mounted with drawings, 330 in all; and the figure seated on the steps on the right holds what may represent a large (?unfinished) drawing of the *Virgin and Child*, which looks appropriately Correggesque. The open, quattrocentesque loggia could be Aretine. Otherwise the setting is markedly Roman (the Colosseum) and learned (statue of Minerva).

D. Graf kindly called to my attention a preliminary, unfinished drawing (Fusconi/Rodino, p.244, no.57) of this composition in the same media and on the same scale in the Kupferstichkabinett, Berlin (Inv. KdZ Nr.16457), but with the architecture and balustrade unresolved. This Berlin drawing is inscribed, *Passari scolaro di Carlo Maratti/10*; and it is stamped *P*, cut off lower right, presumably signifying the collection of Vincenzo Pacetti who acquired it after the death of Bartolomeo Cavaceppi in Rome (1799).

Appropriately the medallion of the young Raphael, above the left column in the Chatsworth drawing, follows, in reverse, Maratti's engraving after Raphael's self-portrait frescoed at the right of *The School of Athens*. The medallion above the right column, less instantly recognisable, is likely, from Resta's interest and the content of this volume, to represent Correggio. Resta devoted three of his albums to Correggio. It is fitting that Passeri should have designed the tailpiece to Vol. XVI, since we have Resta's own statement: 'Il Sig. Ghezzi aprovo il mio parere; essere il Quadretto di mano del Correggio, col di piu, che ivi a tergo scrisse. Lo mandai al Sig. Passeri gia nel 1690 compagno del mio Viaggio Pittorico in Lombardia, e per tale lo riconobbe ancor esso per la prattica delle maniere viste di tanto Autore e meco, e da se.'

It is also appropriate that this drawing should be in the Devonshire collection, most likely from the time of the second Duke. In the British Library, Lansdowne MS.802, are copies put in order by the Richardsons of Resta's notes on the drawings which he sold to the Bishop of Arezzo between 1698 and 1702. Book L. corresponding to Talman's (and Resta's) Vol. III ends, 'Ma torniamo agl'Italiani di Scuola Moderna dalli Carracci restauratori sino a viventi hoggi in Italia senza pregiuditio ne esclusione de Forestiera. Seque il Tomo 4.' Most of these Resta/Marchetti drawings were to be acquired by Lord Somers in 1710, and further Resta volumes followed by direct sale from Resta in 1712. They were all disposed of after Somers's death in 1717. Some found their way to Chatsworth: but evidently not all bear the familiar Resta-Somers miniscule letter and number in pen.

It is noteworthy that the Lord James Cavendish album, now in the British Museum, made up initially by the second Duke from his collection for his second son's encouragement and delectation, has (fol.23 recto) the bust-length portrait of a prelate whose appearance is consonant with Chatsworth 634 as the rubicund and plump Giovanni Matteo Marchetti, Bishop of Arezzo. This drawing bears on the mount an old and plausible ascription to Giuseppe Passeri.

106 Giovanni Francesco Penni, called il Fattore

(Florence 1496?–*c*.1536 Naples)

The Emperor Constantine, addressing his Troops, startled by the Vision of the Cross in the Sky

Pen and brown ink with brown wash over preliminaries in black chalk, heightened with white bodycolour, partly squared for enlargement, 232 × 415mm. There is a vertical crease, and a tear to the upper right. Mounted in full for the 2nd Duke (his mark on lower right corner after repair).

Chatsworth 175

Provenance: Sir Peter Lely (L.2092), as Raphael; his sale, 1688, bought Sonnius; J. van Bergestein; N. A. Flinck (L.959); William, 2nd Duke of Devonshire (L.718), from 1723–4

Literature: *The Autobiography of the Hon. Roger North*, ed. Augustus Jessop, 1887, p.200 (as Raphael); Reveley, p.7 (as Raphael); Ruland, 1876, p.235, i, 4 (as Raphael); Gere and Pouncey, 1983, p.51 (as Penni); Oberhuber-Fischel, 483 (as Penni); Knab, Mitsch, Oberhuber, 1983, no.600 (as Raphael); P. Joannides, 'Opere giovanili di Giulio Romano' in *Paragone*, 425, 1985 (as Penni); K. Oberhuber in Mantua, 1989, pp.84, 85 (as Raphael); Milan, 1989, pp.84–5 (as Raphael)

Exhibitions: London, RA, 1960 (570, as 'school of Raphael'); Washington, etc., 1969–70 and London, V&A, 1973–4 (59); London, BM, 1983–4 (197, as Penni); New York, 1987 (48, as ?Raphael)

The Hon. Roger North, Lely's executor, wrote of the 1688 sale: 'I remember a lord, now a duke said "Damn me, what care I whether the owner bids or not as long as I can tell whether I wish to buy, and for what"... There was half a sheet that Raphael had drawn upon with umber and white, that we called washed and heightened; a tumult of Roman soldiery, and Caesar upon a suggestum with officer appeasing them. This was rallied at first, and some said 6d, knowing what it would come to; but then £10, £30, £58, and my quarrelsome lord bid £70, and Sonnius £100 for it, and had it. The lord held up his eyes and hands to heaven, and prayed to God he might never eat bread cheaper' (*The Lives of the Norths*, ed. Jessop, 1890, pp.199–200). Sonnius was one of the auctioneer's agents. The future 1st Duke of Devonshire was evidently the underbidder for this 'Raphael' at this vast price. His son, the 2nd Duke, was to acquire it in 1723 with his purchase of the Flinck collection.

The drawing remains of importance quite beyond the significance of this collector's anecdote, in that it presumably reflects Raphael's intentions for the *Allocutio* to be painted on the wall of the Sala di Costantino. Giulio Romano, in painting the wall (certainly before the death of Leo x) was to compress Raphael's design and to make major changes, among them the insertion of additional figures. The Chatsworth drawing can hardly be by Raphael himself (*pace* Oberhuber) in some unexamined late phase of his graphic style; for the woodenness of Constantine's gestures and that of the young soldier running forward from the right, not to speak of the empty expressions, betray the morphology and the hand of Penni. Oberhuber's recent arguments from the Louvre modello for the Battle of Constantine shows a disregard of style and of his earlier, more sensible opinion.

107 Baldassare Peruzzi

(Siena 1481–1536 Rome)

Pan walking with a Youth, while three other naked Satyrs remain with a naked Putto

Pen and brown ink with brown wash, heightened with white bodycolour, squared in black chalk, 177 × 240mm (trimmed to an oval). Mounted in full for the 2nd Duke.

106

107

Chatsworth 41

Provenance: Sir Peter Lely (L.2092); William, 2nd Duke of Devonshire (L.718)

Literature: Frommel, 1967–8, pp.101–2, cat.58c 3, pl.XLVIIC

Exhibitions: London, RA, 1960 (569); Washington, etc., 1962–3 and London, RA, 1969 (49); New York, 1987 (89)

Traditionally attributed at Chatsworth to Peruzzi. P. M. R. Pouncey pointed out that this is a modello for one of the four oval frescoes with mythological scenes in the north-east cupola of the loggia of the Villa Madama on Monte Mario just north of Rome. The Villa was designed by Raphael with assistance from Giulio Romano for Cardinal Giulio de' Medici (later Pope Clement VII). The decoration was begun by Giulio and Giovanni da Udine in summer 1520, very soon after Raphael's death.

Although Peruzzi is not mentioned in this connection by Vasari (and no known document associates him with the Villa), his involvement in the decoration of the loggia is established by Pouncey's discovery of this drawing and others which are all surely by him. Frommel (pls.xlvii–xlviii) reproduces all four of these purely decorative ovals by Peruzzi: *Odysseus inviting the Daughters of Lykomedes into the King's Palace* (drawing, formerly also at Chatsworth, sold at Christie's, 3 May 1984, lot 35, now in the J. Paul

Getty Museum, Malibu); *The Discovery of Achilles*; *Salmacis and the Hermaphrodite* (drawing Louvre 10476); and the fourth, for which Chatsworth 41 is a study, for a subject still indeterminate.

108 Studio of Baldassare Peruzzi, reworked by Rubens

The Presentation of the Virgin in the Temple, after Peruzzi

Brown ink with pen and wash, heightened slightly in white, on brown washed paper, and reworked extensively in brown ink with brown wash and white bodycolour, 540 × 836mm.

Chatsworth unnumbered

Literature: P. P. Rubens; N. A. Flinck (L.959); presumably William, 2nd Duke of Devonshire from 1723–4

Literature: G. Vasari, *Vite* (edn. 1771), III, 325, n.1 (as a copy by Annibale Carracci, 'formerly in the Devonshire collection'); Frommel, 1967–8, pp.126–7, no.629; M. Jaffé, *Rubens and Italy*, Oxford, 1977, p.49, n.42, pl.133

Basically, this copies the modello in the Louvre (Frommel, 1967–8, cat.90, pls. LXII and LXIII) drawn by Peruzzi *c.*1518 for his half life-size fresco commissioned shortly after his return from Bologna by Filippo Sergardi, a friend, executor and fellow countryman of Agostino Chigi, for the octagon in S. Maria della Pace, Rome. The fresco, finished by September 1526, is surrounded by a stucco frame to give it the appearance of a *quadro riportato* (as observed by S. J. Freedberg in *Painting in Italy 1500–1600*, London, 1971, p.67). It shows numerous differences especially in the foreground figures. The crowded narrative in a rich architectural setting was evidently inspired by Raphael's example in *The Fire in the Borgo*.

This is one of the largest and most important examples of Rubens in the metropolis transforming to superbly plastic effect a sixteenth-century drawing. His hand is evident on most of the figures except for the almost naked beggar, seated lower left, some background figures, including those on the triangular pediment, and the dog in the foreground. It is especially effective on the horse and groom, on the man giving alms, and on numerous bystanders including those by the portico; whereas Peruzzi's style appears not only in the fanciful combination of architectural elements, but also in the drawing of the two beggars.

Frommel, 1967–8, cat.89, pl.LXIa, illustrates another drawing in the Louvre which copies the finished fresco in S. Maria della Pace, which he attributes to an anony-

mous sixteenth- or seventeenth-century draughtsman. This is of much weaker quality than the Chatsworth drawing. The attribution of that in the 1771 edition of Vasari to Annibale is understandable before the transforming hand of Rubens was intensively studied by the present writer in articles in *Master Drawings* and in *Rubens and Italy*, Oxford 1977. The closest Annibale gets to this sort of work in application of brown ink with brown wash and white bodycolour would be Chatsworth 435 (cat.35).

109 Pier Francesco di Bartolomeo del ser Piero da Vinci, called Pierino da Vinci

(Vinci *c.*1530–1553 Pisa)

Duke Cosimo de' Medici expelling the Vices from Pisa and introducing the Virtues

Pen and brown ink over indications in black chalk (one unfinished figure entirely in black chalk), cut from Vasari's mount and the lower corners chamfered, 165 × 293mm. Mounted in full on an early 18th-century mount. Labelled in brown ink, on the surviving part of the original 16th-century mount: *Piero da Vinci Scult: Fior:*

Chatsworth 707

108

109

A preliminary sketch for the marble relief in the Vatican (photo. Anderson 3951); this is one of very few Pierino drawings recognised to be extant, and the only one with such an ancient and presumably reliable attribution.

110 Polidoro Caldara, called Polidoro da Caravaggio

(Caravaggio *c.*1500–?soon after 1536 Messina)

Vae victis; *Brennus placing his Sword in the Balance*

Pen and brown ink with brown wash, squared in black chalk, 280 × 194mm. Mounted in full for the 2nd Duke.

Chatsworth 143

Provenance: William, 2nd Duke of Devonshire (L.718)

A. E. Popham (1962) classified this as 'Italian, early six-teenth century', and so it remained on the Courtauld Institute list of 1963. But the attribution of this drawing, manifestly an original of *c.*1520–3, not a copy, should not be in doubt. Polidoro with Maturino frescoed the Brennus story on the face of a house near Sant' Agata, Rome (so Vasari, v, p.146). Brennus and the Gallic legions besieged

Rome for about seven months. Another drawing in the series is at Windsor (Inv.5476).

111 Jacopo Carrucci, called Pontormo

(Pontormo 1494–1557 Florence)

A seated Youth wearing a Cap, studied three-quarter length

Black chalk on cream paper, squared in black chalk for enlarge-ment, 264 × 187mm (cut to an arched top). Fully mounted for the 2nd Duke.

Chatsworth 714

Provenance: N. A. Flinck (L.959); William, 2nd Duke of Devon-shire (L.718) from 1723–4

Literature: Strong, 1902, XVI (as 'a characteristic but faded specimen of Pontormo'); Vasari Society, 1925, VI, 9; Berenson, 1938 (no.1957, as Pontormo); J. A. Gere, *Burl. Mag.* XCI, 1949, pp.169–70; Craig Hugh Smyth, *Bronzino as Draughtsman*, New York, 1971, 3–4, fig.4

Exhibitions: London, RA, 1930 (538); London, Arts Council, 1949 (2); Washington, etc., 1962–3 and London, RA, 1969 (8); Florence, 1980 (126, as Bronzino)

A study used by Bronzino in the phase after his return from Pesaro to Florence in 1532 for his painting of a *Youth with a Lute* (Uffizi 1575). The introduction of the lute in this painting was an afterthought by the painter. There

111

is no such indication in Chatsworth 714, in which he holds a piece of stuff (?a glove). The attribution of the drawing to Pontormo was supported successively by S. A. Strong, B. Berenson, A. E. Popham and K. Clark. An attribution to Bronzino was supported by Craig Smyth (op.cit.). On the strength of that another three-quarter-length study of *A seated Man* (Uffizi 6698F), slightly more refined in its finish, has been attributed to Bronzino, rather than to Pontormo (see Annamaria Petrioli Tofani and Graham Smith, *Sixteenth-Century Tuscan Drawings from the Uffizi*, Oxford, 1988, cat.28). Most recently J. Byam Shaw and J. A. Gere (1989) have supported the attribution of Chatsworth 714 to Pontormo, in that the costume study in the Lugt Collection (Byam Shaw 1983, no.27, pl.38), although rubbed and slightly redrawn in the face, is connected with Pontormo's portrait, now in the J. Paul Getty Museum, Malibu, for the *Young Duke Cosimo I de' Medici*, and seemingly by the same draughtsman. Accepting their observation implies that Bronzino was given, or otherwise obtained, Chatsworth 628, likewise essentially of costume, for his early portrait.

112 Giovanni Antonio Licinio, called Pordenone

(1485–1539)

The Almighty supported by Angels

Red chalk, 216 × 213mm (upper corners chamfered). Mounted in full for the 2nd Duke.

Chatsworth 236

Provenance: Sir Peter Lely (L.2092); William, 2nd Duke of Devonshire (L.718)

Literature: Strong, 1902 (38); Tietzes, 1944 (1300); G. Fiocco, *Pordenone*, Udine, 1939, pp.104, 155 and pl.140; Hadeln, 1925 (43); Cohen, 1980, p.65; C. E. Cohen in *Pordenone*, 1984, under cat.no.4.20

Exhibitions: London, New Gallery, 1894–5 (856); Manchester, 1961 (46); Manchester, 1965 (363); Washington, etc., 1962–3 and London, RA, 1969 (52)

Traditionally in the Devonshire collection as Pordenone, this is a study for one or other of the very similar groups in Pordenone's altarpieces in S. Rocco, Venice, or in the Franciscan Church at Cortemaggiore (c.1529), more probably the latter.

113 Giuseppe Porta, called Giuseppe Salviati

(Castelnuovo di Garfagnana c.1520–1575 Venice)

The Legend of Seven Kings paying homage to a Pope

Pen and brown ink with brown wash, heightened with white bodycolour, on blue paper, squared in black chalk, 390 × 500mm.

Inscribed by the artist *PIVS.IIII.|PONT.MA* on the socle of the statue of St Paul

Chatsworth 16

Provenance: Sir Peter Lely (L.2092); William, 2nd Duke of Devonshire (L.718)

Exhibitions: London, RA, 1960 (559); Washington etc., 1962–3 and London, RA, 1969 (53)

Formerly ascribed in the Devonshire collection to Francesco dei Rossi (Salviati), this is probably the modello for a fresco commissioned by Pius IV for the Sala Regia of the Vatican, for which his pupil Giuseppe Porta was paid 300 scudi in 1565 (Carlo Ridolfi, *Le Maraviglie d'Arte*, ed. von Hadeln, I, Berlin, 1914, p.243, n.3). This was never even begun, doubtless because Pope Pius IV, who had commissioned the work, and whose name is inscribed on the pedestal of the nearer statue, died on 9 December that year. The perception of the probable connection of Chatsworth 16 with the Sala Regia commission is due to P. M. R. Pouncey.

114 Francesco Primaticcio

(Bologna 1504–1570 Fontainebleau)

Hercules surprised with Omphale

Pen and brown ink with brown wash, the outlines indented for transfer, 225 × 396mm. Mounted in full for the 2nd Duke.

Chatsworth 182

Provenance: N. A. Flinck (L.959); William, 2nd Duke of Devonshire (L.718), from 1723–4

Literature: Dimier, 1900, p.471 (238)

Exhibitions: Washington, etc., 1962–3 and London, RA, 1969 (54); Manchester, 1965 (364); Sheffield, 1966 (35); Tokyo, 1975 (36)

Traditionally in the Devonshire Collections as Primaticcio. Miscalled in Braun's catalogue *The Capture of Samson*, this marvellous night scene is a design for one of the frescoes decorating the Porte Dorée which was at one time the principal entrance of the Château de Fontainebleau. It was etched in reverse by Léon Davent (B. XVI.325.50).

112

113

115 Camillo Procaccini

(Bologna *c*.1555–1629 Milan)

Head of a bearded Man, looking up to the right

Black and red chalks on grey paper, 235 × 175mm. Mounted in full for the 2nd Duke.

Chatsworth 399

Provenance: N. A. Flinck (L.959); William, 2nd Duke of Devonshire (L.718) from 1723–4

Exhibitions: Washington, etc., 1969–70 and London, V & A, 1973–4 (10, as 16th-century Emilian); Florence/Paris, 1976 (5, as Titian)

Camillo Procaccini is the traditional attribution in the Devonshire collection for this head. Other large 'character' heads in this medium are attributed to him in the Accademia, Venice, and at Windsor Castle, although none is so fine in handling. Byam Shaw classed it as Emilian,

perhaps by Cavedone. It is more likely to be by Camillo Procaccini: compare *The Penitence of St Peter*, a painting by Procaccini, which may be identical with a *San Pietro che piange al cantar del gallo* recorded by Malvasia (*Felsina Pittrice*, Bologna (1678) 1841, I, p.218) in the church of San Pietro con la rete o Cornaredo, Milan. In 1585 was published posthumously *Le Lacrimo di San Pietro*, a religious poem by Luigi Tansillo da Nola (1510–68), which was also translated into Spanish.

The attribution by Bert W. Meijer (1976) to Titian is a fair tribute to the exceptional quality and strength of Chatsworth 399: but the chief comparisons which he makes in his catalogue entry to the anonymous woodcut of *St Roch* after Titian and to the fresco of *St Christopher* in the Doge's Palace do not convince of a Venetian authorship, let alone Titian's.

114

115

116 Biagio Pupini delle Lame

(Bologna doc. 1511–1575 Bologna)

Recto: Panel from the Arch of Constantine

Verso: Virgin and Child with St John, after Parmigianino

Pen and brown ink with brown wash, heightened with white bodycolour on blue paper, 411 × 274mm (recto); 405 × 263mm (verso)

Inscribed on the verso, in pen and black ink, R. *Urbino di questa bonda al manco*, and what appears to be a price, written upside down, *.£.3*, rather than an unrecorded collector's mark

Chatsworth 906

Provenance: Sir Peter Lely (L.2092); William, 2nd Duke of Devonshire (L.718)

Formerly kept at Chatsworth as 'school of Raphael', but the *recto*, in the combination and use of media, in the fold style and in the silhouetting by pen, is patently by Pupini. Chatsworth 1059 may be compared, even to the summary description of fingers. On the verso is a characteristic copy (incomplete) after the *Madonna della Rosa*, cf. Chatsworth 349.

116 *recto*

116 *verso*

117 Raffaello Sanzio, called Raphael

(Urbino 1483–1520 Rome)

Study for The Transfiguration

Red chalk, over indentations with the stylus, 246 × 350mm.

Chatsworth 904

Provenance: William, 2nd Duke of Devonshire (L.718)

Literature: Reveley, p.7; Ruland, 1876, pp.30, 85; Strong, 1905, p.118 ('probably made in the school, perhaps by the master's own hand'); Fischel, 1948, (as Penni); Knab, Mitsch, Oberhuber, 1983, no.603 (as Raphael); K. Oberhuber, 'Raphael: le rouge et le noir' in *Drawing: Masters & Methods: Raphael to Redon*, London, 1992, p.109 (as Raphael)

Exhibitions: London, BM, 1983 (174); New York, 1987 (37)

An early trial by Raphael for the upper zone of *The Transfiguration*, corresponding in all essentials, save that the figures are nude, with that part of the altarpiece as eventually carried out for Cardinal Giulio de' Medici. The earliest known reference to the commission is in a letter of 17

January 1517 to Michelangelo from Raphael's unfriendly rival in Rome, Sebastiano del Piombo.

A studio drawing in the Albertina (Knab, Mitsch, Oberhuber, 1983, no.70) which must be either a modello for the composition *c.*1518, or a copy of one, is made up (apart from the half-figure of God the Father) of exactly the same elements as this Chatsworth study. This important late drawing at Chatsworth was curiously neglected by nineteenth-century scholars: it was omitted by Passavant, overlooked by Morelli, not mentioned by Crowe and Cavalcaselle, and not included by Fischel in his 1896 volume. Only in the late twentieth century has it been properly extolled.

117

118 Raffaello Sanzio, called Raphael

(Urbino 1483–1520 Rome)

Nude studies for St Andrew and another Apostle in The Transfiguration

COLOUR PLATE VIII

Red chalk over indentations with the stylus on cream paper, 328 × 232mm. Fully mounted for the 2nd Duke.

Chatsworth 51

Provenance: Sir Peter Lely (L.2092); William, 2nd Duke of Devonshire (L.718)

Literature: Reveley, pp.7, 8; Ruland, 1876, p.28, no.61; Crowe and Cavalcaselle, ii, p.488; Fischel, 1898, no.336; Hartt, 1958, p.87; Oberhuber, 1962, p.57; J. Pope-Hennessy, *Raphael*, New York, 1970, p.75, pl.62; Knab, Mitsch, Oberhuber, 1983, no.605 (as drawn in black chalk); Joannides, 1983, no.426

Exhibitions: Leeds, 1868 (2647, as Raphael); Pittsburgh, 1986–7 (64, as Raphael)

For so crucial a work, commissioned by Cardinal Giulio de' Medici, to be painted in competition with Sebastiano del Piombo, who was aided in his design by Michelangelo, Raphael took in his preliminary studies of *c*.1517 comparable care to that which he had taken for the *Disputà* a decade earlier. The figures were first studied nude, in red chalk; afterwards the draperies, in black. Preceding the Chatsworth drawing, Raphael sketched the St Andrew in red chalk, over preliminaries in black chalk, in a drawing now in the Albertina (Joannides, op.cit., no.425).

119 Raffaello Sanzio, called Raphael

(Urbino 1483–1520 Rome)

Study for the Disciple at the extreme left of The Transfiguration

COLOUR PLATE IX

Black chalk, on greyish paper, over the pounce marks of an auxiliary cartoon, 375 × 276mm (folded horizontally, as are the other known auxiliary cartoons for *The Transfiguration*). Mounted in full for the 2nd Duke.

Chatsworth 67

Provenance: William, 2nd Duke of Devonshire (L.718)

Literature: Ruland, pp.29, 77; Fischel, 1898, p.140, no.344; Crowe and Cavalcaselle, ii, pp.310 and 489 (as by G.F. Penni); F.Hartt, 'Raphael and Giulio Romano, with notes on the Raphael school' AB, xxvi, 1944, p.87; Oberhuber, 1962, p.142; Oberhuber-Fischel, 1972, p.70, n.194; Knab, Mitsch, Oberhuber, 1983, no.613; Joannides, 1983, no.434

Exhibitions: London, 1949 (19); Manchester, 1961 (51); London, BM, 1983 (178); Pittsburgh, 1986–7 (63)

One of Raphael's ultimate preparations in 1520 for the altarpiece which was fully planned, but not quite finished at his death a few months later, it has been described by Joannides: 'The combination of breadth and precision, relief and texture is incomparable in this auxiliary cartoon; the hair ... acts as a metaphoric halo ... the moustache is drained of detail by the fall of light while retaining plastic form'. Carmen Bambach Cappel has urged abandonment of Fischel's term for such elaborately advanced studies ('auxiliary cartoons') in favour of 'full-scale figure studies on pounced marks'. Two other such studies are in the British Museum (Pouncey and Gere, 37 and 38), one of the heads and hands of two contiguous figures is in the Ashmolean (Parker, 568), and one is in the Albertina (cat.iii, 1932, no.79; 1983, no.45).

120 Raffaello Sanzio, called Raphael

(Urbino 1483–1520 Rome)

A Woman seated on a Chair reading, with a Child standing by her Side

Metalpoint on grey preparation, heightened with white body-colour, 190 × 140mm. Mounted in full for the 2nd Duke.

Chatsworth 728

Provenance: Sir Peter Lely (L.2092); William, 2nd Duke of Devonshire (L.718)

Literature: Passavant, II, 1836, p.451; Strong, 1902 (49); Fischel, VIII, 1942 (375); Knab, Mitsch, Oberhuber, 1983, no.444; Joannides, *Paragone*, 425, 1985 p.29

Exhibitions: Paris, 1935 (566); London, Arts Council, 1949 (14); London, RA, 1953 (58); Washington, etc., 1962–3 and London, RA, 1969 (57); London, BM, 1983–4 (137)

A life study of a woman and child in contemporary costume, drawn by Raphael about the period of his preparation for *The Mass of Bolsena*. A drawing in Oxford (London, British Museum, 1983 (138)) is closely related in style, technique and genre of subject. In Chatsworth 728 a third figure is adumbrated standing in the right background, as though on the threshold of a further

120

room. Both studies were most likely made for the purpose of being engraved by Marcantonio Raimondi or one of his pupils (B.XIV.54.48).

121 Raffaello Motta, called Raffaellino da Reggio

(Codemondo, Reggio Emilia 1550–1578 Rome)

Recto: The Entombment

Pen and brown ink with brown wash, over preliminaries in black chalk, heightened with white bodycolour, 180 × 160mm.

Verso: Two studies for an 'Ecce Homo'

Pen and brown ink over red chalk, 167 × 103mm.

Inscribed on the verso in pen and brown ink, in a 16th-century hand, *Raepheael da Regio*

Chatsworth 737

Provenance: William, 2nd Duke of Devonshire (L.718)

Literature: Reveley, p.59; Gere and Pouncey, 1983, p.146

The recto of this sheet was used as the basis for a chiaroscuro woodcut by Andrea Andreani in 1585 (B.XII.44.24). The traditional attribution, corresponding to the lettering of the chiaroscuro, is to be respected for this beautiful, highly emotive drawing. According to Baglione, Raffaello came from Reggio to Rome during the pontificate of Gregory XIII (1572–85). Also connected with the Andreani woodcut are two other drawings: Louvre inv. 6675 and Uffizi, 914S (Gere, Uffizi exhibition 1966, no.80, fig.55). As Reveley wrote, drawings by Raffaellino are 'extremely scarce and greatly valued'.

122 Guido Reni

(Calvenzano 1575–1642 Bologna)

A terrified nude Man, prone on rocky Ground

COLOUR PLATE V

Red chalk 290 × 435mm. (the sheet has been trimmed at the sides and the top).

Inscribed on the mount in pen and brown ink by J. Richardson
Guido

Chatsworth 490

Provenance: Dukes of Devonshire by 1868, and probably by the early 18th century

Exhibitions: Leeds, 1868 (2731, as *Prometheus* by Reni)

The traditional attribution to Reni of this study, of which the body, the legs, and probably both arms are manifestly from the life, while the head and its expression are idealised, should not have been doubted, as it was in the Courtauld Institute List of 1963. The suggestion by the compiler of the Leeds exhibition entries that Prometheus is represented is less likely than a fallen giant for *The Fall of the Titans*. In character and style, especially in the gestures and in the emphatic silhouetting of the limbs, there are marked similarities to the Windsor life study, also in red chalk, for a *Falling Giant* (Kurz, 1955, no.364). That is a preparation for one of the figures in the centre of the chiaroscuro woodcut of 1638 by Bartolomeo Coriolano after Reni (B.XII.114.12). Reni's plans for his first *Fall of the Titans* can be assumed on grounds of style to have been of the early years of the *seicento*. Presumably he knew of the engraving after Giulio Romano's treatment of the subject, and, as a young man, wished to emulate him.

Malvasia describes 'un altro pensiero de' Giganti fulminati, disegnato in tela di chiaroscuro a olio …', adding that the work greatly improved on the woodcut by Coriolano after the earlier painting, for in this chiaroscuro Reni 'pretendendo avere corretto e miglio-

121 *recto*

121 *verso*

rato inquesti molte cose'. He says further 'qual disegno oggi è posseduto da' Signori Sacchetti in Roma'. However the seventeenth-century inventory in the Archivio Sacchetti refers to a charcoal drawing ('La caduta dei Giganti disegno di Carbone alto p.m. 10 1/2, lung. p.m. 7.9 con la cornice intagliata, di colore e noce e oro di Guido Reni'). The Chatsworth drawing may well connect with the early project. Immediately following that is likely to be the first Coriolano woodcut (and preceding the editions of 1638, 1641, and 1647, the last dedicated to the Duke of Modena, with addition of Winds and Giants).

In the 1696 inventory of the Bonfiglioli collection, the most famous in *seicento* Bologna, which was drawn up after the death of Silvestro Bonfiglioli (1637–96), there was 'un disegno di un Gigante' by Reni. That could be the Windsor drawing, and among those purchased by Consul Smith, eventually passing to the English Royal Collection, from the heirs of Zaccaria Sagredo in Venice. However, since it is clear that important Bolognese drawings left the Bonfiglioli albums perhaps even years before the transfer of the collection in 1728 to Venice, the reference could be to the Chatsworth or to yet another drawing.

Reni returned to the theme *c.*1636–7 in his painting in Pesaro (Pepper, 1984, cat.163).

123 Guido Reni

(Calvenzano 1575–1642 Bologna)

The Head of a young Woman, turned to glance over her left Shoulder

Red chalk, 300 × 220mm. There is repaired damage in her hair behind her right temple, and pinholes at the corners to fix the drawing to a board. Mounted in full for the 2nd Duke.

Chatsworth 485

Provenance: Sir Peter Lely (L.2092); William, 2nd Duke of Devonshire (L.718)

Literature: S. Pepper, *Burl.Mag.*, 1971, p.380; Johnston, 1974, no.50; Pepper, 1984, n.33.3

Exhibitions: Washington, etc., 1962/63 and London, RA, 1969 (65); Sheffield, 1966 (41); Tokyo, 1975 (54); Vienna, 1981 (27 and p.57); Frankfurt, 1988/89 (B8)

A study from life for a figure in *The Birth of the Virgin*, the altarpiece of the Cappella dell' Annunziata, the private chapel of Paul V in the Quirinal. The first payments to Reni for his work in the chapel were of 1609, although the frescoes were painted by him and his assistants between January and September 1610. The Chatsworth drawing is therefore datable 1609.

124

124 Guido Reni

(Calvenzano 1575–1642 Bologna)

The youthful St John the Baptist preaching

Red chalk, 255 × 194mm. Mounted in full for the 2nd Duke.

Chatsworth 480

Provenance: William, 2nd Duke of Devonshire (L.718)

Surprisingly this beautiful drawing has no mention in the literature on Reni, and it has remained unpublished. The lyrical form, the rhetoric of the raised arms are manifestly inspired by Raphael's painting commissioned by Cardinal Pompeo Colonna and given by that prelate to the Florentine physician Jacopo da Carpi. The care which the draughtsman has taken to work out and support the pose are characteristic of Reni's classicism. These distinguish his strenuous efforts from those of his more facile follower, Simone Cantarini, whose emulative endeavour can be observed in a drawing of the same theme at Christ Church in Oxford (Byam Shaw, 1976, no.1017; formerly as Reni). It may be connected with the preparations for the painting published by R.Longhi, *Paragone*, IX, 1958, pp.68–70, in the collection of conte Leonardo Vitetti, Rome (formerly Duke of Westminster's collection at Grosvenor House).

125

125 Girolamo Romani, called il Romanino

(Brescia 1484/7–1562 Brescia)

An Executioner about to decapitate a bearded Saint

Pen and brown ink with brown wash, heightened with white bodycolour, over red chalk on blue paper, 267 × 192mm. Mounted in full for the 2nd Duke.

Chatsworth 759

Provenance: N. A. Flinck (L.959); William, 2nd Duke of Devonshire (L.718) from 1723–4

Literature: Strong, 1902 (67, as by Callisto da Lodi); Brescia, 1965, p.234

Exhibitions: Leeds, 1868 (2700, as 'Giorgione, A Decapitation'); London, New Gallery, 1894–5 (850, as 'school of Giorgione'); Washington, etc., 1969–70 and London, V & A, 1973–4 (60, as Romanino); London, RA, 1983–4 (D.48)

An early work by Romanino. The 1965 Romanino catalogue claimed that F. Kossoff made the convincing reattribution. At Chatsworth A. E. Popham is recorded as having come to the same opinion, independently and earlier. As D. Scrase pointed out (London, RA, 1983–4) this drawing is cut from a larger sheet, on which the full modello for the martyrdom was set out. The stocky thighs and imperfectly articulate ankles are characteristic of Romanino's provincial beginnings. The painterly use of brown and white washes on blue paper characterize his early accomplishment.

126 Girolamo Romani, called il Romanino

(Brescia, 1484/7–1562 Brescia)

The Pyre raised before Hannibal's Troops at the fall of Saguntum

Pen and brown ink with brown wash, 194 × 268mm. Mounted in full for the 2nd Duke.

Inscribed lower right, in a ?17th-century hand, *Raefael*

Chatsworth 402

Provenance: N. A. Flinck (L.959); 2nd Duke of Devonshire, from 1723–4

The text is Livy, xxi. 14; 'The leading men ... casting it into a fire which they had hurriedly made up for this purpose, many threw themselves into the same flames. A tower that had long been battered had collapsed, and through the breach a cohort of Phoenicians had rushed in and signalled guards and sentinels.' Saguntum (Sagunto) is a town near the coast of Hispania Interior (now Eastern Spain on the river Palancia south of the Ebro); the incident was the immediate cause of the 2nd Punic War (218–201 BC) between Carthage and Rome.

The subject, which had been supposed in modern times to be of an allegorical kind, is identifiable from the inscription 'Sagontom obsessom', penned by the elderly Romanino at the foot of Uffizi n.8199 S (exhibited, *Disegni Italiani*, Uffizi, 1967, fig.21). That drawing uses the same fierce hatchings, impatient ductus and brutal deformations to

126

render the narrative of the heroic citizens of Saguntum, allies of Rome, burning their goods in the piazza rather than let them fall into the hands of the Carthaginian army under Hannibal. Chatsworth 402, on the Courtauld Institute List of 1963 as Camillo Procaccini, represents with even more vigour the burning of those who died in the siege, while Hannibal's troops look on. The name of Raphael, the supreme narrator, presumably became attached because of the way in which the pyre blazes at the left of the composition. That could be a reminiscence of the drawing of *God the Father appearing to Moses* for the frescoed vault of the Stanza d'Eliodoro. On the suite of Roman histories frescoed in the Casa del Gambero, Romanino had help from his young collaborator, Lattanzio Gambara.

127 Salvator Rosa

(Arenella, Naples 1615–1673 Rome)

Study for an Allegory of Justice

Pen and brown ink with brown wash, 170 × 110mm (the upper corners are chamfered). Mounted in full for the 2nd Duke.

Chatsworth 613

Provenance: William, 2nd Duke of Devonshire (L.718)

Literature: Reveley, p.132 (as Rosa, 'Enchantress in his best manner'); Vitzthum, 1970, p.83; Paris, 1971, p.20; Mahoney, 1977, no.54.2

The traditional and correct attribution in the Devonshire collection is to Salvator Rosa. Other drawings connected with this composition, datable *c*.1650, are Leipzig 7450.24.16A (Mahoney, 54.1), Louvre 9734 (Mahoney, 54.3), and the National Galleries of Scotland, RSA 199 verso (Mahoney 54.4). Rosa wrote of this painting (Salerno, 1963, pl.63) for the first time in 1651 in a letter to his friend Ricciardi. A drawing in the Teylers Museum, Haarlem, studies the figure in an attitude very similar to Chatsworth 613.

128 Giovanni Battista dei Rossi, called Rosso Fiorentino

(Florence 1495–1540 Paris)

Ignudo on the Sistine Vault, after Michelangelo

COLOUR PLATE X

Red chalk on cream paper, 413 × 279mm. The lower right corner has been repaired by Flinck (and perhaps at the same time damage to the left edge). Mounted in full for the 2nd Duke.

Inscribed on the verso *Buonarotti* (according to a pencilled note by Mrs S.A. Strong in the Chatsworth album of photographs (Braun no.25))

Chatsworth 900

127

Provenance: Sir Peter Lely (L.2092); N.A.Flinck (L.959 on the repair); William, 2nd Duke of Devonshire (L.718), from 1723–4

Literature: Passavant, 1836, II, p.142 (as by Michelangelo); Waagen, 1854, III, p.354 (as by Michelangelo); Morelli, 1892, p.130 (as by Pontormo, on the strength of the Braun photo)

Exhibitions: Leeds, 1868 (as by Michelangelo); Pittsburgh, etc., 1987–8 (68, as by Rosso)

Traditionally given in the Devonshire collection to Michelangelo, but classed at Chatsworth since 1929 just as 'after Michelangelo', this drawing struck me there (1984) as a superb tribute by Rosso, drawn presumably soon after he went in 1524 to Rome. The annotated typescript of F. Thompson's 1929 catalogue on deposit in the British Museum revealed in 1988 A.E. Popham's note: 'This copy might well be by Rosso'. It can be compared to the Uffizi drawing of a *Nude Man in profile* (P. Barocchi, *Il Rosso Fiorentino*, Rome, 1950, pl.184), especially for the hand and arm. Rosso in reaching for expressive pictorial effects in chiaroscuro has characteristically flattened the plastic sense of the original figure: but to a brilliant result.

129

His own *ignudi*, to be executed in stucco for the Galerie de François I at Fontainebleau many years later, patently benefited from such youthful study of Michelangelo (cf. *Revue de l'Art*, 16/17, 1972). Passavant and Waagen accepted the tradition of Michelangelo's own hand in this drawing, Waagen remarking the 'soft and masterly modelling'.

129 Giovanni Battista dei Rossi, called Rosso Fiorentino

(Florence 1495–1540 Paris)

Draped female Figure bearing a Bundle on her Head

Red chalk, 274 × 136mm. Mounted in full for the 2nd Duke.

Provenance: N. A. Flinck (L.959); William, 2nd Duke of Devonshire (L.718)

Literature: Strong, 1902 (712); K. Kusenberg, *Le Rosso*, Paris, 1931, p.139, no.5; P. Barocchi, *Il Rosso Fiorentino*, Rome, 1950, p.200, n.3; Longhi, 1951, p.59; Parker, 1956, under no.236; Carroll, 1976, no.F.3

Exhibitions: Washington, etc., 1962–3 (66); Manchester, 1965 (367); Cambridge, 1988 (15)

As Carroll noted, the *Draped female Figure* may be a study for the full-length woman silhouetted against the sky in a compositional drawing that seems to conflate more than one episode from the Old Testament account of the Israelites' wanderings in the Wilderness of Sinai (British Museum ff.1–18; Carroll, 1976, F.36). This figure once may have been attributed to Parmigianino (see Carroll); but it was associated with Rosso's name by both Loeser and Colvin, and by tradition at Chatsworth it has been kept, classed, and exhibited as his. The attribution to Rosso before 1523, published by Kusenberg, was queried by Longhi and rejected by Carroll but followed by all other commentators. Carroll took both it and the British Museum drawing away from Rosso declaring them to be early works of Bandinelli on the spurious basis of comparison with a drawing in the Uffizi of a *Saint Blessing* (Carroll, 1976, no.F.16), which he incorrectly identified as a study for Bandinelli's statue of St Peter of 1515–17 (Cambridge, 1988, cat.9). There was however an association between the two artists in about 1516–17 as Vasari relates. The Chatsworth and British Museum drawings show Rosso in a Bandinellian idiom.

130 Andrea Sacchi

(Rome 1599–1661 Nettuno)

Arcadian Scene

Red chalk, with brown washes on the trees and rocks, heightened with white bodycolour on the figures and on other elements of the landscape, on paper washed pink, squared in black chalk, 241 × 360mm. Mounted in full for the 2nd Duke.

Chatsworth 565

Traditionally attributed in the Devonshire collection to Sacchi. Eugénie Strong suggested that this depicted a scene from Ariosto: Astraea, called Justice, cloudborne, holds her scales while menacing with the thunderbolt of her father Jupiter the ithyphallic satyr who wields an axe

130

to one side of a wheel, representing the ingenuity of man, while his satyress bends to gather something from the ground in the animal skin which she wears as an apron. Another satyr crouches in a cave on the left; at the right Cupid bearing a torch advances, a dove flies and a woman on whom the sun shines, lies asleep. As Dr J.Montagu has suggested to me, this scene of the goddess forbidding the destruction of the wheel is of the shape and complexity to be the model for a thesis.

131 Francesco de' Rossi, called Salviati

(Florence 1510–1563 Rome)

Aurora, after Michelangelo

Black chalk, 370 × 230mm. Lifted (1986) from its 18th-century mount.

Inscribed on the verso in pen and brown ink in an early 18th-century hand *P.G.No20*

Chatsworth 14

Provenance: N.A.Flinck (L.959); presumably William, 2nd Duke of Devonshire from 1723–4

Exhibitions: Pittsburgh, etc., 1987–8 (71)

Another view of Michelangelo's marble *Aurora*, recumbent below Duke Lorenzo in the Medici Chapel of San Lorenzo, drawn in red chalk apparently by the same draughtsman standing with his back to the altar is in the British Museum (Wilde 102). That London drawing was classed by Wilde as 'by a very competent draughtsman working in the second half of the century or later' and placed by him with 'copies from sculptures'. But comparison may be made with British Museum 1946–7–13–250, a *Nude Female* drawn in black chalk, and with Uffizi 253F, a copy drawn in red chalk after Duke Giuliano in the Medici Chapel (the latter drawing attributed to Salviati by G. Sinibaldi). The silhouetting, the shading, the texture, the spatulate toes and the manner of crooking the fingers, all point to the same authorship, that of Francesco Salviati, to whom the present drawing has traditionally been ascribed at Chatsworth. Salviati's use of the British Museum drawing is to be noted in the *Female Nude, partly draped, reclining in a Landscape* (Uffizi 608; pen and brown ink and brown wash).

131

132 Andrea d'Agnolo, called del Sarto

(Florence 1486–1530 Florence)

Two studies of a Man suspended by his left Leg

COLOUR PLATE XI

Red chalk on cream paper, 206 × 192mm. Mounted in full for the 2nd Duke.

Chatsworth 710

Provenance: N. A. Flinck (L.959); William, 2nd Duke of Devonshire (L.718)

Literature: J. Shearman, *Andrea del Sarto*, Oxford, 1965, II, p.324; Samuel Y. Edgerton Jr., *Pictures and Punishment*, Ithaca/London, 1985, pp.114–19, fig.27

Exhibitions: Manchester, 1961 (57); Washington, etc., 1962–3 and London, RA, 1969 (3)

Studies for paintings of three captains who had fled from Florence during the siege of 1530 and had been declared traitors. Andrea had undertaken to paint their effigies on a wall of the Mercanza Vecchia, as well as those of three civilian traitors on the Palazzo Vecchio. They were to be represented according to Florentine custom suspended by one leg, as a warning: but the figures had been whitewashed by the time Vasari wrote in 1568 (ed. Milanesi, v, pp.53–4). Only this and some drawings in the Uffizi (Berenson, 118a, 118b, 118c and 125) survive to record this gruesome commission; Uffizi 330F being the closest to Chatsworth 710. According to Vasari, although Andrea painted the figures by his own hand, he preferred that his name should not be mentioned and that the commission should be in the name of his pupil, Bernardo del Buda. Vasari also records (ed. Milanesi, VI, p.63) that the sculptor Tribolo modelled the three figures in wax for his friend Andrea.

133 Bartolomeo Schedoni

(Modena 1578–1615 Parma)

A Mother and Child

Black chalk, with brown wash, slightly heightened with white, on faded blue paper, 410 × 318mm. Mounted in full for the 2nd Duke.

133

134

Chatsworth 552

Provenance: N. Lanière (L.2883); N. A. Flinck (L.959); William, 2nd Duke of Devonshire from 1722–3

Literature: Campbell Dodgson, OMD, 1, 1926, p.19 (?Schidone); M. Jaffé, 'Another Schedoni Drawing', in *Festschrift to Erik Fischer*, Copenhagen, 1990, p.219, fig.2

Exhibitions: Sheffield, 1966 (44); Washington, etc., 1969–70 and London, V&A, 1973–4 (67)

Traditionally in the Devonshire collection as Guercino, but reattributed tentatively to Schedoni by Campbell Dodgson. Datable *c*.1609–10 from congruence of style with the Städel drawing published by the present writer in 1990.

134 Andrea Meldolla, called il Schiavone

(Zara (Dalmatia) 1522–82 Venice)

The Worship of the Golden Calf

Pen and brown ink, with brown and grey washes, with extensive use of white bodycolour (oxydised) on blue paper, 213 × 330mm. Fully mounted for the 2nd Duke.

Chatsworth 306

Provenance: Sir Peter Lely (L.2092); P. H. Lankrink (L.2090); William, 2nd Duke of Devonshire (L.718)

Literature: Reveley, p.43 (as Parmigianino); Richardson, 1980, p.121, cat.161

Exhibitions: London, New Gallery, 1894–5 (866)

Traditionally in the Devonshire collection as Parmigianino. His influence on this Dalmatian working in Venice is apparent. In F. L. Richardson's view, which is surely correct, 'but for a finer than usual pen line, an utterly typical large-scale Schiavone drawing of the more elaborate variety'.

135 Sebastiano del Piombo

(Venice *c*.1485–1547 Rome)

A reclining Apostle

Black chalk with brown wash on faded blue paper, heightened with white bodycolour, squared in red chalk, 237 × 444mm. Strips have been added along most of the left and upper edges to mend tears. Mounted in full for the 2nd Duke.

Chatsworth 39

Provenance: William, 2nd Duke of Devonshire (L.718)

135

136

Literature: Strong, 1902 (47); Berenson, 1938 (2478); L.D. Düssler, *Sebastiano del Piombo*, Basle, 1942, p.167; L. Palluchini, *Sebastian Viniziano*, Milan, 1944, p.52; M. Hirst, *Sebastiano del Piombo*, Oxford, 1981, p.59

Exhibitions: London, RA, 1930 (840); London, Arts Council, 1949 (21); Washington, etc., 1962–3 and London, RA, 1969 (68); London, RA, 1983–4 (D.57)

Sebastiano's study for St James on the right of the fresco of *The Transfiguration*, commissioned in 1516 for S. Pietro in Montorio, Rome, by Pierfrancesco Borgherini whose features may have been represented; as Berenson pointed out, they resemble those of the donor in the *Madonna and Child with Sts Joseph and John the Baptist* (London, National Gallery, no.1450).

136 Francesco Solimena

(Canale si Serino/Naples 1657–1747 Barra/Naples)

Heliodorus driven from the Temple

Pen and grey wash, over preliminaries in black chalk, 380 × 547mm. Mounted in full for the 2nd Duke.

Chatsworth 626

Provenance: William, 2nd Duke of Devonshire

Literature: W. Vitzthum, 1970, p.86

Exhibitions: Sheffield, 1966 (45); Washington, etc., 1969–70 and London, V&A, 1973–4 (63); Tokyo, 1975 (65)

Traditionally in the Devonshire collection as Solimena, this magnificent drawing is his large study drawn for the huge fresco inside the entrance wall of the Gesù Nuovo at Naples, which is signed and dated by him, 1725. The Chatsworth drawing surely preceded the painted *bozzetti* in the Toledo Museum of Art (*Civiltà del '700 a Napoli 1734–1799*, I, cat.75) and in the Louvre (F. Bologna, *Solimena*, 1958, p.272, fig.166); and it differs from these and from the fresco in the figures in the background and in architectural details. Instead of the naked beggar in the lower left corner of the drawing, both the Louvre oil sketch and the fresco show a boy, with a dog to his left (a dog only appears in the Toledo sketch). In Chatsworth 626 the area of the main entry to the church is ruled off.

137 Parri Spinelli

(Arezzo *c.*1387–1453 Arezzo)

Recto: Christ and the Woman taken in Adultery

Verso: Pilgrims kneeling at a Shrine

Pen and brown ink, over preliminaries in metalpoint, 288 × 208mm. The lower left corner and margin of the recto have been repaired

Chatsworth 703

137 *recto*

137 *verso*

Literature: Vasari Society, 2nd series, VI, 2, 3; Berenson, 1938 (1837D); Degenhart and Schmitt, 1969, I (212); Maria Fossi Todorow, *L'Italia dalle origine a Pisanello*, Milan, 1970, pl. XX; Ames-Lewis, 1981, p.82, fig.58

Exhibitions: London, RA, 1953 (1); Washington, etc., 1969–70 and London, V&A, 1973–4 (65); Nottingham/London, 1983 (49)

Traditionally in the Devonshire collection as Spinelli, and unmistakably his penwork. Degenhart and Schmitt (211) pointed out that the recto formed the right half of a composition completed on the recto of a sheet in the Uffizi, no. 23E. A similar double sheet by Parri, with a continuous composition recto, and two independent studies verso, is intact in Uffizi 8E (Degenhart & Schmitt, 213).

138 Pietro Testa

(Lucca 1612–1650 Rome)

The Goddess Diana as Huntress

Pen and brown ink on cream paper, 310 × 217mm. Mounted in full for the 2nd Duke.

Chatsworth 623

Provenance: N. A. Flinck (L.959); William, 2nd Duke of Devonshire (L.718) from 1723–4

Literature: Harris, 1967, p.52; Roli, 1969, p.116; Hartmann, 1970, p.170; Brigstocke, 1978, pp.118, 144; Blunt, 1980, pp.25–6

Exhibitions: London, Wildenstein, 1955 (80); Washington, etc., 1962–3 and London, RA, 1969 (70); Philadelphia/Cambridge (Mass.), 1988–9 (18)

In a composition reminiscent of Pietro da Cortona, Diana, goddess of the moon and of hunting, rests with her hounds after the chase. Bow in hand she sits contemplating the deer she has shot. Behind her at the left a figure looks up, eyes shielded from the afternoon sun which is high above the point of the obelisk that symbolises its rays. The lassitude of the goddess, like that of Adonis in the Albertina *Venus and Adonis*, conveys sweet melancholy, as Elizabeth Cropper (1988–9) has emphasized. Here, however, the remains of the past establish the sense of permanence in change. The fanciful cityscape of *Roma antiqua* includes not only the obelisk but also allusions to the Quirinal Horse-Tamers, the Colosseum and the Torre delle Milizie. The hounds and the dead hind derive directly from Testa's drawings for his etching of *Venus and Adonis* of c.1631–71 (B XX.222.25).

138

139 Pellegrino Tibaldi

(Puria di Valsolda 1527–1596 Milan)

Allegorical design for a sopraporta in the Sala Paolina of the Castel S. Angelo, Rome

Pen and brown ink with brown wash, 350 × 228mm. There is a hole in the knee of the seated captain. Mounted in full for Lord Somers, with the missing base made up.

Inscribed on the drawing in pen and brown ink *li quattro maestri d esemplari del Pelegrino/Vasari 10 Perino 20 Cechino 30 M.Angelo 40/ PELEGRINO/TIBALDO/imitato da(?un) maestro di..*; and in the hand of J. Richardson the elder, following Resta, on the mount for Lord Somers, in pen and brown ink, *e.23* and *Prospero Fontana*

Chatsworth 181

Provenance: P. Sebastiano Resta (as Prospero Fontana); Giovanni Matteo Marchetti (died 1704), Bishop of Arezzo, from 1698; sold by his heir, the cavaliere Orazio Marchetti of Pistoia; Lord Somers from 1710 to 1716; his sale, London 1717; William, 2nd Duke of Devonshire (L.718)

Although born in Lombardy, Pellegrino Tibaldi's artistic formation began in Bologna where his father worked as an architect. He was in Rome by the mid-1540s. There is no obvious explanation for Resta's attribution to Prospero Fontana. Vasari and Baglione give accounts of the collaboration of Pellegrino Tibaldi and Marco Pino da Siena with Perino del Vaga in the fresco decoration of the Sala Paolina. The drawing corresponds closely to the overdoor fresco, with idiosyncratically different expressions to the figures, different actions and different fruit in the swags (Parma Armani, 1986, p.218, fig.266). The scene shows the Muses Erato and Thalia, with *The Blinding of Elymas* enframed in the tondo.

This drawing should be considered with Perino's design for the Sala della Giustizia in the Castel S. Angelo, composed of comparable elements drawn in a similar technique, but the draughtsmanship and the inscriptions differ (see Popham and Wilde, no.979; *Castitas* and *Concordia*).

140 Titiano Vecellio, called Titian

(Pieve di Cadore (?) 1477–1576 Venice)

Landscape with a riderless Horse pursued by a Serpent

Pen and brown ink, on cream coloured paper, 199 × 298mm. Fully mounted on an 18th-century mount.

Chatsworth 751

Provenance: presumably Rembrandt van Rijn; presumably 1st or 2nd Duke of Devonshire

139

140

Literature: Passavant, 1836, II, p.146 (as Titian); Waagen, 1854, III, p.358 (as Titian); Wethey, 1987, cat.38 (as Titian); W.R. Rearick, 'Titian Drawings: a progress report' in *Artibus et historiae*, no.23 (XII), Vienna, 1991, pp.21–2 (as Titian)

Exhibitions: London, New Gallery, 1894–5 (867, as 'attributed to Titian'); Venice, 1976 (47, as Titian); Pittsburgh, etc., 1987–8 (74, as Titian); Amsterdam, 1991 (15)

The horse clambering up the bank has a bridle, but there is no rider; and behind the horse in the water is a serpent in pursuit. The *poesia* remains unexplained: but the poetic pitch, not to speak of such noble passages as the middleground trees with their reflections and the relation of the distant mountain to the cumulus boiling in the sky, are eloquent of Titian *c.*1565, with a creativity and touch far beyond the powers of Domenico Campagnola to whom this drawing was attributed at Chatsworth in the first half of the twentieth century (dott. Frizzoni and conte Gamba, visiting Chatsworth, considered it to be a seventeenth-century copy after Campagnola; R. Walker, in his Harvard doctoral thesis of 1941 on Campagnola, included it as by that artist, p.15, n.99).

M. Winner, 1973, pp.221–4 signalled a copy in the Berlin Kupferstichkabinett, attributed to Carracci (KdZ 17598; pen and brown ink, 188 × 303mm) which was convincingly attributed to Rembrandt *c.*1650–2 in Washington, 1990 (38); P. Dreyer noted another in the Munich Print Room, Inv.Nr.2376, attributed to Domenichino; and knowledge of the Munich copy may have led A. E. Popham in 1962 to accept Domenichino's authorship for the Chatsworth drawing. As Oberhuber pointed out, the cloud recalls the motifs of comparable force in Titian's drawing of *The Landscape with St Jerome* (his no.12) and in the woodcut of *The Crossing of the Red Sea* (M. Muraro and D. Rosand, *Tiziano e la silografia veneziana del cinquecento*, Vicenza, 1976, no.8). A similar horse had already appeared in a Titian design, galloping across the distance in the woodcut *Landscape with a Milkmaid and a Youth sowing* of *c.*1523 (Wethey, 1987, fig.91).

The warmth and density of the boskage at the right is such as we find in the drawing in John J. Steiner's collection (Oberhuber, 1976, no.36 *bis*). Passavant wrote of two landscapes at Chatsworth by Titian, 'most spiritedly drawn with the pen. On the one, a piece of water, out of which a horse is coming'. The other, which was likewise attributed to Campagnola in the first half of the twentieth century, was tentatively re-attributed to Titian by

141 *recto*

141 *verso*

Byam Shaw in the 1969–70 exhibition (68), and correctly so. Waagen supported the attribution, evidently of long standing, of both these drawings at Chatsworth to Titian ('poetical in conception, and very spiritedly drawn with the pen').

141 Pietro Buonaccorsi, called Perino del Vaga

(Florence 1500–1547 Rome)

Recto: Studies of an Eagle, a Goose, a Jug, a Jar, and of human Figures (including two for a Rape of Lucretia*)*

Verso: Studies of an Eagle, a domed Building, and of human Figures (including a Madonna and Child under a Canopy and a Supplicant kneeling before ?a King and Queen)

Pen and brown ink with brown wash, 201 × 284mm. Mounted in full.

Inscribed in brown ink, on *verso Perino. 8* (the digit may refer to a lot number at auction)

Chatsworth 1050

Provenance: Sir Peter Lely (L.2092); presumably 1st or 2nd Duke of Devonshire

A highly characteristic sheet of studies by the restless pen of the young Perino.

142 Pietro Buonaccorsi, called Perino del Vaga

(Florence 1500–1547 Rome)

The Banquet of Dido and Aeneas

Pen and brown ink with brown wash, heightened with white, on blue paper, 226 × 172mm. Mounted in full for the 2nd Duke.

Chatsworth 163

Provenance: Sir Peter Lely (L.2092); William, 2nd Duke of Devonshire (L.718)

Literature: Reveley, p.19 (as 'The Feast of the Gods'); B. Davidson, 'The Navigatione d'Enea tapestries designed by Perino del Vaga', AB, 1990, pp.39–41, fig.6

Exhibitions: London, RA, 1960 (579, as 'Banquet Scene')

Stylistically this drawing, always attributed to Perino, belongs to his work in Genoa. B. Davidson has identified the subject: Cupid, disguised as Ascanius, embraces Dido enflaming her with love, while other Trojans, led probably by Achates, enter from the right bearing gifts (*Aeneid* I, 695ff.). She has shown that this rapid sketch to arrange limbs and lighting was followed by a more finished drawing in Hamburg (her fig.5), which is actually signed with Perino's monogram on the seat at the left, and which may be regarded as a *modello* for the first of six tapestries to be woven in silk and wool as decoration for the first *salone*

to be decorated to the order of Andrea Doria for his palace at Fassolo. The banquet scene was evidently inspired by the small scene, lower right, in the border of Marcantonio Raimondi's *Quos Ego* engraved after Raphael (B.XIV.264.352), a print which Perino knew well in Rome, and of which he probably owned an impression.

The six tapestries with illustrations to *Aeneid* I were delivered in time for the 1636 visit to Genoa of the Emperor Charles V, a passionate collector of tapestry. The cartoons never appear in the Doria inventories, and were presumably kept by the Flemish weavers. The 1636 set survived in the palace until the nineteenth century. Variants of the composition of the banquet scene are to be found in the Oesterreichisches Museum für Angewandte Kunst in Vienna and in the Palacio de las Cortes, Madrid (Davidson, 1990, figs.7 and 8). Vasari records that Perino made drawings for 'la maggior parte della Eneide con le storie di Didone, che se ne fece panni d'arazzi'. The *Navigatione d'Enea* suite, as Davidson suggests, may precede the other suite designed by Perino for the *piano nobile* of Andrea Doria's palace. There the Neptune *salone* was painted soon after Perino's arrival in 1528. The tapestries would have followed virtually immediately and before the *Furti di Giove* suite, also designed by Perino.

142

143

143 Pietro Buonaccorsi, called Perino del Vaga

(Florence 1500–1547 Rome)

The Hunt of the Calydonian Boar

Pen and brown ink with brown wash, heightened with white bodycolour, 198 × 260mm. Mounted in full for the 2nd Duke as an oval.

Chatsworth 157

Provenance: Sir Peter Lely (L.2092); William, 2nd Duke of Devonshire (L.718)

Literature: Morelli, 1892, p.148; Parma Armani, 1986, p.154, n.54, fig.240

Exhibitions: Leeds, 1868 (2708, as Perino del Vaga); Washington, etc., 1962/3 and London, RA, 1969 (47); Sheffield, 1966 (30)

Design for one of six oval intaglios of rock crystal which were to be engraved by Giovanni Bernardo di Castelbolognese and set into a silver gilt casket ordered for Cardinal Alessandro Farnese from the Florentine goldsmith Manno di Bastiano Sbarri and made between 1548 and 1561 (Naples, Museo di Capodimonte). Although there is no contemporary record of Perino having made these designs c.1544 for the Cassetta Farnese, the attributions of the extant original drawings to him is trustworthy. A less finished design for the subject of Chatsworth 157 is in the Musée des Beaux-Arts, Besançon (No.1398D).

144 Pietro Buonaccorsi, called Perino del Vaga

(Florence 1500–1547 Rome)

Studies of an Eagle's Head

Pen and brown ink, 261 × 192mm. Fully mounted for the 2nd Duke.

Chatsworth 168

Provenance: William, 2nd Duke of Devonshire (L.718)

A. E. Popham in the 1930s thought of Baldassare Peruzzi; but by 1962 he had reverted to the traditional attribution, apparently unknown to him. In their passionate ferocity these studies may be compared with those of the eagles, wings outspread, which are penned with other studies either side of Chatsworth 1050, a sheet traditionally ascribed to Perino (his name is inscribed in an old hand on the *verso*) and highly characteristic of him. Those on the present drawing do not connect with any known painting; but one or other could have been used for the attribute of St John the Evangelist.

145 Francesco Vanni

(Barontoli, Siena 1563–1610 Siena)

Two Scenes from the Life of St Catherine of Siena

Red chalk, 201 × 292mm. Mounted in full for the 2nd Duke.

Inscribed in pen and brown ink, in a (?)late 17th-century hand, *Franco Vanni*

Chatsworth 376

Provenance: William, 2nd Duke of Devonshire (L.718)

Literature: L. Bianchi, *Caterina da Siena nei disegni di Francesco Vanni incisi da Pieter de Jode*, Rome, 1980, p.23, fig.3

Exhibitions: Avignon, 1992 (43)

The full-sized model for the engraving by Pieter de Jode for scenes 4–6 of the *Legenda Major* in the set of twelve historiated plates and a frontispiece which were published together on 1 October 1597 by the Sienese printer Matteo Florini. On the left, St Catherine receives the habit from St Dominic (Vita 53). On the right, she puts the demons to flight (Vita 63 and 109). Above she is transported on a white cloud after she had retired to her grotto.

146 Giorgio Vasari

(Arezzo 1511–1574 Florence)

Allegory of Justice

Pen and brown ink with brown wash, on cream paper, 290 × 221mm. Mounted in full for Lord Somers by J. Richardson the elder.

Inscribed in pen and brown ink, by the artist: on the book, XII; and below the vices, *crudetta*; *ignoranza*; *corringo*; *busgia*; *tradimento*; *maledicem*; *timore*; and by a later hand for Lord Somers *e.i.*

Chatsworth 177

Provenance: P. Sebastiano Resta; Giovanni Matteo Marchetti (died 1704), Bishop of Arezzo, from 1698; sold by his heir, the cavaliere Orazio Marchetti of Pistoia; Lord Somers from 1710

144

until at least 1716; his sale, London, 1717; William, 2nd Duke of Devonshire (L.718)

Exhibitions: Arezzo, 1981/2 (IV. 28b, pp.80–90, fig.142)

Always attributed in the Devonshire collection to Vasari, following Resta, except for T. P. P. Clifford's suggestion of Francesco Salviati. On 6 January 1543, Vasari was commissioned by Cardinal Alessandro Farnese to paint the subject on a 'tavola grande, alta braccia sei et largha 4½' (Vasari-Frey, II, p.860). Two mediators were appointed, the banker Bindo Altoviti and Paolo Giovio, Bishop of Nocera. On 21 January Giovio was able to send the cardinal a drawing accompanied by a detailed explanation by Vasari himself. 'Giustizia' in this proposal was 'nuda dal mezzo in su' sitting on the pandects of Justinian, and identified with Astrea. The seven vices are naked and bound at her feet, chained to her belt. Her right arm embraces the neck of an ostrich, 'lo struzzo, il quale ... smaltiscie il ferro, si come si purga per lei ogni ignominia; et ha le ali parissime ... posto dalli Egyptii nelle piramide'. These last words reveal Vasari's source in the *Hieroglyphica* of Horapollo taken up also by Valerian. The prodigious digestion of the ostrich was referred to by Pliny. Vasari's letter of January 1543 gives other details applicable

145

neither to Chatsworth 177, nor to the finished painting in Naples, Museo di Capodimonte, Inv.84214, which was ready for delivery a year later, on 5 December 1544. Chatsworth 177 seems therefore to have been an earlier trial of the composition drawn in January 1543.

147 Giorgio Vasari

(Arezzo 1511–1574 Florence)

Lorenzo the Magnificent petitions Ferdinand, King of Naples for Peace

Pen and brown ink with brown wash over preliminaries in black chalk, heightened with white bodycolour, 145 × 342mm. Mounted in full for the 2nd Duke.

Chatsworth 176

Provenance: an unknown collector (*u–sc*); N. A. Flinck (L.959); William, 2nd Duke of Devonshire, from 1723–4

Literature: F. Stampfle, 'A ceiling design for Vasari', MD, VI, 1968, pp.266–7

Exhibitions: Arezzo, 1981/2 (V, 43, p.144, fig.154)

Designed for one of the hemicycles on the ceiling of the Sala di Lorenzo il Magnifico of the apartments of Leo X in the Palazzo Vecchio, Florence, this is closer to the painting (Stampfle, fig.3.) than is the study for the whole ceiling (Pierpont Morgan Library: Stampfle, pl.32). The programme for showing Lorenzo as a diplomat, warrior and humanist is set out in detail in a letter addressed to Vasari, presumably by Cosimo Bartoli, probably sometime before 23 April 1556 (Karl Frey, *Der literarische Nachlass Giorgio Vasaris*, Munich, I, 1923, pp.437–8). The decorations were finished in 1562.

In her entry for the 1981 exhibition catalogue, Laura Corti names in Lorenzo's suite Paulantonio di Tommaso Soderini, Pier Capponi, Giovanni de'Medici; and behind the king, the Florentine Diotisalvi Neroni.

147

146

148 Paolo Caliari, called Veronese

(Verona 1528–88 Venice)

The Supper at Emmaus

COLOUR PLATE XII

Pen and black ink with brown wash, heightened with white bodycolour, over preliminaries in black chalk on blue paper, 421 × 576mm. Mounted in full for the 2nd Duke.

Chatsworth 277

Provenance: Sir Peter Lely (L.2092); William, 2nd Duke of Devonshire

Literature: Tietzes, 1944 (2055, as by Veronese's shop); Cocke, 1984 (35, as by Veronese)

Exhibitions: London, New Gallery, 1894–5 (853, as Paolo Veronese); Washington, etc., 1962–3 and London, RA, 1969 (71, as 'attributed to Paolo Veronese' and 'perhaps by Paolo Farinati'); Washington, 1988–9 (5, as by Veronese)

This develops the primary group of *Christ and two Pilgrims* tried in a Parmigianesque drawing which belongs to the Kupferstichkabinett, Berlin (Washington, 1988(4)). Both drawings are dated by Rearick in the Washington catalogue *c*.1549. The Berlin drawing was regarded by the Tietzes as a copy: but this would not account for the nervosity of its black chalk preliminaries or for its vibrant revisions. Niccolò dell'Abate seems also to have influenced Veronese's stylisations at this early stage of his draughtsmanship. No painting by him of this subject is known to survive earlier than the Louvre version of the mid 1550s: but it seems more likely that a painting was at least intended than a presentation drawing which was Rearick's suggestion.

149

149 Paolo Caliari, called Veronese

(Verona 1528–88)

Allegory to celebrate the Publication of the Holy League, 1571

Pen and brown wash, heightened with white bodycolour, over preliminaries in black chalk, on green prepared paper, 437 × 583mm. Mounted in full.

Chatsworth 278

Literature: Waagen, 1854, III, p.358; Coutts, 1986 (the penwork added by a later hand); Crosato, 1986 (as shop work); Tietzes, 1944 (2165, 'a typical shop production'); Cocke, 1984, 150 (n.62, as Veronese)

Exhibitions: Washington, etc., 1969–70 and London, V & A, 1973–4 (73); London, Hayward Gallery, 1975 (283); Venice, 1986 (4); Washington, 1988–9 (53)

Traditionally in the Devonshire collection as Veronese, this vastly important drawing was preceded by a drawing in Berlin which is Veronese's only known drawing in red chalk (Washington, 1988 (52)). Emperor, Pope and Doge, seated left with their respective supporters (courtiers, cardinals and a quartet of senators) behind them and their symbolic beasts (eagle, wolf and lion) below, receive the appealing figure of Faith holding a chalice, while St Mark with Sts Peter and Mark, cloudborne, throw down laurel branches of victory to a trio of putti in the hall below, who festoon a halberd. Drummers and soldiers in the colonnade include one with a wheel; and further allegorical figures, including Neptune, are at the right.

The allegory celebrates the grandeur of the public celebration in Venice of the formation of the Holy League against Suleyman the Magnificent on 2 July 1571, as Boucher first brought out in his entry in the Andrea Palladio catalogue of 1975. The Holy League had been signed on 25 May by the Papacy, the Empire, Spain and Venice. While the ruling of the elaborate architectural setting may well have been entrusted to an assistant, the principal figures and the finishing touches are masterly. There is some damage through the centre, and some of the

150

contours have been re-inforced (e.g. the three putti holding arms, right centre). In this finished chiaroscuro drawing Veronese abandoned the unfamiliar medium of red chalk which he had used for the Berlin trial of the scenography. Cocke (Washington, 1969–70) first proposed correctly that the important historical act celebrated by this allegory might be *The Publication of the Holy League* rather than *The Peace of Cateau Cambrésis, 1559.*

150 Federico Zuccaro

(S. Angelo in Vado 1542/43–1609 Ancona)

Scene of Falconry: the Combat of a Hawk and a Heron

Pen and brown ink over preliminaries in black chalk and occasionally red chalk, with brown wash, 358 × 403mm. Mounted in full for the 2nd Duke.

Chatsworth 202

Provenance: N. A. Flinck (L.959); William, 2nd Duke of Devonshire (L.718), from 1723–4

Literature: Gere and Pouncey, 1983, p.185 (under no.289)

Exhibitions: Washington, etc., 1962–3 and London, RA, 1969 (74); Sheffield, 1966 (48); Tokyo, 1975 (45)

152

The fight between hawk and heron recalls Ghirlandaio. This is a design for a stage hanging prepared by Federico Zuccaro for the festivities on the occasion of the marriage of Francesco de' Medici and Joanna of Austria in Florence in 1565, and which is described by Vasari ('una grandissima tela che copriva la scena in testa della sala': ed. Milanesi, vii, p.100). Federico represents himself on a diminutive scale on a trestle in front of a tree stump in the act of painting the curtain. The play was performed in the Sala dei Cinquecento of the Palazzo Vecchio on 26 December 1565.

The *modello* signed by Federico and dated 1565, *ETATS SVE XXV*, is in the Uffizi 11074F (exhibited Uffizi 1966, no.48, fig.33 and illustrated by G. Briganti, *Il Manierismo e Pellegrino Tibaldi*, Rome, 1945, fig.101). There are other drawings in the British Museum, in the Albertina and elsewhere. The British Museum drawing precedes the Chatsworth drawing. On 21 September 1565 Vasari reported to Vincenzo Borghini that Federico still

had 10 days to complete his scene (Frey, Vasari, der literarische *Nachlass*, ii, 1930, pp.209 ff.). Federico had spent most of the previous year in Venice. The hanging, which has disappeared was described as 'una caccia con gran numero di figure, & a cavallo, & a piedi, con cani, & vocelli, che cacciavano in un grandissimo, & bellissimo paese' (*Descrizione dell' Apparato della Commedia ... recitata in Firenze il giorno di S. Stefano 1565*, p.6).

151 Federico Zuccaro

(S. Angelo in Vado 1542/43–1609 Ancona)

Head and Shoulders of a bearded Man wearing a Cap

COLOUR PLATE XII

Black, red and brownish yellow chalks, 285 × 205mm. There is a triangular repair midway down the left margin. Mounted in full for the 2nd Duke, with strips of gold paper added later for enframement.

Chatsworth 908

Provenance: N. A. Flinck (L.959); William, 2nd Duke of Devonshire from 1723–4

Exhibitions: Washington, etc., 1962–3 and London, RA, 1969 (75); Manchester, 1965 (399)

The drawing is in superb condition (except for a wedge-shape missing from the left edge), and there is no justification for A. E. Popham's comment (1962) that it has been 'touched up'. It is indeed a characteristic portrait drawing by Federico; a comparable one, identified by the present author, is or was in the Rosenbach Foundation at Philadelphia.

152 Taddeo Zuccaro

(Sant'Angelo in Vada 1529–1566 Rome)

The Adoration of the Shepherds

Pen and brown ink with brown wash, heightened with white bodycolour, 394 × 510mm. Mounted in full for the 2nd Duke.

Chatsworth 194

Provenance: Sir Peter Lely (L.2092); P. H. Lankrink (L.2090); N. F. Haym (L.1971); presumably 2nd Duke of Devonshire

Literature: Gere, 1969, cat.19

Exhibitions: London, RA, 1960 (597); Washington etc, 1962–3 and London, RA, 1969 (76); Manchester, 1965 (400); Sheffield, 1966 (49)

The attribution is traditional. There are variants of this composition in the Uffizi. The composition may originally have been intended for the Mattei Chapel in S. Maria della Consolazione, Rome. A preparatory study is in the Nationalmuseum, Stockholm. The Windsor drawing may be a study for the right half of the same composition. The picture was partially copied by G. B. Ricci in his picture in S. Marcello al Corso, Rome (Venturi, IX.5, fig.534).

153

153 Taddeo Zuccaro

(Sant'Angelo in Vada 1529–1566 Rome)

Circe seated, the bewitched Argonauts transmogrified

Black chalk with brown wash, heightened with white bodycolour, 422 × 287mm. Mounted in full for the 2nd Duke.

Inscribed in black chalk, lower left, *Taddeo Zucchero*

Chatsworth 195

Traditionally attributed in the Devonshire collection to Taddeo. The animals, especially the way in which the stag at Circe's feet is illuminated, and the treatment of Circe's drapery particularly from the waist down, point to his authorship. The scene inset upper right is also characteristic of Taddeo. The drawing was omitted by Gere, 1969.

DUTCH AND FLEMISH SCHOOLS

(Nos 154–192)

154 Paulus Bril

(Antwerp 1554–1626 Rome)

Roman Landscape, with ruined medieval Buildings overgrown by Trees

Pen and brown ink with brown and grey washes, 275 × 424mm.

Dated lower left, *1615*, and inscribed (?signed) below centre *P.Bril.*

Chatsworth 698

Provenance: William, 2nd Duke of Devonshire (L.718)

Exhibitions: London, RA, 1930 (542); Washington, etc., 1969–70 and London, V&A, 1973–4 (78)

Formerly attributed to Claude, this magnificent late example of Bril's work in Rome is important not least in defining Claude's relation as a draughtsman to him.

155 Paulus Bril

(Antwerp 1554–1626 Rome)

Fantastic Landscape with a Chapel or Hermitage perched on a rocky Escarpment

Pen and brown ink with brown wash, 199 × 276mm.

Signed in pen and brown ink, lower left.

Chatsworth 672

Provenance: William, 2nd Duke of Devonshire (L.718)

Characteristic of Bril's fecund fantasy in his early landscapes drawn south of the Alps.

156 Jan Brueghel I

(Brussels 1568–1625 Antwerp)

The Arch of Septimius Severus, Rome, after Matthijs Bril

Pen and brown ink (faded almost to yellow); slightly wrinkled and a few holes, 194 × 275mm, squared by indentation. Fully mounted on an early 18th-century mount.

Signed and dated *BRVEGHEL/1594 S.P.Q.R.*, in the position

154

155

that Matthijs Bril wrote *PROPAGAVIT/S.P.Q.R.* on his drawing.

Chatsworth 846

Provenance: presumably William, 2nd Duke of Devonshire

Literature: H. Egger, *Römische Veduten*, II, 1931, p.13, pl.14; Münz, 1961, no.A.25, pl.176; Lugt, 1949, no.356, pl.XIX; Winner, 1961, p.191; Winner, 1972, p.122; S. Bedoni, *Jan Brueghel in Italia e il Collezionismo del Seicento*, Florence/Milan 1983, p.31, no.16; M. Wolff in *The Age of Bruegel: Netherlandish Drawings in the Sixteenth Century*, National Gallery of Art, Washington, 1986, p.80; M. Schapelhouman, *Nederlandse Tekeningen omstreeks 1600 in het Rijksmuseum*, The Hague, 1987, p.10, under no.4.

Exhibitions: London, 1927 (548); Berlin, 1975 (111); Pittsburgh, etc., 1987–8 (79)

The original drawing, from which Brueghel made this fine copy, is in the Louvre (inv.no.20.955; pen and brown ink, 207 × 275mm). F. Lugt (1949, no.356) discovered on the *verso* of that an inscription by Paul Bril, *dit is een van die beste desenne die Ick van matijn broeder nae het leeven hebbe* (this is one of the best drawings which I have by Mattijs my

brother, done from life). Bril's view, one of a series of his drawings after Roman ruins, is taken from beside the church of S. Adriana, with his back to the Curia. On the triumphal arch built by Septimius Severus in 203 AD is to be seen the defensive tower built in the Middle Ages, which disappeared in the course of the seventeenth century. To the left are the columns of the Temple of Saturn; to the right, in the distance, is the Capitol.

Another copy, slightly inferior, monogrammed with the initials *GP* and dated 7 May 1596 is in the Courtauld Institute of Art (Witt Collection) of London University (reproduced by W. Gaunt, *Rome Past and Present*, London, 1926, pl.v). A third copy, formerly attributed to Willem van Nieulant, dated 1601 and decidedly inferior, is in the Rijksprentenkabinet, Amsterdam (inv. no.A.184). The evidently popular subject was etched in reverse by van Nieulant (Hollstein 6) in his set of four *Views of Rome*, published at first in Antwerp, then with C. Danckerts in Amsterdam. The engraver introduced a staffage of animals and human figures. Paul Bril, with fraternal piety, kept together these Roman *vedute* drawn by his brother

156

and teacher, who had died in Rome in 1583. He showed them evidently to his friend and fellow countryman Jan Brueghel in 1593–4 and to his pupil van Nieulant in 1600–4.

157 Jan Brueghel I

(Brussels 1568–1625 Antwerp)

Studies of Peasants from the Life

Pen and brown ink, with brown wash, 199 × 145mm; trimmed on the left.

Chatsworth 676

Exhibitions: Berlin, 1975 (121)

A splendid autograph sheet of studies. The study of the man with a sack slung over his shoulder was used in two paintings in English private collections: the *Village Street* of 1605 (Sir Francis Glynn), and, in three quarter view, the *Woodland Road* of 1607 (Earl of Warwick). Chatsworth 676 is datable before 1605 and close to the Brussels sheet of studies (Berlin, 1975 (120)).

158 Pieter Bruegel the Elder

(Breda? 1535/40–1569 Brussels)

View of the Ripa Grande, Rome

Pen and two shades of brown ink, 208 × 283mm.

Inscribed in the sky in pen and brown ink, by the artist *a rypa*, and, lower left, by a later hand *bruegel*

Chatsworth 841

Literature: Egger, 1911, p.38, pl.70; *Vasari Society*, 2nd series, 6, 11; Egger, 1932, I, Taf.74; C. de Tolnay, *The Drawings of Pieter Bruegel the Elder*, London, 1952, no.4; L. Münz, *Bruegel, The Drawings*, London, 1961, A.24 (as Jan I Brueghel); Haverkamp-Begemann, 1964, 57; Winner, 1985, 90–1

Exhibitions: London, RA, 1927 (527); London, Arts Council, 1949 (23); Manchester, 1961 (67); Los Angeles, 1961; Washington, etc., 1962–3 and London, RA, 1969 (77); Brussels, 1973 (275); Berlin, 1975 (26); Richmond, etc., 1979–80 (78); Washington, 1986 (26)

All authorities except Münz (*op.cit.*) accept the traditional attribution to Pieter Bruegel the Elder, who is known to have been in Rome some time between 1552 and 1553,

157

158

and who evidently visited the city's main port on the right bank of the Tiber near the Porta Portese. The drawing shows the old Customs House and the romanesque tower of S. Maria de' Turri. All the buildings shown were destroyed in the eighteenth century to make way for the vast Ospizio di S. Michele. This seems to be the only surviving drawing by Bruegel of Roman buildings, but he must also have drawn at least the Colosseum to judge by his paintings of the Tower of Babel (Vienna and Rotterdam). He was the first to depict such a *veduta* from a low viewpoint.

159 Denys Calvaert, called Dionisio Fiammingo

(Antwerp *c.*1540–1619 Bologna)

The Supper at Emmaus

Red chalk and wash, heightened with white bodycolour, 186 × 137mm. Fully mounted on an early 18th-century mount.

Chatsworth 374

Provenance: William, 2nd Duke of Devonshire (L.718)

Exhibitions: Pittsburgh, etc., 1987–8 (82)

A. E. Popham, who rejected (1962) the traditional attribution at Chatsworth to Francesco Vanni, proposed another, manifestly correct. This excellent example of Calvaert's draughtsmanship is, because of the gestures – especially that of Christ in benediction, being reversed – to be understood as preparation for an engraving, albeit one untraced. That the engraving was executed is indicated by a drawing now in a Bolognese private collection, the composition of which reverses and considerably modifies that of the present drawing, especially in the seating and posture of the disciples, in the omission of the onlookers behind Christ, and in the still life of the foreground. This second drawing was catalogued for sale by Julien Stock, with the agreement of P. M. R. Pouncey, as by Calvaert himself (Sotheby's, 27 June 1974, lot 158; red chalk, heightened with partly oxidised white, 196 × 140mm, inscribed in red chalk *DIONISIO CALVA*). The inscription was taken as a signature, and the dry manner was presumably taken as comparable to drawings in the Louvre attributed to the master. Assessing its quality and status only from a photograph, I find the drawing in Bologna rather to be a heavy-handed copy after the missing engraving, whereas the style and the technique of the Chatsworth drawing resembles that of the *Marriage at Cana* (BM inv.no.1895–9-15-1014; A. E. Popham, *Catalogue of Drawings by Dutch and Flemish Masters ... in the British Museum*, v, 1932, p.548, no.1; 256 × 201mm), which Calvaert signed and dated 1591. Keith Andrews ('The Marriage at Cana – A Trio by Denys Calvaert', *Burl. Mag.*, CXXVII, 1985, p.757) shows that the drawing in the British Museum served as the *modello* for an engraving in reverse, dated 1592 by Philippe Thomassin (Hollstein, IV, p.85, no.12). This may be taken as a pointer to the likely date of the Chatsworth drawing.

159

160 Denys Calvaert, called Dionisio Fiammingo

(Antwerp *c.*1540–1619 Bologna)

Holy Family with the young St John and St Michael Archangel

Black chalk and brown wash, heightened with white body-colour, 499 × 297mm. Squared for enlargement in black chalk. Fully mounted on an early 18th-century mount.

Chatsworth 397

Provenance: William, 2nd Duke of Devonshire (L.718)

Literature: A. Emiliani, et al., *Bologna 1584: Gli Esordi dei Carracci e gli Affreschi di Palazzo Fava*, Bologna, 1984–5, under nos.22 and 50 (ill.).

Exhibitions: Pittsburgh, etc., 1987–8 (81)

At Chatsworth as by Lorenzo Sabbatini (1530–1577); and indeed the commission *c.*1564 of the altarpiece (oils on canvas, 350 × 220cm) for the cappella Malvasia in S. Giacomo Maggiore, Bologna, went to him. The overall invention, undoubtedly his, was acknowledged in lettering on the engraving made after the drawing in the same sense by the young Annibale Carracci (B.12): *Laurentius Sabad: Bononien. inven:/Ani:Cara:f.1582.*

The existence of this print (457 × 294mm) led Diana De Grazia-Bohlin (*Prints and Related Drawings by the Carracci Family*, Washington, 1979 (ed.1984), pp.225–6) to attribute the present drawing to Annibale by fancied analogies to the first two Jason scenes frescoed in Palazzo Fava and to the *Baptism* which he painted for SS. Gregorio e Siro. However, there are in it no convincing analogies to the style of the young Annibale, let alone to his draughtsmanship. *Pentimenti* in defining the cross of the young St John, the archway above which the Madonna and Child are seated, the right hand and forearm of Satan, and elsewhere, indicate rather that this sheet was not drawn as a *modelletto* for a print, but as a *modello* for the altarpiece itself. The confusion may have resulted from the drawing style, which while projecting Sabbatini's invention, is foreign to his personality.

Philip Pouncey put to me that this drawing accords well with the style of Sabbatini's leading assistant at this time, Denys Calvaert, to whom Malvasia, 1678 (p.163) credited *l'inarrivabilmente graziosissimo arcangelo* in the altarpiece which was finished in 1570. Close scrutiny shows that the St Michael was painted by the same hand as the remaining figures; that the execution overall was effectively by Calvaert for Sabbatini; and that the penultimate stage, assuredly approved by Sabbatini, is apparent in Calvaert's *modello*.

160

PLATE I

15 Federico Barocci

PLATE II

34 Annibale Carracci

PLATE III

44 Giovanni Benedetto Castiglione

PLATE IV

48 Cavaliere d'Arpino

PLATE V

62 Pietro Faccini

122 Guido Reni

PLATE VI

76 Giovanni Francesco Barbieri, il Guercino

PLATE VII

105 Giuseppe Passeri

PLATE VIII

118 Raphael

PLATE IX

119 Raphael

PLATE X

128 Rosso Fiorentino

PLATE XI

132 Andrea del Sarto

PLATE XII

148 Paolo Veronese

151 Federico Zuccaro

PLATE XIII

163 Anthony Van Dyck

177 Rembrandt van Rijn

PLATE XIV

186 Peter Paul Rubens

PLATE XV

203 Hans Holbein the Younger

PLATE XVI

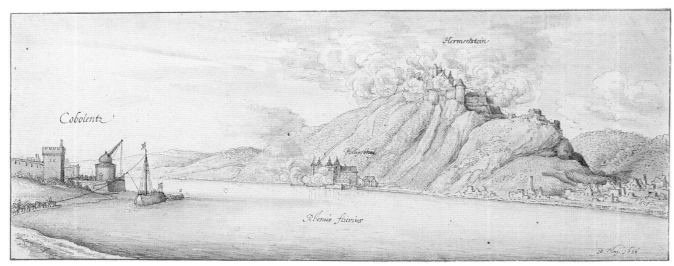

205(a) Wenceslas Hollar

218(a) Jacques Callot

161

161 Anthony Van Dyck

(Antwerp 1599–1641 London, Blackfriars)

Cattle

Pen and brown ink, with a little brown wash, 318 × 515mm.

Inscribed below in an 18th-century hand *Ant. van Dyck* [partly cut off]

Chatsworth 964

Engraved by Paul Pontius in Rubens's 'Livre à Dessiner' (Rooses, v, 1229, 16)

Provenance: N. A. Flinck (L.959); presumably William, 2nd Duke of Devonshire from 1723–4

Literature: M. Rooses, *L'Oeuvre de Rubens*, no.1584 (as Rubens); Held, 1959, pp.12–13, fig.21 (as 'P. P. Rubens?')

Exhibitions: London, RA, 1938 (609, as Rubens); Washington, etc., 1969–70 and London, V&A, 1973–4 (79, as Van Dyck); London, BM, 1977 (200, as Van Dyck)

The old inscription is trustworthy. This is superb in quality and is the original of *c*.1618–20 on which two copies in the British Museum are based (A.M.Hind, *Catalogue of Dutch and Flemish Drawings*, II, nos.118 and 122). The first of these London drawings was treated by Glück and Haberditzl, no.136, as an original study by Rubens for the *Landscape with Cows* (Munich, Alte Pinakothek) of

c.1636–8; but it is noticeably inferior to the present drawing in the rendering of the bushes to the left and centre, and in the slighter indications of the animals at the upper left and right. Hind no.122 is altogether inferior. In fact only the cow on the left of the Chatsworth drawing, with her head turned away, and the lightly sketched one, seen from the back, upper right, correspond to any in the Munich painting, although two of the cows appear also in the Berlin *Landscape with a Duck Hunter*.

A convincing contrast to this drawing by Van Dyck is a pen drawing by Rubens of a *Woman Milking* (Held, 1959, cat.no.88, pl.104). The hatching and cross-hatching are directed in that almost wholly to plastic effect; and the peculiarly tense nervosity of Van Dyck's approach is absent, as is his trick of trailing lines of dots for decorative purposes.

162

162 Anthony van Dyck

(Antwerp 1599–1641 London, Blackfriars)

Head and Forequarters of a Horse

Black chalk, heightened with white chalk, 337 × 314mm.

Chatsworth 1009

Literature: M. Rooses, 'Oeuvre de P. P. Rubens, Addenda et Corrigenda: Dessins', *Rubens-Bulletijn*, 5, Antwerp, 1900, p.203 (as Rubens); A. J. J. Delen, *P. P. Rubens: Een Keuze van 26 teekeningen*, Antwerp, 1944, fig.24 (as Rubens); H. Vey, *Van-Dyck-Studien*, pp.61 ff; Vey, 1962, no.18 (as Van Dyck); New York, 1991, p.76, fig.5 (under cat.no.10)

Exhibitions: London, RA, 1953 (271); London, RA, 1953–4 (524); Nottingham, 1960 (59); Antwerp/Rotterdam, 1960 (12); Manchester, 1961 (80)

A study for Van Dyck's early painting in Antwerp of *St Martin dividing his Cloak with a Beggar*, commissioned for the parish church of Saventhem, Brussels, and still in place over the altar on the east wall to the right of the high altar. A contemporary version of this composition, undertaken for Rubens and in Rubens's mortuary inventory of 1640, was painted by Van Dyck using this same life study of the saint's horse, a study in the tradition of the Carracci reforms of drawing as emulated and redefined by Rubens.

163 Anthony Van Dyck

(Antwerp 1599–1641 London, Blackfriars)

Unfinished Landscape of Meadows and Trees, a square Tower in the Distance

COLOUR PLATE XIII

Pen and brown ink with grey, blue and green watercolours, 228 × 330mm.

Chatsworth 1003

Inscribed on the verso, in pen and brown ink, possibly by N. A. Flinck *16 lanschappen van van Dyck*, and on the mount by a Netherlandish early 18th-century hand *Ant:van Dyck*

Literature: Hind, 1932–3, pp.63–5; A. P. Oppé, *Burl.Mag.*, LXXIX, 1941, p.190 and pl.IIa; Vey, 1962, no.306

Exhibitions: London, RA, 1938 (584); Rotterdam, 1948–9 (94); London, Arts Council, 1949 (27); Antwerp/Rotterdam, 1960 (120); Manchester, 1961 (78); Washington, etc., 1962–3 and London, RA, 1969 (83)

Probably sketched from nature during Van Dyck's residence in England after 1632. To finish, Van Dyck would have used touches of watercolour.

164 Anthony Van Dyck

(Antwerp 1599–1641 London, Blackfriars)

Michelangelo, after Federigo Zuccaro

Red and black chalks, pen and brown ink with brown wash, 250 × 188mm.

Chatsworth 684

Literature: Michael Jaffé, *Van Dyck's Antwerp Sketchbook*, London, 1966, n.129, pl. CXLVIII

About twenty years later this pattern was to be used (except for a crossing of the forearm over the right wrist) by Van Dyck for his *Iconography* portrait of *Aubertus Miraeus Bruxellienso, Decanus Antwerpiensis*, engraved by Paul du Pont. Captain Drury-Lowe, Locko Park, has a portrait of Michelangelo attributed to Bugiardini, which refers to a prototype closer than Musée de Grenoble no.380 to the Chatsworth drawing.

Denucé, p.102, records *Een conterfeytsel van Michiel Angel, get no.496 as opde caemer boven den winckel* in the Inventory of the picture-dealer Herman de Neyt, who died at Delft, 8 September 1642; and p.163, *Het Contrefeytsel van Michiel Angeli selffs*, no.363 as *Opde Schilders Caemer* in the Inventory of the painter Johannes Wildens, who died 30 December 1653. These portraits recorded in Antwerp collections may be identical with each other and with the portrait which was copied by the young Van Dyck.

The Museum Boymans-van Beuningen has an elaborate variant of the Chatsworth drawing, which is classified as nr.14 'school of Rubens', formerly as 'J. de Wit after the

164

portrait by Federigo Zuccaro in the Capitoline Museum, Rome' (black and red chalks and graphite, with black, grey and olive-green washes, also work with the point of the brush and the pen, 269 × 223mm). This Rotterdam drawing (ex collection Boymans) was probably the drawing in the J. de Wit sale, Amsterdam 1755.

A comparable case of Van Dyck copying a sixteenth-century portrait by an Italian master is a hitherto unpublished pen and ink drawing in the Musée Atger, Montpellier (inscribed *Ritratto fatto Dal Penello d'oro de Tintoreto Vetio/ Arteficiosissimus*, in pen and brown ink, not by Van Dyck). The original of this is the painted three-quarter length *Portrait of a Man* in the Metropolitan Museum, New York (inv.no.41.100.12). The technique of pen and brown ink over preliminaries in black chalk, with extensive use of brown wash was to be employed by Van Dyck in his preparations of 1627–35 for the *Iconography*, e.g. the *Erycius Puteanus* in the British Museum, and the *Jacob van Broeck* in the collection of Mr and Mrs Eugene Victor Thaw, New York (New York, 1991, cat.nos.56 and 57).

165 Anthony Van Dyck

(Antwerp 1599–1641 London, Blackfriars)

Recto: Sacra Conversazione

Verso: Man brandishing a Sword

Pen and brown ink, and grey and brown washes on cream paper, 207 × 277mm, cut irregularly.

Inscribed on the *verso* by the artist in pen (not entirely decipherable) *A so[...]; ave Maria q[...] par pien di dolcette il Core Cante rag[...]; soy/nog amoor non sey; piene di bel; d'amor bel mie la[...].* Also a column of figures

Chatsworth 986

Provenance: N. A. Flinck (L.959); William, 2nd Duke of Devonshire, from 1723–4

Literature: *Vasari Society*, IV, p.84, no.22; Vey, 1962, no.98, figs.133 and 135

Exhibitions: London, Arts Council, 1949, no.24; Genoa, 1955, no.106; Nottingham, 1957, no.32; Nottingham, 1960, no.41; Antwerp/Rotterdam, 1960, no.50; Pittsburgh, etc., 1987–8 (89)

Recto: a study for an important composition – a *sacra conversazione* with Sts Anthony of Padua, Francis of Assisi, Sebastian, Jerome, Catherine and George – drawn by Van Dyck perhaps even before he went to Italy 1621–7, which was inspired by his recent interest in Lorenzo Lotto (the figure of St George on the right) as well as by his longer-standing attraction to the scenographic taste of Paolo Veronese.

Verso: probably a study for St Peter cutting off the ear of Malchus in a *Betrayal of Christ* of Van Dyck's first period in Antwerp.

166 Anthony Van Dyck

(Antwerp 1599–1641 London, Blackfriars)

Portrait of Pieter Brueghel the Younger (Brussels 1564/65–1638 Antwerp)

Black chalk, 245 × 198mm.

Chatsworth 995

Provenance: N. A. Flinck (L.959); William, 2nd Duke of Devonshire from 1723–4

Literature: *Vasari Society*, 1st series, III, 1907–8 (17); Hind, 1915, 10; Mayer, 1923, pl.1; Delacre, 1932, 51–3,69, pl.15; Gerson and ter Kuile, 1960, pl.111; Vey, 1962, no.242

Exhibitions: London, RA, 1938 (586); Rotterdam, 1948–9 (84); Nottingham, 1960 (49); Antwerp/Rotterdam, 1960 (79); Manchester, 1961 (76); Washington, etc., 1962–3 and London, RA, 1969 (80); Eastbourne, 1979 (6); New York, 1991 (55)

A preparatory study from life for the etching, in reverse, by Van Dyck himself in the *Iconography* (Mauquoy-Hendrickx, 1956, p.154, no.2), but substantially different in pose. Van Dyck drew another study which served directly for his print. This is lightly squared and incised. It belongs to the State Hermitage Museum in St Petersburg (black chalk, 254 × 180mm).

167 Anthony Van Dyck

(Antwerp 1599–1641 London, Blackfriars)

Portrait of Inigo Jones (London 1573–1652)

Black chalk, 241 × 197mm.

Inscribed on the mount by Lord Burlington *Van Dyck's original drawing, from which the Print by van Voerst was taken in the/Book of Van Dyck's Heads. Given me by the Duke of Devonshire./Burlington*

Chatsworth 1002A

Engraved by Robert van Voerst for the *Iconography* (Mauquoy-Hendrickx, 72)

Provenance: N. A. Flinck (L.959); William, 2nd Duke of Devonshire from 1723–4; given by the 3rd Duke to Richard, 3rd Earl of Burlington (1694–1753); after his death, his heir Charlotte, by her marriage to the future 4th Duke, brought it back to the Devonshire Collections

Literature: Cust, p.276, no.105; Delacre, 1932, pp.92–3, fig.24; M. Delacre, *Le Dessin dans l'oeuvre de Van Dyck*, Brussels, 1934, pp.92–3 and pl.24; Vey, 1962 no.271.

Exhibitions: Antwerp/Rotterdam, 1960 (87); Manchester, 1961 (77); Washington, etc., 1962–3 and London, RA, 1969 (82); Eastbourne, 1979 (41); New York, 1991 (72)

Jones was the leading architect and theatrical designer of his day. The drawing returned to the Devonshire Collections at the same time as the designs for masques by Inigo Jones (see Stephen Orgel and Roy Strong, *Inigo Jones, The Theatre at the Stuart Court*, 2 vols, London, Berkeley and Los Angeles, 1973).

It was mounted in an album of Jones's theatrical designs on its return to the Devonshire Collections, from which it was removed in 1960. Jones must have sat to Van Dyck in London, either 1632–3 or after Spring 1635. The head in a painted portrait by Van Dyck (State Hermitage Museum, St Petersburg; canvas, 64 × 53cm) appears also to be *ad visum*.

A copy of Chatsworth 1002A is at Weimar (Delacre, 1932, pl.25).

165 *recto*

165 *verso*

Vandyke's original Drawing, from which the Print by Van. Voerst was taken, in the
Book of Vandyke's Heads. Given me by the Duke of Devonshire.

Burlington

167

168

168 Hendrick Goltzius

(Mühlbrecht, near Venlo 1558–1616 Haarlem)

Landscape with Peasants by a Hut

Pen and dark brown ink, 357 × 468mm. Mounted in full.

Signed in pen and brown ink in monogram *HG/ Ao 1593* and numbered, upper left: *4*

Chatsworth 1065

Literature: A. E. Popham, *Burl.Mag.*, 1962, p.396, fig.41; Washington, 1986, under cat.no.59, fig.2

Exhibitions: Manchester, 1965 (313); Washington, etc., 1969–70 and London, V & A, 1973–4 (86)

First published by Popham (1962), reviewing E. K. J. Reznicek, *Die Zeichnungen von Hendrick Goltzius*, Utrecht, 1961, which omitted Chatsworth 1065. The landscape in this, the earliest by Goltzius which we know, and in the Lisbon drawing dated the same year (Reznicek, *op.cit.*, no.437) is dominant, and the 'dashing penwork

imitates Venetian drawings and woodcuts from Titian's circle'. The mood, however, is contemplative. The figure of the shepherdess in the right foreground, her back turned, became a characteristic device of Goltzius (cf. the pen drawing of a *Couple viewing a Waterfall*, Stockholm, Nationalmuseum).

169 Jan Gossaert, called Mabuse

(Mauberge *c.*1478–1532 Breda?)

Adam and Eve

Pen and black ink, heightened with white bodycolour, on paper prepared grey, 348 × 239mm.

Chatsworth 935

Provenance: N. A. Flinck (L.959); presumably William, 2nd Duke of Devonshire from 1723–4

Literature: Strong, 1902, LIV; Strong, 1905, p.134 ('a good

169

example of Hans Baldung Grien'); Popham, 1926, p.14; Max J. Friedlaender, VIII, 1930 (1); Krönig, 1936, pp.70,146; H. Schwarz, *GBA*, 1953, pp.155–6; Von der Osten, 1961, p.455

Exhibitions: Rotterdam, 1936 (43); London, Arts Council, 1949 (31); Manchester, 1961 (82); Washington, etc., 1962–3 and London, RA, 1969 (87); Brussels, 1963 (289); London, NG, 1975; Richmond, etc., 1979–80 (77); Washington, 1986 (67)

Traditionally in the Devonshire Collections as Hans Baldung Grien (on the evidence of S. A. Strong), this highly finished drawing is in a technique much used in the early sixteenth century. It is one of several drawn by Gossaert of this subject. Others are in the Albertina, in the Staedelsches Kunstinstitut and in the Rhode Island School of Design (see Rotterdam, 1965). In Chatsworth 935 Gossaert abandoned the concepts of Dürer, which had influenced him in his earlier representations of *c*.1509 and *c*.1512, except for Eve's long, flowing hair in the *Small Passion* of 1509–11, and the embrace. The crossed legs of Adam, leaning against a tree, reflect the engraving of the subject by Marcantonio Raimondi.

The drawing is datable *c*.1515. Schwarz suggested that the Adam might have been a self-portrait (cf. the engraving by Hieronymus Wierix and the presumed portrait in the Currier Gallery, New Hampshire, Rotterdam, 1965, no.33). The authors of that catalogue point also to the 1526 medal by Hans Schwarz, overlooked by Schwarz in 1953. The identification is far from certain.

170 Maerten van Heemskerck

(Heemskerk 1498–1574 Haarlem)

The Triumph of Christ

Pen and brown ink, 179 × 265mm. Fully mounted on an early 18th-century mount

Inscribed by the artist in brown ink *Marten van Heemskerck inventoor/.1565.* On the back of the mount, in graphite *L.22*

Chatsworth 666

Engraved in reverse, by Philips Galle (see Thomas Kerrich, *A Catalogue of Prints Which Have Been Engraved after Martin Heemskerk*, p.82, no.6; Hollstein, VIII, no.346), lettered *M.l.Ve, PG.F., 6/Praeterunt cuncta et fugiunt labentis annis/Christus at aeternum ducit solidumque triumphum, /Invida quem non alla potest anolere vetustas,/Indigetum casta septus sine fine corona*

Provenance: William, 2nd Duke of Devonshire (L.718)

Exhibitions: Pittsburgh, etc., 1987–8 (101)

171

In this model for the last of the *Six Petrarchan Triumphs*, Christ, cloud-borne, is carried by the symbols of the four Evangelists. His progress is witnessed by Sts Peter, Mary, Andrew, John, and others. A flight of angels trumpets to awake the dead. A furious Leviathan appears at the left, a human victim in his maw. Death, Time, Love, and others lie stricken in the foreground.

The engraver followed his model faithfully, except for omitting the signature and date; but the angel of St Matthew has his mouth closed; the shaded area of sky behind the figures is packed with cherubic faces, the clouds being more fanciful; and the attribute (a flagon?) of the kneeling man (the Baptist?) second from the left in the drawing is omitted. The date of the drawing gives not only a *terminus post quem* for the engraved series but a close dating for that series, for which the *Triumph of Chastity*, a pen drawing, similarly signed and dated, is also at Chatsworth (no.669).

171 Valentin Lefèvre

(Brussels ?1642–?1680–82 or later, ?Venice)

Presentation of the Infant Christ to the High Priest

Pen and brown ink with brown wash, 238 × 270mm; squared beneath in black chalk

Chatsworth 281

Provenance: unidentified (?English) collector of the first half of the 18th century (L.1160); William, 2nd Duke of Devonshire (L.718)

Literature: Julien Stock, *Disegni Veneti di collezioni inglesi*, exh. cat., Venice, 1980, p.48 (under cat.no.54); Ugo Ruggeri, 'Drawings by Valentin Lefèvre', *MD*, XXVI, no.4, 1988, cat.no.34, pl.18

This drawing was attributed in the Devonshire collection to Paolo Veronese; and the Venetian use of wash and the scenographic taste in presenting a crowd is indeed conspicuous. The authorship, as Byam Shaw (1952) first perceived, is however that of Valentin Lefèvre. His reinterpretation of Veronese's motifs was influenced by the work of Giovanni Coli and Filippo Gherardi, two painters from Lucca at work in Venice between 1663 and 1668 in the Library of S. Giorgio Maggiore where Lefèvre himself was active, as Ruggeri (*loc.cit.*) suggests, during those very same years. The Fleming was sensitive to this reinvention in the baroque mode of Veronese's art.

Close stylistic comparison may be made with a drawing of *Chronos* from the collections of Sir Thomas Lawrence and T. P. P. Clifford (pen and brown ink with brown wash, squared in chalk, 190 × 145mm), which bears an (18th-century?) inscription to *Filippo Gherardi Lucchese*. The Devonshire *Presentation in the Temple* agrees closely in style, especially in the rendering of the draperies and in the articulated screening of the background by Sansovinesque architecture, with the Düsseldorf *Continence of Scipio* (Ruggeri, pl.2) which is one of very few drawings recognised as preliminaries for a Lefèvre painting (see U. Ruggeri, 'Valentin Lefèvre interprete di Paolo Veronese', *Interpretazioni Veneziane. Studi di storia dell' arte in onore di Michelangelo Muraro*, ed. D. Rosand, Venice, 1984, p.422, fig.4). Ruggeri (1988, cat.no.35, pl.19) illustrates from an English private collection a fragment of a preliminary study of a *Woman seen from the back*, closely connected with the Chatsworth drawing. Although we have no knowledge of a *Presentation in the Temple* painted by Lefèvre corresponding to these preliminary studies, one might be inferred, not least from the squaring of the Chatsworth drawing.

Without dated paintings or drawings it is hazardous to guess the date of these two drawings in English collections: but the style of pen and wash in the Chatsworth drawing is close to that of Lefèvre's copy (formerly London market) drawn after Veronese's *Supper in the House of Simon*, the vast canvas presented by the Serenissima in 1664 to Louis XIV, the painted copy being in the casa parrochiale of S. Francesco della Vigna. Very tentatively it may be supposed that the Chatsworth drawing is of the 1660s.

172 Sir Peter Lely

(Soest 1618–1680 London)

A Knight of the Garter bowing

Black chalk and oiled chalk, heightened with white, on blue paper (faded to grey-blue), 468 × 373mm.

Chatsworth 281

Provenance: Earl of Warwick (L.2600); Warwick sale, 1896; acquired for Spencer Compton, 8th Duke of Devonshire

Literature: John Woodward, *Tudor and Stuart Drawings*, London, 1951, p.49; E. Croft-Murray and Paul Hulton, *British Museum. Catalogue of British Drawings*, I, London, 1960, p.409.

Exhibitions: London, RA, 1953 (436); Washington, etc., 1962–3 and London, RA, 1969 (114)

One of the best preserved of a series of drawings (at least 30 are extant) showing the actual participants in the ceremony on St George's day (23 April) of the oldest order of European chivalry. They must date from between 1663 and 1671. They are assumed to have been drawn for use in forming tapestry cartoons, on the example of the oil sketch painted *en grisaille* in Charles I's day by Van Dyck. One of very few drawings added to the Devonshire Collections since the early eighteenth century.

173 The Master of 'The Months of Lucas'

(?Lucas van Nevele, Brussels)

Petit Patron for the full-scale tapestry Cartoon of January

Black chalk and brown wash, extensively hatched with gold to indicate the areas for silver gilt threading, on brownish paper, 368 × 467mm. Mounted in full.

Chatsworth (loose, unnumbered drawing)

Provenance: John Talman (?); 3rd Earl of Burlington (?); 4th Duke of Devonshire (?)

Literature: Edith A. Standen, 'Drawings for 'The Months of Lucas' Tapestry Series', *MD*, IX, 1975, pl.5

Exhibitions: Pittsburgh, etc., 1987–8 (92)

A set of twelve tapestries, reputedly commissioned by Colbert, were in Louis XIV's 1684 inventory as *fabrique de Bruxelles, dessein de Lucas*. Félibien ends his account of Lucas van Leyden (with whom this Lucas is not to be confused) by recording *douze pièces dans le Garde Meuble du Roi, où sont représentés les douze mois de l'année*. Gobelins copies, presumably faithful, were woven between 1682 and 1770.

Five pieces of a sixteenth-century weaving have been identified in United States collections (ex Barberini, Charles M. Ffoulke, and Mrs E. H. Harriman collections): *April* (Nelson-Atkins Gallery, Kansas City); *May* (Norton Simon Foundation, Pasadena); *September* (Portland Art Museum, Oregon); *October* (Joslyn Memorial Art Gallery, Omaha); and *December* (Denver Art Museum, Colorado). But the luxurious *editio princeps* for France was melted down in 1797 for the gold in the floater threads.

Two other of Lucas's *petit patrons* are at Chatsworth: *February* (Washington, etc., 1969–70, no.89, as 'School of Barend van Orley. *Winter Scene in a Castle, with Ladies and Gentlemen Playing Cards and Dominoes*'); and *March*, with ladies, gentlemen and children skating on a frozen lake before a castle. Of other drawings at an earlier stage of preparation, one is in the Cooper-Hewitt Museum, New York, and two were in the collection of the late Harry Sperling, New York.

Deriving ultimately from the Chatsworth *January* is a Gobelins tapestry, woven in 1732–7, adapting the design

172

173

to an upright, which was identified by Dr. Standen in the Metropolitan Museum of Art (gift of John D. Rockefeller, Jr., 1944). The Janus-headed divinity at the centre is flanked by Bacchus and Ceres, as in the January scene from the slightly earlier suite of Flemish designs in Palazzo Doria, Rome. *Choreas ducit Januarius* accounts for the dancing couples with their candles (Erik Duverger, 'Een 17de-eeuws Brugs wandtapijt uit een reeks van de Maanden voor het Gruuthuismuseum', *Artes Textiles*, x, 1981, p.305, fig.2, illustrates and discusses a weaving of *January* by Mathieu Mommerqué of Paris *c.*1747, in the Musée National du Château de Pau). This indoor scene seems to rival, more or less consciously, the famous engraving of 1519 by Lucas van Leyden of the outdoor scene, *The Dance of Mary Magdalene*.

The *Months of Lucas* suite of the mid-1520s was evidently of regal importance; and it has been suggested that it was commissioned to celebrate the marriage in 1526 of Charles V to Isabella of Portugal. They have been recognised as the leading pair of dancers (see George L. Hunter, *The Practical Book of Tapestries*, Philadelphia/London 1925, pp.129–130 and 180, pl.XXI-b: the floor tiles in this Gobelins weaving being patterned with the imperial two-headed eagle).

The most plausible suggestion hitherto of the authorship of the cartoons, Lucas van Nevele, was put forward by E. Duverger in the exhibition catalogue of 'Bruges et la tapisserie', Bruges/Mouscron 1987, p.413, n.5. Duverger discusses a weaving at Bruges of *The Months* after the *editio princeps* at Brussels, without reference to the *petits patrons* at Chatsworth.

174 Rembrandt Harmensz. van Rijn

(Leyden 1606–1669 Amsterdam)

An Actor in his Dressing-Room

Pen and brown ink, 183 × 150mm.

Inscribed on the *verso*, in pen and brown ink, by an eighteenth-century collector *Rembrandt*

Chatsworth 1018

Provenance: N. A. Flinck (L.959); presumably William, 2nd Duke of Devonshire from 1723–4

Literature: HdG 832; Benesch, I, 1954, no.120, fig.132; H. van de Waal, *Steps Towards Rembrandt*, Amsterdam/London, 1974, pp.73ff.; Dudok van Heel, *Amstelodamum*, 66, 1979, pp.83–7

Exhibitions: London, RA, 1953 (316, 'the pose suggests a study of an actor or studio model, rather than of any particular religious subject'); Manchester, 1961 (89, 'St Augustine in his study'); Washington, etc., 1962–3 and London, RA, 1969 (88, again as 'St Augustine'); Richmond, etc., 1979–80 (93, as 'An actor in his dressing-room')

This brilliant study was dated by Benesch *c.*1636, but 1638 is much more probable. De Waal changed the traditional title convincingly to that of an actor about to perform the part of the Bishop Gozewijn in *Gijsbrecht van Aemstel* by Joost van den Vondel. This poetic tragedy, written in 1637, was produced in 1638, the likely date of Chatsworth 1018. Rembrandt is known to have been in

174

touch with Vondel. He may well have attended rehearsals and visited the actors in their dressing-rooms. Other drawings of his depict individual actors and scenes from the play, for example that of the same actor standing on stage as Bishop Gozewijn belonging to the Herzog Anton Ulrich-Museum, Brunswick (pen and brown ink, heightened with white bodycolour, 209 × 165mm; Benesch no.122).

Dudok van Heel (1979) identified the actor as Willem Bartelsz. Ruyters (1587–1639). He appears also in Benesch, 1954, nos.121 and 123. B. Albach, 'Rembrandt en het toneel' in *De Kroniek van het Rembrandthuis*, 31, 1979, 2, pp.2–32, examines the interest of Rembrandt in the stage.

175 Attributed to Rembrandt Harmensz. van Rijn

(Leiden 1606–1669 Amsterdam)

David's Charge to Solomon

Pen and brown ink and brown wash, 219 × 209mm.

Inscribed on the *verso* in pen and brown ink, lower centre (by the same hand as Chatsworth 1015, 1018 and 1019) *Rembrandt*

Chatsworth 1016

Literature: *Vasari Society*, 1st series, III (22); HdG, 830 (as Rembrandt of the early 1640s); Münz, *Die Graphischen Künste*, NF II, 1937, p.103 (as Flinck); Benesch, VI, p.384, no.A.81 (as attributed to Rembrandt); Ben Broos, *Gemeentemusea van Amsterdam, III, Rembrandt en tekenaars uit zijn omgeving*, Amsterdam, 1981, under no.39, fig.a (as Rembrandt and Samuel van Hoogstraten, *Isaac blessing Jacob and David's Charge to Solomon*), reviewed by P. Schatborn, *Oud Holland*, 1982, pp.256–7 (uncertainly attributed to Rembrandt)

Exhibitions: London, RA, 1929 (613); London, RA, 1938 (542); Washington, etc., 1969–70 and London, V & A, 1973–4 (91)

Byam Shaw (1969) was rightly unconvinced by Benesch's rejection of this drawing, of which there is an old copy in Berlin. First, Benesch claimed that it is based in reverse on the etching *David in Prayer* of 1652, and therefore must be later than 1650. David in the print, like Solomon in the drawing, kneels and is seen from the back. In both there is a four-poster bed and a general resemblance of perspective. The etching could as well be carrying reminiscence of the drawing. Second, Benesch considered that the Chatsworth drawing derived from two drawings by Rembrandt of *Isaac blessing Jacob*, Benesch 891 (Chatsworth 1015) and 892 (Lady Melchett); but these 'mature drawings' are closer to one another than either is to Chatsworth 1016, which Benesch wished to attribute to Aert de Gelder. Byam Shaw (1969) inclined to Hofstede de Groot's view of Chatsworth 1016; and M. Royalton-Kisch more or less supports this with a dating 1640–42.

175

176

The latter has called my attention to a photograph in the Rijksmuseum of another copy in the Goutard Collection at Legou (France) in the same media, 212 × 202mm; to Samuel van Hoogstraten's version of the subject which depends on Chatsworth 1016; also to a drawing of the 1640s by N. Maes at Rotterdam which shows he knew Chatsworth 1016 (Jeroen Giltaij, *The Drawings by Rembrandt and his school in the Museum Boymans-van Beuningen*, Rotterdam, 1988, no.113).

Schatborn corrected the view of Broos that the subject of Chatsworth 1016 is also *Isaac blessing Jacob*. M. Royalton-Kisch (1991) has called my attention to Benesch no.477 (Musée Bonnat, Bayonne), a *Study of a Man kneeling* for B.92, an etching signed and dated 1640. This shows the same fluency of pen strokes as Chatsworth 1016.

176 Rembrandt Harmensz. van Rijn

(Leiden 1606–1669 Amsterdam)

The Rijnpoort at Rhenen in Gelderland

Reed pen and blackish brown ink with some brown wash, rubbed with the finger, 120 × 176mm.

Chatsworth 1043

Provenance: N. A. Flinck (L.959); presumably William, 2nd Duke of Devonshire

Literature: Lippmann, I, 72; HdG, 857; Lugt, 1920, pp.161–2 (identifying the Rijnpoort); Benesch, 1957, VI, no.1301, fig.1531; C. Boschma, 'Rembrandts tekeningen van de Rhenense stadspoorten', *Oud-Holland*, 81, 1961, pp.91–6; P. Schatborn, 'Mek Rembrandt naar buiten', *Kroniek van Rembrandthuis*, 1990, pp.31–9; Washington, 1990, under no.53

Exhibitions: Stockholm, 1956 (144); Washington, etc., 1962–3 and London, RA, 1969 (95); Chicago, 1969 (126); Washington, 1990 (52); Berlin/Amsterdam, 1991 (29)

Dated by Benesch *c*.1652–3, who points to a Louvre drawing (22.916) of the same medieval gate (destroyed 1673 by the French) from a slightly different view (Benesch, no.1300) but with less variety. The buildings to the left of the entrance to the gate are similar, but the throughway is especially different. Instead of the *chiaroscuro* in Chatsworth 1043, there is a blackish hole in the Paris drawing, which generally reflects Rembrandt's absorption in the work of Titian. As the light falls from different angles in the two drawings, Lugt noted that one was made in the forenoon, the other in the afternoon. On the other hand Rembrandt may have visited Rhenen twice.

It is more than probable that Rembrandt accompanied Hendrickje Stoffels when in 1649 she attended a baptism in her native Bredevoort not far from the German border. On their journey he would have been attracted by the medieval city gates of Rhenen, and in Chatsworth 1043 he has brought out the weathered, picturesque character of the buildings, with a high finish to the city side of the massive Rijnpoort. A dating of 1649 seems plausible.

177 Rembrandt Harmensz. van Rijn

(Leiden 1606–1669 Amsterdam)

A thatched Cottage by a large Tree, a Figure seated outside

COLOUR PLATE XIII

Reed pen and two shades of brown ink, 175 × 267mm.

Chatsworth 1046

Provenance: N. A. Flinck (L.959); presumably William, 2nd Duke of Devonshire

Literature: HdG, 859; Benesch, 1957, VI, no.1282, fig.1510

Exhibitions: London, RA, 1929 (612); London, RA, 1938 (555); London, Arts Council, 1949 (42); Washington, etc., 1962–3 and London, RA, 1969 (96); Washington, 1990 (12)

Dated by Benesch *c*.1652, and by the Washington, 1990, catalogue 1648–50. The Lubomirski Museum, Lwow, has another drawing of the same motif (Benesch, 1283), which has rightly been doubted as the work of the master; the name of the pupil or follower has been suggested as Willem Drost (Washington, 1990, p.98, fig.1).

178 Rembrandt Harmensz. van Rijn

(Leiden 1606–1669 Amsterdam)

Copse at the Head of the Amsteldyke near Trompenburg

Reed pen and brown ink, 132 × 207mm. Fully mounted.

Chatsworth 1023

Provenance: N. A. Flinck (L.959); William, 2nd Duke of Devonshire, from 1723–4

Literature: Lippmann, 1, 64; HdG, 837; *Vasari Society*, III, no.23; Lugt, 1920, p.100, pl.59; Benesch, 1957, VI, no.1219; P. Schatborn, 'De Geschiedenis van een tekening', *Kroniek van het Rembrandthuis*, 28, 1976, pp.19–27, fig.3; Berlin/Amsterdam, 1991, under no.22, fig.22b; London, BM, 1992, p.166; Royalton-Kisch, 1992, p.123, fig.24

Exhibitions: Amsterdam, 1935 (63); Pittsburgh, etc., 1987–88 (105); Washington, 1990 (68)

Upstream from Kostverloren and just below the Omval, the copse near the Trompenburg Estate (named for Admiral Cornelis Tromp) is on the same road as the subject of Chatsworth 1025 (Benesch 1268). A sketch of *c*.1649, the present drawing was developed in Chatsworth 1022 (here cat.no.179) and in a Louvre drawing (Edmond de Rothschild Bequest, pen and brown ink with brown wash, 148 × 269mm, Benesch, 1220; Royalton-Kisch, 1992, fig.25). This outline version, evidently drawn before the motif, renders details with greater precision than Chatsworth 1022: the cross-bar at the top of the gate sits firmly on its support, as do the orb finials, whereas in the more finished version the orbs are omitted and the

remaining indication of the cross-bar seems insecurely supported. In Chatsworth 1021 the trees are taller and the foliage described across the trunk is convincingly natural, whereas in Chatsworth 1022 above the gate the clumps of foliage are more conventionalised. In fact in Chatsworth 1023 the tree trunks, clearer in their individual structure (which is particularly noticeable in the row next the road), seem attached to particular areas of foliage, whereas in Chatsworth 1022 they support an undifferentiated mass.

This blurring or suppression of detail in the interests of a calculated composition becomes more obvious still in the Paris drawing (where a later hand has added some of the wash). Both that and Chatsworth 1022 were inventions skilfully recast by Rembrandt in his studio on the basis of Chatsworth 1023, noted from the motif, to make it more subtly picturesque. The wooden gate with a roof appears in Benesch no.817 (*ex* Lubomirski), a black chalk drawing dated by P. Schatborn 1645 by the stylistically related etching, *A Boathouse among Trees* (B.231).

179 Rembrandt Harmensz. van Rijn

(Leiden 1606–1669 Amsterdam)

View on the Amstel: the Road on the Amsteldijk leading to Trompenburg

Pen and brown ink with brown wash, touched with white body-colour, on paper prepared with horizontal strokes of brown wash, 130 × 217mm.

Chatsworth 1022

Provenance: N. A. Flinck (L.959); William, 2nd Duke of Devonshire, from 1623–4

Literature: Lippmann, 1, 54; HdG, 836; Benesch, no.1218; P. Schatborn, 'De Geschiedenis van een tekening', *Kroniek van het Rembrandthuis*, 28, 1976, pp.19–27, fig.4; Royalton Kisch, 1992, p.123, fig.23.

Exhibitions: Richmond etc., 1979–80 (894); Washington, 1990 (69).

This carefully composed view of *c*.1649–50 is taken near the Trompenburg estate outside Amsterdam. Based on Chatsworth 1023 (here cat.no.178), it is an elaborated and populated version probably done up for sale.

The inn, 'Het Molentje', takes its name from the mill on the opposite bank. For other comments, see under cat. no.178.

178

179

180 Rembrandt Harmensz. van Rijn

(Leiden 1606–1669 Amsterdam)

A Man sculling a Boat on the Bullewijk, with a View towards Ouderkerk

Reed pen and brown ink with brown wash, touched with white bodycolour, 133 × 200mm.

Chatsworth 1033

Provenance: N. A. Flinck (L.959); presumably William, 2nd Duke of Devonshire

Literature: Lippmann, I, 59; HdG, 847; *Vasari Society*, 1910–11, 6, no.22; Lugt, 1920, 125–6; Benesch, VI, no.1232; White, 1984, p.110, fig.90

Exhibitions: London, RA, 1929 (604); London, RA, 1938 (554); Stockholm, 1956 (135); Washington, etc., 1969–70 and London, V&A, 1973–4 (94); Richmond, etc., 1979 (95); Washington, 1990 (13)

Dated by Benesch, followed by White, c.1650. Washington, 1990 preferred the late 1640s. The locus had been identified by Frits Lugt (*loc. cit.*). Once the Amstel reaches Ouderkerk, the river becomes more open, and there are fewer trees and houses; but to the north-east there is a small tributary known as the Bullewijck. In the distance is the spire of Ouderkerk's church. Rembrandt rejoiced in the restfulness of the scenes where the reach is at once narrower and more lethargic than the main stream. The motif of a farmstead protected by trees from the wind and shaded from the sun appears to have been particularly dear to Rembrandt.

181 Rembrandt Harmensz. van Rijn

(Leiden 1606–1669 Amsterdam)

View over the River IJ from the Diemerdijk

Pen and brown ink with brown wash on greyish paper, heightened with some white bodycolour, 76 × 244mm; the top originally curved, but at some time trimmed.

Chatsworth 1030

Provenance: N. A. Flinck (L.959); presumably William, 2nd Duke of Devonshire

Literature: HdG, 844; Benesch, 1957, VI, no.1239, fig.1465; White, 1984, p.106, fig.84

Exhibitions: London, RA, 1929 (609); London, RA, 1938 (587); London, Arts Council, 1949 (35); Amsterdam, 1969 (84); Washington, etc., 1962–3 and London, RA, 1969 (91); Berlin/Amsterdam, 1991 (28)

Placed by Benesch c.1650–1 and by White c.1650, the drawing must have been made before the dyke was breached on 5 March 1651. This open landscape attracted Rembrandt on more than one sortie from Amsterdam. Instead of going north-east, as was his wont, immediately outside the Anthoniespoort, he continued along the Diemerdijk towards Diemen. At the end of the dyke he reached the IJ. When he made this drawing he was sitting at a bend of the Diemerdijk, where a few inns were situated. To the left he saw the spit jutting into the IJ from outside the dyke. In the right foreground is the oak facing, which starts here and runs along the dyke. Across the river can be seen the villages of Nieuwendam, Schellingwou and, to the right and further inland, Ramsdorp with its tower. Rembrandt 'wonderfully suggests the width of the river with its translucent quality set against the opacity and solidity of the river banks' (White, *loc. cit.*).

182 Peter Paul Rubens

(Siegen 1577–1640 Antwerp)

Ecorché Head, with the Features of the Emperor Galba

Pen and brown ink, 130 × 174mm.

Inscribed on the *recto*, at points of the flayed head to correspond with annotations deriving ultimately from Andreas Vesalius, *De Humanis Corporis Fabrica*, II, Basel, 1543, p.175, which deals with the 'Secundae Musculorum Tabulae Characterum Index'. Rubens provides fresh illustration for Vesalius's second plate. He confines his tabulation to A-I, although he letters the head A-K. His legend abbreviates the Vesalian text, which by the first decade of the 17th century, as Dr. Roger French has pointed out to me, was old-fashioned in anatomical circles. It reads:

A   *Temporalis Musculus* (the first sentence only from Vesalius, p.175, A)

B   *Os Jugale. Foramen illud loco auricula Auditorius est meatus* (quotes the first, and paraphrases the second sentence from Vesalius, B)

C   *Musculus a Mandendo mansorius dictus et Maxillam Momentium secundus* (adapts Vesalius, C)

D   *Musculus buccarum motibus subserviens* (the first clause only from Vesalius, D)

E   *Musculus sinister an Inferior Maxilla in os u referens productus* (follows Vesalius, E, omitting only *maginum*)

F   *Musculus a Pectoris odde in os u referens Insertus* (copies Vesalius, F)

G   *Musculus sinister a Superiori pectoris ossis/sede principium ducens et aliquando quasi sub F. latet Ipse in humchorem Cartila/gines scuti imaginem rappresentantis/Insertus* (follows Vesalius, G, only to *ducens*)

HH   *Musculus a superiori Scapule Costa/ad Os u properans* (follows Vesalius, HH, first clause only, omitting *imagini simile*)

H   *Superius etiam denotat Glandulas ad auris/Radicem et Internam Interioris Maxillam/sedem hic repositas* (not in Vesalius)

I   *A pectoris Ossis & Clavicula principium/bucens et maxillarem Temporis/Ossis processum insertus* (follows Vesalius, I, omitting *sumens musculus* from the first clause)

The dynamic conflation of anatomical study instituted by Vesalius, thus plagiarised, with his own penetrating study of an antique head, is typical of Rubens's double-pronged approach to authority in art.

180

181

Inscribed on the *verso*, in chalk: [*fi*]*nished finished finished Pe.turerus* [?]/ *bital* [?] *garter* [?]/... *tuisque* [?].

Chatsworth (loose, unnumbered drawing)

Provenance: Inigo Jones (?); Richard, 3rd Earl of Burlington; William, 4th Duke of Devonshire

Literature: Jaffé, 1966, p.43, pl.XI; Jaffé, 1977, p.31, fig.291

Exhibitions: Pittsburgh, etc., 1987–8 (98)

This Vesalian type of drawing of *c*.1605–8 was evidently intended to illustrate the anatomy book which was one of Rubens's unfulfilled projects. It is based on a larger-scale study datable to the same period of his work in Rome, which is derived from the same antique marble of Galba (collection of M. Paul Eeckhout, Ghent; red chalk, 233 × 115mm).

Both studies were identified and successively published by the compiler: this drawing, formerly in a volume of sketches by Inigo Jones bound for Lord Burlington, in Jaffé, 1966, p.43, pl.XI; and the Ghent drawing formerly as 'anonymous Italian', in 'Rubens in Italy: Part II,' *Burl. Mag.*, CX, 1968, pp.184–7, fig.19. Copy drawings in the MS Johnson (210b, 213b) now in the Courtauld Institute, London University, confirm the identification of Rubens's source as a marble of Galba, an antique most probably in the artist's own collection. Finding this drawing in the Inigo Jones album at Chatsworth suggests that it may

have lain there because it had belonged to Jones, and that it came with the Burlington inheritance to the 4th Duke. P.-J. Mariette (*Abecedario*, V, p.141) knew other Rubens *écorchés* in the collection of Pierre Crozat, 'qui sont beaux, dit il, mais peu interessants'.

183 Peter Paul Rubens

(Siegen 1577–1640 Antwerp)

Two Franciscan Friars

Black and white chalk, with some red chalk on the faces, on a greyish paper, 560 × 403mm.

Chatsworth 964A

Literature: Glück-Haberditzl, no.113; Held, 1959, no.93; Burchard-d'Hulst, 1963, no.125; Vlieghe, 1972, no.102C; Kusnetsov, 1974, no.96; Held, 1986, no.136

Exhibitions: Brussels, 1938–9 (45); Rotterdam, 1939 (35); Paris/ Brussels, 1949 (90); London, Arts Council, 1949 (43); Helsinki/ Brussels, 1952–3 (28); Antwerp, 1956 (73); Manchester, 1961 (95); Washington, etc., 1962–3 and London, RA, 1969 (99); London, BM, 1977 (75)

Study for the *Last Communion of St Francis* (Antwerp, Musée Royal no.305), painted by Rubens for the altar of the saint in the church of the Recollects at Antwerp, on

182

183

184

the commission of Jaspar Charles. The figure stretching out his arms is for the monk supporting the dying saint; the cowled monk is for a head in the background on the left edge of the altarpiece.

Between the figures Rubens inserted some folds and a belt relating to the right figure, which proves that this magnificent study has not been cut on the right.

184 Peter Paul Rubens

(Siegen 1577–1640 Antwerp)

Five Groups of Figures for a Last Supper (Christ announcing his Betrayal)

Pen and brown ink with touches of brown wash, 283 × 444mm.

Chatsworth 1007A

Provenance: presumably William, 2nd Duke of Devonshire

Literature: Rooses, *Rubens Bulletijn*, v, Antwerp, 1897, pp.202–3 (as Rubens); Held, 1959, p.96, under no.7 (as Rubens); Burchard-d'Hulst, 1963, no.35 (as Rubens); Jaffé, 1977, pp.29–30 and 57ff; Müller Hofstede, 1977, no.26; Held, 1986, no.18

Exhibitions: Antwerp, 1899 (116, as Van Dyck); London, Wildenstein, 1950 (40, as Rubens, but *verso* sketches identified as for a *Hercules*); Antwerp, 1956 (25, as Rubens); London, BM, 1977 (24); Washington, National Gallery of Art, 1983–4, no.12 (as Rubens, *c.*1611–12); Pittsburgh, etc., 1987–8 (93)

The pen style and the morphology are those of Rubens early in his Mantuan service, *c.*1601–4; and comparisons may be made with the Brunswick drawing for the *Mocking of Christ*, which he painted in 1601–2 in Rome for the Cappella di Sant'Elena of S. Croce in Gerusalemme, and with the Berlin drawing for *A seated Ecclesiastic*.

A second, closely subsequent sheet of studies, with only three groups of figures, was on the *recto* of another drawing in the Devonshire collection (formerly Chatsworth 1006; sold Christie's, London, 3 July 1984, lot 53). The inspiration for the gesture of the young apostle second from the right in the upper right group, with both hands raised across his breast, derives from Marcantonio Raimondi's engraving of the *Last Supper* after Raphael (B.26), and this print was almost certainly known to Rubens in Antwerp; but not until he had experienced Caravaggio's art during his first visit to Rome is he at all likely to have conceived, on the inspiration of the *Calling of St Matthew* in S. Luigi de' Francesi, the back view of the youth seated on the stool at the left. The two apostles, upper right, imply that he had seen Leonardo's *Last Supper* in Milan. No painting of the *Last Supper* appears to have been executed by Rubens in Italy: but this does not justify Müller Hofstede's view that these were *Ideenskizzen* with no painting in mind. In 1611 he was commissioned to paint a large one in horizontal form for the Benedictine Abbey of St Winoksbergen, Antwerp; but although he supplied a design, he did not proceed with the work.

His earliest known painting of *St Sebastian* (Rome, Galleria Corsini) appears to have been started during his second period in Rome, carried north in October 1608, and finished in Antwerp. It shows no resemblance to the earlier Laocoon-like studies on the *verso* of this drawing. The sheet developing these *Last Supper* studies, formerly at Chatsworth, shows on the *recto* an apostle pointing self-searchingly at his own head; and one of the head studies on the *verso* of the present drawing connects with this motif. Neither sheet can reasonably be dated after the studies drawn by Rubens for his Oratorian commissions in Rome and Fermo.

185

185 Anon. 16th-century Swiss and Peter Paul Rubens

(Siegen 1577–1640 Antwerp)

A fashionable young Woman holding a Shield

The original in pen and indian ink on white paper; Rubens's additions in pen and brown ink with brown wash, heightened with white and ochre bodycolours and some green wash, 261 × 210mm.

Chatsworth 838

Provenance: P.P.Rubens; his heirs until 1657; N.A.Flinck (L.595); presumably William, 2nd Duke of Devonshire from 1723–4

Literature: *Vasari Society*, v, 1909–10, 29 (as school of Holbein); F. Thöne, 1940, 64; Lugt, 1943, p.108; E. Schilling, 1950, p.251; Held, 1959, no.168, pl.178 and infra-red fig.44; Held, 1986, no.233

Exhibitions: Washington, etc., 1969–70 and London, V&A, 1973–4 (104)

Thöne was the first to mention Rubens's name in connection with this drawing. Not having seen the original, he was uncertain whether it was an unfinished work retouched by Rubens or an outright copy by Rubens. Lugt correctly stated that it had been reworked by Rubens. Schilling followed Lugt, adding that the original was a work by Daniel Hopfer. Byam Shaw pointed out a closer affinity to the bold, early designs by Hans Holbein the Younger for glass-painting. Of the original design for glass nothing remains visible except the architecture, the hat plumes, the sleeve of the right arm, and the pattern on the underskirt. The remainder of the figure has been reworked with some extensive changes. Originally the woman wore a cap under the feathered hat, from which barely a hair escaped. The visible hand is worked by Rubens's brush. The exposed flesh has been reworked and the shape of her hands changed. Originally she stood behind the shield of which the outline coincides with the long fold running obliquely from her right hand towards her left foot (her right hand held a loop attached to the shield). The changes in her dress, in her stance with respect to the shield, and in her demure expression are entirely due to Rubens; so are the 'horn' and 'curl' of the shield; and the highlights on the pilaster on the left.

Photographs taken for Held allow the charge on the shield to be descried (two pitchers and a housemark), presumably of some Swiss family. The original drawing is likely to have been the work of a sixteenth-century Swiss designer of stained glass working under Holbein's influence in Basel.

Rubens's reworking is sensibly dated by Held *c*.1625–35. For other examples of Rubens's practice of reworking earlier drawings, see cat. nos.108 and 189.

186 Peter Paul Rubens

(Siegen 1577–1640 Antwerp)

A peasant Girl churning Butter

COLOUR PLATE XIV

Black and red chalk on the woman's face and bodice, some pen lines on her cap and curls, 333 × 255mm.

Chatsworth 984

Provenance: presumably William, 2nd Duke of Devonshire

Literature: *Rubens Bulletijn*, v, 1900, p.204; *Vasari Society*, I, 3rd series, 1907, no.16; Glück-Haberditzl, no.210; Glück, 1933, p.182; Held, 1959, no.95, fig.103; Held, 1986, no.120

Exhibitions: Antwerp, 1899 (116, as Van Dyck); London, RA, 1938 (605); Brussels, 1938–9 (46); Rotterdam, 1939 (44); Rotterdam, 1948–9 (44); London, Arts Council, 1949 (46); London, Wildenstein's, 1950 (54); Helsinki/Brussels, 1952–3 (44); Washington, etc., 1962–3 and London, RA, 1969 (101)

Dated by Glück-Haberditzl *c*.1635; by Burchard in the 1950 exhibition catalogue, *c*.1630; and by Held, *c*.1618–20. The last suggestion seems to put forward the earliest plausible dating for this study for a figure which does not occur in any extant painting by Rubens. The application of red and black chalk to the face is comparable, as Held points out, to no.183 above, the drawing of *Two Franciscans* for the *Last Communion of St Francis* of 1618–19.

187 Peter Paul Rubens

(Siegen 1577–1640 Antwerp)

A dying Tree, its Trunk covered with Brambles

Red and black chalks, pen and brown ink, with some coloured wash, 352 × 298mm.

Inscribed by Rubens *afgevallen bladern ende op sommighe plaetsen schoon gruen grase door kyhen* ('fallen leaves and in some places pretty green grasses peep through')

Chatsworth 1008

Provenance: presumably William, 2nd Duke of Devonshire

Literature: *Vasari Society*, 2nd series, vi, no.12; Glück-Haberditzl, no.135; Held, 1959, p.145 and fig.17; Vergara, 1982, pp.83–4; Held, 1986, no.116

Exhibitions: London, Arts Council, 1949 (48); Washington, etc., 1962–3 and London, RA, 1969 (102); London, BM, 1977 (199)

This study is related to a drawing in the Louvre (Held, 1959, no.131), used by Rubens in his *Wild Boar Hunt* (Dresden) of *c*.1615–20 (KdK, 1931, pl.184). Held has cast doubt on the inscription being in Rubens's Flemish script: but there seems no other plausible explanation of this wholly characteristic observation of nature written on his drawing.

187

There is a similar, although lighter drawing in the Princes Gate Collection of the Courtauld Institute (A. Seilern, *Catalogue*, 1955, no.63; exhibited London, BM, 1977 (198)).

188 Roelant Savery
(Courtrai 1574–1639 Utrecht)

Thatched Dwellings, partly in Ruins, on a Mountainside

Pen and black ink, with some work in black chalk only, 175 × 288mm.

Inscribed on the *verso* in brown ink (by the same hand as

Chatsworth 457, Annibale Carracci's *Riposo*, which belonged to Jabach) *Rol. Savery/M.No 9*

Chatsworth 1095

Provenance: presumably Everhard Jabach; presumably William, 2nd Duke of Devonshire

Exhibitions: Pittsburgh, etc., 1987–8 (99)

Probably a leaf from a Bohemian sketchbook kept by Savery during his service to the Emperor Rudolf II in Prague. There is a slight sketch of a building in black chalk on the *verso*. A comparable drawing by Savery of this period, in pen and ink with coloured washes, is a *Village Street with Cottages* in the National Galleries of Scotland

188

(D.1706; Andrews, 1985, fig.508). The Chatsworth draw-ing shows particularly well Savery's developed taste for the ruinous and the vertiginous, such as we see also in the Utrecht drawing (Centraal Museum, inv.no.6729) of *Steps Up to a Ruin* which is signed *Roland Savery* and inscribed on the *verso*: *dit is van Savrij*.

189 Dierick Vellert (Antwerp, active 1511–1544) and Peter Paul Rubens (Siegen 1577–1640 Antwerp)

The Exhumation of St Hubert

Originally in pen and black ink, developed with point of brush and brown wash and white heightening, on dark brown pre-pared paper, 285mm in diameter.

Chatsworth 353

Provenance: N. A. Flinck (L.959); presumably William, 2nd Duke of Devonshire, from 1723–4

Exhibitions: Pittsburgh, etc., 1987–8 (100)

Evidently, as Campbell Dodgson realised in 1925, a design for a roundel of stained glass, probably to be executed in silverstain and paint. The original drawing is typical of Vellert *c*.1520, especially in the character of the architec-tural setting, which shows his emphasis on vertical linearity (at the right a beam projects towards us without support), and in the type and staging of the figures in rela-tion to that (not least their hats).

Lambotte, and later A. E. Popham (1962), suggested the possibility of his authorship of this drawing, which had been classed since 1929 simply as 'sixteenth-century Flemish' and previously, according to Eugénie Strong (1909), as 'Lelio Orsi, Scene of Burial'. However, it was not realised that the original drawing must have been rub-bed and crumpled by the early seventeenth century. The damages during the first century of the drawing's existence, most conspicuous on the left, were more than made good in entirely characteristic fashion by Rubens, who not only added (or entirely recreated) the torch-bearer, but also extensively corrected the typical insecuri-ties of the young Vellert's poses, especially of the man kneeling to raise the corpse. By his enhancements in white body colour and brown wash, Rubens has brought out the dramatic quality of the scene in the church by night.

This scene has been called hitherto at Chatsworth the 'Enterment of a Monk at Night, Attended by a Bishop'; but, as Dr Hilary Wayment has proposed to me, it surely represents the *Exhumation of St Hubert*, and the roundel could well have been intended for the palace of the Prince Bishop of Liège, Erard de la Marck. St Hubert had been the first bishop of Liège from 722 to 727. The scene was depicted by a follower of Rogier van der Weyden as taking place in the choir of a Gothic church (London, National Gallery, no.783). St Hubert's body had been exhumed in 743 by St Floribert, and again on 30 September 825. The National Gallery's painting, which was in the chapel of St Hubert in St Gudule, Brussels, c.1623, refers to the second occasion.

Vellert shows Louis le Débonnaire, King of the Franks, carrying his sceptre on the right, and the bishop of Liège on the left. The extraordinary flaring illumination, a concentration of which particularly dramatises the group of the bishop and his torchbearer, is redolent of the lessons absorbed by Rubens from the drawings of Jacopo Tintoretto, such as the latter's study of *Venus and Vulcan* in the Berlin Kupferstichkabinett (inv.no.4193). His work on the Vellert sheet likely postdates his return in 1608 from Italy, and should be placed c.1610–15. The delineation of the profile of the torchbearer can be matched, by reversal, in the St Elizabeth of Rubens's oil sketch for the *Visitation* wing of the Arquebusiers triptych for Antwerp Cathedral (repr. Held, 1980, cat.no.357).

190–191 Sebastian Vrancx

(Antwerp 1573–1647 Antwerp)

Set of Views in Rome and the Campagna (c.1597–1601)

Pen and brown ink with grey and brown washes, over preliminaries in graphite.

Inscribed with dates by the draughtsman in the strapwork cartouche and on nine of the succeeding views (one date being partially cut off; see below)

Chatsworth 1107

Vrancx made his Italian journey in the latter half of the 1590s, being then in his twenties. He was to be named as a master in the Antwerp Guild of St Luke in 1600/1

189

190

and was to join the Antwerp Guild of Romanists in 1610. It may well have been his intention to publish, but he did not complete, an album or portfolio of picturesque views of antique ruins in and about Rome, on a more ambitious scale than Willem van Nieulandt's set of 19 etchings of Roman ruins.

Also at Chatsworth (no.1142) is (and apparently has always been) kept Vrancx's design for a cartouche inscribed in a circle: *Anno./1597/A di 20 di Lulio/in Roma* (his lettering framed with strapwork and grotesques). This is to be compared with the earlier cartouche inscribed by him in an ellipse: *Desen boeck hoori/toe Sebastian/vrancx anno/1594* (Frankfurt, Staedelsches Kunstinstitut), which shows a similar combination of strapwork frame with foliage and fruit swags, but with male satyrs instead of sphinxes. Also comparable is the later cartouche inscribed by him in a circle: *Anno/1609/SV* (in monogram; St Petersburg, Hermitage, in pen and brown ink, 210 × 293mm).

Beyond the cartouche of 1597 there are forty-four sheets of *vedute*, one of which (Chatsworth 1126), showing *S. Maria delle Febbre*, is inscribed: *Anno 1598*. Another, showing the *Temple of the Tiburtine Sibyl at Tivoli*, is inscribed: *Anno 1599* (Chatsworth 1098). Seven others showing Campagna views are dated 1601 (Chatsworth 1100, 1104, 1109, 1112, 1113, 1118 and 1128). One drawing of *Ruins on the Palatine* (Chatsworth 1117) is half-finished in pen and wash, the goatherds and their flock being sketched only in black chalk. Others, still wholly in black chalk, are of *Trajan's Column and S. Maria di Loreto* (Chatsworth 1139) and of the *Forum Romanum*, a lively scene with figures (Chatsworth 1116).

The project may have been interrupted by Vrancx's return home sometime between 1601 and 1610, and probably nearer the earlier date. The highest number in his numeration of these views is '40' (Chatsworth 1098).

Half a century later, four years after Vrancx's death, ten of the more finished drawings were selected by Wenceslas Hollar for a series of etchings on a much reduced scale. Two of these little prints are dated 1651, five are undated and three are dated 1675. Not all the views are identified in the lettering of the prints; and one, which shows the *Entry to the Colosseum* (Chatsworth 1145), is labelled *Thermae of Diocletian*.

This Vrancx series has only been mentioned with other Roman views (e.g. Chatsworth 1130 and 1132) which were likewise removed from 'a large oblong green volume' in which T. Ashby saw them before 1916 (mentioned by Ashby in footnotes to his Roxburghe Club publication that year of the C. W. Dyson Perrins Manuscript by Etienne Dupérac). It is however of particular interest to Vrancx's development and, with those by the brothers Bril, by Willem van Nieulandt and by Jan Breughel the Elder, among the earliest such *vedute* drawn by a Netherlander. A landscape of fantasy, including antique ruins and distant mountains, was drawn by him in the living tradition of Paulus Bril (pen and brown ink over traces of red chalk, signed and dated on the *verso*: *sebastian vrancx/in. et fecit Roma/1597*; Sotheby's, London, 22 November 1974, lot 2). Another drawing of a *Landscape with Roman Ruins, a Mule Train crossing the hilly Foreground*, closer in subject to the Chatsworth series and particularly similar in the rendering of the foliage and cumulus clouds, was inscribed on the *recto* by the draughtsman: *1597/ Sebastiano Vrancx*. It was evidently also drawn by him in Rome (Schwarz sale, Vienna, 24 April 1918, lot 53, repr.).

The Chatsworth series show some advance in truth to natural appearances. The young Vrancx did not keep pedantically to the recording of actual situations. Not only did the rocky grottoes of the Aniene Valley at Tivoli tickle his fancy, but such a well-known *mirabilium* of Rome as the Basilica of Constantine would be transformed as it suited his sense of fantastic landscape (Chatsworth 1103). Nor did he avoid following the work of Paulus Bril's pupil Willem van Nieulandt or drawings by (or attributable to) Bril himself (or even a drawing by Toeput).

Hollar did not choose to engrave any of those Vrancx

subjects which he would have known in van Nieulandt's etchings of Roman ruins.

Seemingly always kept with this series, and presumably acquired at the same time, is an exceptionally fine watercolour by Vrancx of *Tivoli with the Temple of the Tiburtine Sibyl and the Falls* (Chatsworth 1107, here cat. no.190). Despite his apparent failure to find a publisher in his lifetime, as a Romanist he made at least one of these forty-four views available in Antwerp to a fellow draughtsman: the drawing of *S. Maria delle Febbre by Old St Peter's* (Chatsworth 1126) dated 1598. This, or the last original of it, was copied by Balthasar Lauwers, although it was itself a copy from the same late sixteenth-century original that was available also to Cornelis Vroom, to whom Chatsworth 54 has been convincingly attributed by An Zwollo.

190 Sebastian Vrancx

View of Tivoli with the Temple of the Tiburtine Sibyl and the Falls

Pen and brown ink with brown and blue washes, 284 × 436mm. Mounted in full on a 20th-century mount.

Chatsworth 1107

A masterly panorama in watercolour, which entitles Vrancx to more consideration as a landscape artist than he has generally received. It appears to have been kept at Chatsworth always with Vrancx's set of views; although larger than any of them, it is by the same hand.

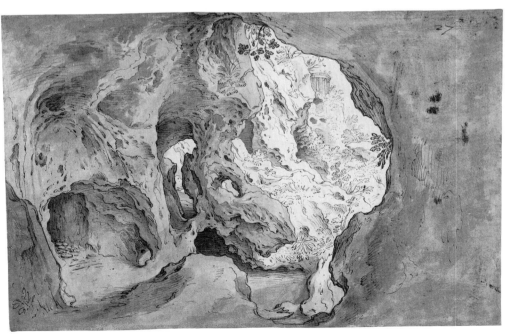

191

192

191 Sebastian Vrancx

Fantastic rock Formations made by the River Aniene in the Grottoes below the Temple of the Tiburtine Sibyl at Tivoli

Pen and brown ink, with brown and grey washes, 278 × 420mm. Mounted in full on a 20th-century mount.

Inscribed (by the artist?) in brown ink *27*

Chatsworth 1101

A mannerist revel in curious rock formations, of breathtaking originality. There are several others in this series of picturesque views of ruins and other *mirabilia* in Rome and the Campagna drawn by Vrancx *c.*1598–1601, presumably with an eventual publication in mind. He drew for that a frontispiece showing an extensive view looking down on the Piazza del Popolo, habitually the first introduction for a northern artist to the metropolis (Chatsworth 1131).

192 Caspar Adriensz. van Wittel, called Gasparo Vanvitelli

(Amersfoort 1653–1736 Rome)

View of Santa Madinella, near Civitavecchia

Pen and brown ink with brown, grey and blue washes, 222 × 339mm.

Inscribed by the artist in pen and brown ink *Santa Madinella vicino Civitavecchia*

Chatsworth 1147

Provenance: Richard, 3rd Earl of Burlington; William, 4th Duke of Devonshire

A fortified harbour in a bay, with figures and shipping. A drawing of *c.*1680, probably acquired by Lord Burlington on his tour of 1714.

GERMAN SCHOOL

(Nos 193–207)

193 Circle of Albrecht Altdorfer

(Regensburg? 1482/5–1535 Regensburg)

Landsknechten, Musketeers and Artillery, opposed by Cavalry, battle to defend a Castle by a Bridge over a wide River issuing from a Lake

Pen and ink, heightened with white bodycolour on a dark brown ground, 280 × 429mm.

Chatsworth 934

Provenance: N. A. Flinck (L.959); presumably William, 2nd Duke of Devonshire from 1723–4

Literature: C. Dodgson, *Vasari Society*, 1st series, 1911/12, VII, p.26; Buchner and Feuchtmayr, 1924, p.250, fig.154 (as Ruprecht Heller)

Exhibitions: Manchester, 1961 (140, as attributed to Rupert Heller); Washington, etc., 1969–70 and London, V&A, 1973–4 (102, as Bavarian School *c*.1530); Tokyo, 1975 (87); Jerusalem, 1977 (41)

Formerly attributed in the Devonshire Collections to Altdorfer, but, as J. Byam Shaw (1969) realised, not by his hand, although, as Campbell Dodgson remarked in the *Vasari Society* publication, it is reminiscent of the *Battle of Arbela* (Munich, Alte Pinakothek). Dodgson reported that Ernst Buchner had suggested an attribution to Ruprecht Heller, by whom there is a comparable painting of the *Battle of Pavia* (Stockholm, Nationalmuseum) signed and dated on the original frame: *Rupert Heller 1529*. Artillery was first used decisively at Pavia.

Chatsworth 934 typifies the manner of the so-called Danube School inspired by Altdorfer and Wolf Huber in the first half of the sixteenth century, exaggerating Altdorfer's technique.

194 Jost Amman

(Zürich 1539–1591 Nuremberg)

Lion Mask

Pen and indian ink with white bodycolour with the point of the brush, on dull red prepared paper, 143 × 104mm. Fully mounted.

Chatsworth 88B

193

194

Provenance: presumably William, 2nd Duke of Devonshire

Exhibitions: Pittsburgh, etc., 1987–8 (110, as by Jost Amman)

In the annotations of 1925 to the *First Rough Draft for a Catalogue of the Chatsworth Drawings* by Eugénie Strong (August 1909), Campbell Dodgson and A. E. Popham classed this decorative fantasy as 'style of Jost Amman *c.*1560.' Later E. Schilling, followed by I. Q. van Regteren Altena, K. T. Parker, and J. Byam Shaw, attributed it to Amman himself. Convincing comparison may be made with Louvre inv. no. 18.4.9.8., a pen drawing of *St Nicholas Mounted on an Ass*, which is signed and dated 1588 (Demonts, 1937, I, no.15). It may also be compared to the *Head of a bearded Man wearing a plumed Cap* formerly in the collection of Victor Koch (see Kurt Pilz, *Das Graphische Werk des Jost Amman*, dissertation, Nüremberg 1930, pp.320–1, no.156; *idem*, *Fränkische Heimat*, vol.19, no.1, Nüremberg 1940, pl.12) which is monogrammed and dated in pen and black ink by the draughtsman: *IA 1572*. That offers a fairer suggestion for dating Chatsworth 88B.

195 Hans Baldung Grien

(Gmünd 1484/85–1545 Strasbourg)

St Nicholas of Bari, robed as Bishop of Myra

Brush in brown ink and white bodycolour, with some accents of rose bodycolour, on paper washed brown, 282 × 160mm (after trimming). Fully mounted.

Inscribed indecipherably (with a signature?), lower right

Chatsworth 834

Provenance: a late seventeenth- or early eighteenth-century English collector (L.2098); presumably William, 2nd Duke of Devonshire

Literature: Demonts, 1937, I, under no.33 (as a copy of Baldung); Léna Widerkehr in *Dessins de Dürer et de la Renaissance germanique dans les collections publiques parisiennes*, exh. cat., Musée du Louvre, Paris, 1991–2, p.142 (under no.131, as a copy of the Louvre drawing)

Exhibitions: Pittsburgh, etc., 1987–8 (111, as by Baldung)

Demonts, following Gabor von Terey (*Verzeichnis der Gemälde des Hans Baldung gen. Grien*, Strasbourg, 1894, III, no.204), insisted that Louvre no.1886 (298 × 192mm), drawn in a similar technique and acquired for France from Eberhard Jabach in 1671, is the original, presumably because it bears *HGB* in monogram over the date *1515*.

However, the Windsor *St Conrad* (von Terey, p.61), similarly monogrammed and dated 1520, has rightly been regarded as studio work. Although the originator of the Louvre design is most plausibly Baldung in 1515, when he made a number of *chiaroscuro* drawings, and although Demonts may also be correct in seeing a resemblance in the figure to the features of the then bishop of Strasbourg, Wilhelm Graf von Honstein, the further statement of Demonts that the Chatsworth drawing is monogrammed *HK* (Hans Hug Kluber, 1535–1578?) does not stand up to scrutiny. Moreover, careful comparison of the two drawings shows how in several significant respects the Louvre version is laboured and insensitive: in the impossible lighting of the rear portion of the mitre; in the lack of vitality in the silhouettes of the pluvial; in the stodgy, mechanical use of the streaks and fringes of the white heightening; and in the misunderstanding of the figurines of haloed saints which are niched below the scrolled crook of the pastoral staff. It seems that the Louvre draughtsman, having had the artistic problems resolved by the Chatsworth drawing, had then to produce a *modelletto* for a *chiaroscuro* woodcut.

One who was no more than an able imitator of the Louvre drawing would hardly have strayed from the number of balls decorating the scroll of the staff and the face of the mitre; nor would any such person have so disregarded the stiff schemata of shading as well as of lighting the folds. The delicate use of the media in Chatsworth

195

834 is markedly closer to such incontravertible Baldung drawings as the Albertina *Witches Scene* and the Berlin *Death and the Maiden*, both monogrammed '*HGB 1515*', also the Weimar *Lucretia stabbing herself*, monogrammed *HGB 1519*. The Chatsworth drawing has been cropped along the top and at the right as well as along the bottom, losing thereby most of an inscription (also a signature?); and in respect of this last, it might have been cropped so as to pass in England as a Dürer. Nevertheless, it has priority over the Louvre drawing as a Baldung original of his Freiburg period. Unfortunately the catalogue of the 1991–2 exhibition at the Louvre overlooked the 1987–8 exhibition at Pittsburgh and, without apparently direct knowledge of Chatsworth 834, repeated the erroneous observation and judgement of Demonts. The argument of primacy for the Chatsworth drawing is set out again here.

196

196 Hans Sebald Beham

(Nuremberg 1500–1550 Italy)

St Catherine of Alexandria

Pen and indian ink, 162 × 105mm. Fully mounted in the 1920s.

Inscribed with the artist's monogram and date *HSB 1537*

Chatsworth (loose, unnumbered drawing)

Provenance: Sir Peter Lely (L.2092); presumably William, 2nd Duke of Devonshire

Literature: C. Dodgson, *OMD*, September, 1937, p.30, pl.29; Albert J. Elen, *Missing Old Master Drawings from the Franz Koenigs Collection, claimed by the State of the Netherlands*, The Hague, 1989, p.91, under no.100*

Exhibitions: Pittsburgh, etc., 1987–8 (112)

This fine drawing of Beham's maturity in Frankfurt was classed at Chatsworth among the prints (VIII.24) until its true graphic quality was recognised in the 1920s by Campbell Dodgson. It was presumably prepared, as P. Day points out, for a woodcut which was not executed.

A seeming replica (almost certainly a contemporary copy), monogrammed (the place where the date appears on the Chatsworth drawing is trimmed away) was in the Koenigs Collection, among those drawings still missing from the Museum Boymans-van Beuningen. An accidental blot of ink on the saint's overskirt, near her right thigh, seems to be the sole difference except for the far more significant difference that the draughtsman in the Koenigs version has made, in a moment of inattention, an impossible right thumb out of the knop fastening the quillion of her sword. The Koenigs drawing was unknown to Dodgson.

197 Jörg Breu the Younger

(Augsburg *c.*1510–1547 Augsburg)

A fashionable Party in the Grounds of a moated Castle

Pen and brown ink with brown wash, 278 × 414mm.

Inscribed by the artist, lower right, *das erst/stueck* and dated 1534 above left centre.

Chatsworth 664

Literature: Campbell Dodgson, *Vasari Society*, 1st series, VIII, p.31; H. Leporini, *Die Stilentwicklung*, 1925, p.72; H. Röttinger, in *Wiener Jahrbuch*, XXVIII, pp.31ff.

Exhibitions: London, RA, 1953 (245); Washington etc., 1969–70 and London, V&A, 1973–4 (106)

Campbell Dodgson (*loc. cit.*) thought that the inscription meant that the composition would be extended (presumably to the right). Byam Shaw (1969) regarded the drawing as a sketch for a large woodcut. Similar buildings and figures occur in the *Dives and Lazarus* of 1535 (M. Geisberg,

197

Der deutsche Einblatt – Holzschnitt in der ersten Hälfte des XVI Jahrhunderts, Munich, 1930, no.397) and in the *Venetian Banquet* (on three blocks, Geisberg nos.402–4). J.K. Rowlands has pointed out to me (1992) that this drawing is closest in execution to the sketches in Johann Böschenstein's treatise on the dance, written in 1537 (Augsburg, Staats- und Stadtbibliothek, 4' Cod.278; see *Welt im Umbruch*, Augsburg, 1980, I, pp.220–1, no.155 repr.).

The scene is an amusing mixture of elements from the Venetian and the German Renaissances.

198 Hans Burgkmair

(Augsburg 1473–1531 Augsburg)

Wolfgang von Maen

Black chalk with some touches with the brush in brownish ink, 352 × 272mm, top corners chamfered; considerably rubbed, the lower right corner is missing and made up. Several major losses on the right, and some minor.

Inscribed in pen and brown ink *M.D.XVIII*.

Chatsworth 933

Literature: Strong, 1902, no.9; *Vasari Society*, 1st series, IV, 1908–9, p.29; L. Kaemmerer, *Mitteilungen des Österr. Vereins fur Bibliothekwesen*, Vienna, IX, 1905, p.42

Exhibitions: London, Arts Council, 1949 (50); Manchester, 1961 (147); Washington, etc., 1962–3 and London, RA, 1969 (103); Jerusalem, 1977 (42); Richmond, etc., 1979–80 and London, RA, 1980–1 (89)

Formerly attributed to Dürer, Kaemmerer identified the sitter in this bust-length portrait as the chaplain to the Emperor Maximilian, one who was likely to have accompanied him in 1518 to the Diet at Augsburg where Burgkmair was then working.

Despite the condition, this remains a magnificent example of Burgkmair's portrait drawing.

198

199 Albrecht Dürer

(Nuremberg 1471–1528 Nuremberg)

An old Man, three quarter length, gesticulating

Pen and brown ink, with some corrections in white bodycolour and some black chalk, 198 × 140mm.

Chatsworth 642C

Provenance: P. H. Lankrink (L.2090); presumably William, 2nd Duke of Devonshire

Exhibitions: Washington, etc., 1969–70 and London, V&A, 1973–4 (103, as 'German School?')

The mark of Lankrink (1628–92) rules out the former attribution at Chatsworth to P. L. Ghezzi (1647–1755); also the second Duke of Devonshire obtained his Ghezzi drawings more or less directly from that artist (Chatsworth nos.310, 311, 312). A. E. Popham (1962) suggested Quentin Massys, presumably because of the grotesque element reminiscent of Leonardo's caricatures, but there are no comparable drawings by him. De Gheyn has also been suggested. Rather, as Byam Shaw (1969) was the first to suggest, the loose penwork is reminiscent of Dürer's more summary sketches of early date. A comparable grotesque appears in Dürer's *Christ among the Doctors*, dated 1506 (Lugano, Thyssen-Bornemisza Collection). He

was seeing Leonardesque *grotesquerie* on his second visit to Italy. The penwork can be compared closely to a drawing by Dürer in the same technique of a *Kluge Jungfrau* in Vienna (Albertina, D.42) which according to Meder is datable to Dürer's first return from Venice.

Pasted into Volume X of the Chatsworth Inigo Jones drawings (vol. IV of the Walpole Society's *Designs by Inigo Jones*, ed. P. Simpson and C. F. Bell) is a sheet with four heads studied more or less in profile by Inigo Jones (no.143, in pen and brown ink, 202 × 195mm) of which the upper right is manifestly a copy, with the old man's mouth closed, of Chatsworth 642C. Jones therefore is likely to have seen Dürer's drawing in an English collection, probably Lord Arundel's, before Lankrink came from Germany.

200 Albrecht Dürer

(Nuremberg 1471–1528 Nuremberg)

Women's public Bath

Pen and light brown ink, the man's profile on the right in darker ink, 285 × 215mm.

Monogrammed and dated by the artist *AD 1516*

Chatsworth 931

Provenance: William, 2nd Duke of Devonshire (L.718)

Literature: C. Ephrussi, *Les Bains de femmes d'Albrecht Dürer*, Paris, 1881, p.10; Strong, 1902, no.27; F. Lippmann, *Zeichnungen Dürers*, IV, no.398 (recto) and VII, no.904 (verso)

Exhibitions: Washington, etc., 1962–3 and London, RA, 1969 (104); Nuremberg, 1971 (472); Tokyo, 1975 (89); Paris, Marais, 1978 (138)

Winkler (4973) records an old copy of this drawing in the Berlin Kupferstichkabinett. Dürer in 1496, many years earlier in Nuremberg, had drawn a women's bath (Winkler, 152). Visits to these baths were his best opportunity of studying variety in the female nude.

There is an architectural study on the *verso* (see Dürer Society, XI).

199

201

202 Adam Elsheimer

(Frankfurt 1578–1609 Rome)

Salome receiving the Head of St John the Baptist

Gouache, indian ink, heightened with white, on dark paper, 78 × 67mm.

Chatsworth 851C

Provenance: N. A. Flinck (L.959); William, 2nd Duke of Devonshire from 1723–4

Literature: Bode, 1883, pp.307–8; *Vasari Society*, VI, 1925, no.17; H. Weizsäcker, *Adam Elsheimer, Dr. Mailer von Frankfurt*, pp.190, 263, pl.95; Möhle, 1966, no.45, pl.27; Keith Andrews, *Adam Elsheimer*, Oxford, 1977, cat. no.48, fig.93 (enlarged in German edition, Munich, 1985, p.199, no.48, pl.31, erroneously as pl.32 in cat. entry)

Exhibitions: Manchester, 1961 (172); Frankfurt, 1966/67, no.145, fig.106

As Möhle pointed out, this may be *Een teyckeningetje Johannis enthroft van Elshamer*, referred to in the 1680 inventory of Jakob Loys, Rotterdam City Councillor and painter (A. Bredius, *Künstlerinventäre*, 1915–21, V, p.1589, no.22 and under no.23 *Nogh een van dito*). Chatsworth 851C may have been a preliminary study, as Andrews suggested, for a small painting, now lost, which may have served as the pattern for Goudt's engraving (oval, Hollstein 4). If Goudt's print is faithful to the painting, the cloaked figure with the flamboyantly feathered hat, the executioner's

201 Albrecht Dürer

(Nuremberg 1471–1528 Nuremberg)

The Virgin and Child with the infant St John

Pen and brown ink, 286 × 205mm.

Signed, lower right, with the monogram *AD*

Chatsworth 830

Provenance: William, 2nd Duke of Devonshire (L.718)

Literature: Winkler, III, 1938, no.538

Exhibitions: London, Arts Council, 1949 (51); Washington, etc., 1969–70 and London, V&A, 1973–4 (107); Richmond etc., 1979–80 (88)

Closely related in style and in type to the Virgin in the woodcut *The Virgin with many Angels* (B.101) of 1518, and almost certainly of that date. The Child holds up to the Virgin a carnation as a symbol of the Passion. The horizontal hatching is typical of this period in Dürer's draughtsmanship (cf. Chatsworth 931, dated 1516).

Winkler (*op.cit.*) considered that the monogram may have been added by another hand: but J. K. Rowlands (1991) points out that it is convincingly autographic and drawn in correct perspective.

202

large sword, the forward inclination of Salome, and the exclusion of a sixth figure are all modifications from the drawing. However, the rectangular format of the latter is retained in a painting which otherwise copies the Goudt print (Copenhagen, Statens Museum fur Kunst, Inv.559, as 'anon. 17th century', oils on copper, 147 × 108mm).

Stylistically the Chatsworth *gouache* is close to the *Ceres* drawings in Hamburg and Zürich (Andrews, *op.cit.*, cat. nos.50 and 51).

203 Hans Holbein the Younger

(Augsburg 1497/8–1543 London)

Portrait of a Youth in a broad-brimmed Hat

COLOUR PLATE XV

Black and red chalks on cream paper, 245 × 202mm. Mounted in full for the 2nd Duke.

Chatsworth 836

Provenance: William, 2nd Duke of Devonshire (L.718)

Literature: Strong, 1902, p.16, pl.XXVI; Strong, 1905, p.133; *Master Drawings, The Woodner Collection*, London, RA, 1987, under cat.no.54

Exhibitions: London, Arts Council, 1949 (54, as Holbein); London, RA, 1950–1 (133); Washington, etc., 1962–3 and London, RA, 1969 (106); Richmond, etc., 1979–80 (91)

The sitter does not appear to be English. It is surely by Holbein the Younger, as is argued by comparison with the Basel *Man with a slouch Cap*, datable *c.*1528, as was first suggested by K. Oberhuber for a copy in the Woodner Collection. It appears to be the prime original of that version which is also of excellent quality and strong character (exhibited as Holbein by Veronika Birke and Friedrich Piel, *Die Sammlung Ian Woodner*, Albertina, Vienna, 1986, no.54). Ganz (1937, no.17) and Oberhuber have vehemently defended the authenticity of the Woodner sheet.

The Woodner drawing shows more of the young man's bust. The chalk surface has been rubbed, and Ganz detected extensive reworking. Outlines may have been reinforced, e.g. on the chin, the right cheek and the lobe of the ear, which appears oddly drawn in relation to the growth of hairs. Other signs of its revisionary status as a fair copy are evident: the eye cannot connect with the silhouette of the crown of the hat, apparently misunderstood by the draughtsman; the rim and brim of the hat are fussily outlined; on the shoulder the adumbration of the shirt at first followed the rougher indication in Chatsworth 836, and then, with a fresh outline, the linen is heightened with white and made more explicit.

Woltman, Strong, Popham and, most recently, J. K. Rowlands (1991) have upheld the priority and

authenticity of Chatsworth 836, datable 1524–26, before Holbein was introduced by Sir Thomas More on his first visit to England.

204 Hans Holbein the Younger

(Augsburg 1497/8–1543 London)

Six Designs for Pendants or Hat Badges:
(a) *The Fall of Icarus* (b) *The Last Judgement*
(c) *Cupid stung by Bees* (d) *Hagar and Ishmael*
(e) *Diana and Actaeon* (f) *Allegory of Time*

Pen and ink with coloured washes on white paper, diameters: (a) 51mm (b) 47mm (c) 56mm (d) 54mm (e) 50mm (f) 55mm; fully mounted for the 6th Duke together with (g), here attributed to Etienne Delaune (1518–1585)

Inscriptions: (c) *Nocet empta dolore voluptas* (d) *ISMAEL* and *HAGGAR* (f) *Aspetto la Hora*

Chatsworth 837

Literature: Strong, 1902, pl.XVIII; Strong, 1905, p.133, pl.XVIII; Ganz, 1937, V, nos.257–61 and 281

Exhibitions: London, Arts Council, 1949 (53); Manchester, 1961 (151); Washington, etc., 1962–3 and London, RA, 1969 (107)

The six exquisite designs mounted together were drawn during Holbein's second period in England, 1532–43. Although Ganz did not include (g) in his corpus, and A. E. Popham (1949) had suggested for it an attribution to Etienne Delaune, Popham (1962) eventually, as also F. G. Grossmann (1961), catalogued it as by Holbein like the other six drawings. However it is not consonant with Holbein's style, having manifestly closer affinities with the School of Fontainebleau (see *Ecole de Fontainebleau*, Paris, 1972–3, no.72, *La Musique*, a design for tapestry by Delaune); and it is here attributed to Delaune.

205 Wenceslas Hollar

(Prague 1607–1677 London)

(a) *The Rhine at Coblenz with the Castle of Hermenstein (Ehrenbreitstein) on the Philipstal*

COLOUR PLATE XVI

(b) *The Castle, and the Bridge over the Main at Würzburg*

(c) *Lord Arundel's Barges at the Confluence of the Wils and the Danube*

Pen and black ink, with grey, brown, and blue washes; 109 × 280mm (H.4); 114 × 230mm (H.10); 114 × 274mm (H.16).

Inscribed by Hollar, all with a fine pen in black ink *Cobolentz/ Hermenstein/ Philipstal/ Rhenus Fluvius/ 10 Maij 1636* (H.4); *Das*

204 (a–f)

Schlofs zu Würtzburg/ Occidens/Septentrio/Oriens/Meridies [round compass rose] *Moenus fluvius* (H.10); *Vilshoven, Vils fluvius, Danubeus fluvius* (H.16)

Chatsworth H4, 10, 16, S189, 219, 240

Provenance: Thomas Howard, 2nd Earl of Arundel; his daughter-in-law, Viscountess Stafford(?); presumably William, 2nd Duke of Devonshire

Literature: F. Sprinzels, *Wenceslas Hollar and His Drawings*, Vienna, 1938, nos.189, 219, 240 (H.4, H.10, H.16), figs.153, 169, 173; Antony Griffiths and Gabriela Kesnerova, *Wenceslas Hollar: Prints and Drawings from the Collections of the National Gallery, Prague, and the British Museum, London*, London, 1983, pp.21–4; Berthold Roland, *et al.*, *Wenzel Hollar 1607–1677: Reisebilder vom Rhein*, Mainz, 1986/87, no.30 (H.4, inv.no.76)

Exhibitions: Mainz, 1986–7 (30; H.4); Pittsburgh, etc., 1987–8 (113A–C); Koblenz/Bonn, 1992 (33)

On 27 May 1636, soon after Hollar made this drawing of Coblenz, Lord Arundel wrote from Nuremberg to William Petty, his agent in Italy: *I have one Hollarse wth me, who draws and etches Printes in stronge water quickely, and wth a pretty spiritte* (M.S.F. Hervey, *The Earl of Arundel*, London, 1921, p.366). Arundel's rather hopeless mission,

loyally undertaken for Charles I, was to try and secure for the English king's sister and her family their recovery of, or at least succession to, the Palatinate, which had been assigned by the Emperor under the terms of the Peace of Prague to the Duke of Saxony. Hollar joined Arundel's entourage in Cologne, having, as F.G. Grossman suggested (Manchester, 1963, cat.no.D.31), recommended himself by his superb panorama of that city (Chatsworth S.180).

Leaving Cologne on 28 April (old style), the legation progressed by sailing barge up the Rhine to Mainz, branching east up the Main to Frankfurt where they remained from 5–7 May. When there was insufficient wind, the vessel flying the St George's flag was towed by a team of eight horses with postilions, the spare team being towed behind on a raft (H.4).

From Frankfurt, Arundel and his suite went overland, arriving on 10 May at Würzburg, where they are seen crossing the bridge over the Main (H.10); thence via Nuremberg to Regensburg. There they took low, covered barges up the Danube to Linz, where Arundel was to have his first, unsatisfactory, interview with the Emperor. The Earl halted at Vilshoven (H.16). Eventually from Vienna

Das Schloß zu Würtzburg

205(b)

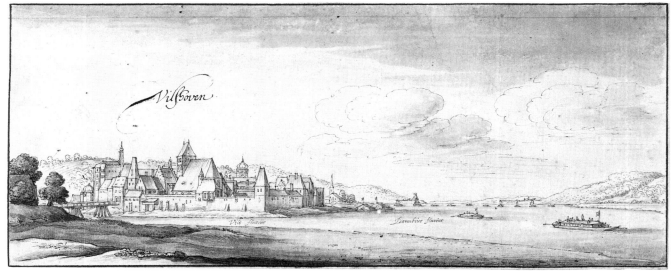

Vilshoven

205(c)

206

he went overland across Moravia to Prague, giving Hollar his last glimpse of his native city.

Another member of the suite, William Crowne, kept a diary of the journey which was printed in 1637. This should be read in conjunction with these Hollar drawings, of which the seventeen others at Chatsworth are likewise his fair copies with watercolours of slighter sketches taken on the spot (e.g. *Drawings from the Springell Collection*, sale, Sotheby's, 30 June 1986, nos.9, 10, 12, 13). Sketches preliminary to H.4 are in the John Rylands Library, University of Manchester (Eng.MS.883, bequest of Mrs Hartland, 1936) and were exhibited for the first time at the Landesmuseum, Mainz (in *Wenzel Hollar 1607–1677: Reisebilder vom Rhein*, 16 November 1986–6 January 1987: cat.nos.28–9). The date 1635 written on these is certainly an error for 1636, the barge with the St George's flag being clearly shown. Hermenstein was the common appellation of Ehrenbreitstein (cf. Chatsworth H.3).

206 Hans Rottenhammer

(Munich 1564–1625 Augsburg)

Banquet of the Gods

Pen and indian ink, with grey wash, extensively heightened with white bodycolour, on buff paper, 231 × 349mm. Fully mounted on an early 18th-century mount.

Chatsworth 690

Provenance: William, 2nd Duke of Devonshire (L.718)

Exhibitions: Leeds, 1868, no.2732 (as by Perino del Vaga); Pittsburgh, etc., 1987–8 (115, as by Rottenhammer)

An important example of Rottenhammer's highly developed and highly finished manner of designing *alla veneziana*. It belongs probably to his time in Augsburg, after 1606. A smaller, very spirited preparatory drawing in the Louvre (18.763; Demonts, 1938, II, no.663, pl.CLXIX), was catalogued without reference to Chatsworth 690. In the Chatsworth drawing both *amorini* disappear from the central foreground; Amor appears alone, reclining at the left; the illumination of the tree trunk, to which the servant boldly gestures, becomes the dominant feature of the background; and there are changes in the attributes of Mars and Oceanus.

207

207 Hans Rottenhammer

(Munich 1564–1625 Augsburg)

Diana and her Nymphs bathing, surprised by Actaeon

Pen and point of brush with brown ink, and brown wash with white heightening, over preliminaries in black chalk, 260 × 202mm. Creased and somewhat faded (a hole in the top horizontal crease). Fully mounted on an early 18th-century mount.

Chatsworth 691

Provenance: N. A. Flinck (L.959); William, 2nd Duke of Devonshire, from 1723–4

Exhibitions: Pittsburgh, etc., 1987–8 (114)

This favourite subject provided opportunities for Rottenhammer, a northern admirer of Tintoretto and Veronese, to display nudes *alla veneziana*. Evidently drawn within Rottenhammer's Venetian period 1596–1606, it appears close in date to his *Diana and Actaeon* in the Victoria and Albert Museum, a painting signed and dated 1597.

FRENCH SCHOOL
(Nos 208–220)

208 Claude Gellée, called Claude Le Lorrain

(Chamagne 1604/05–1682 Rome)

Landscape with a Ruined Temple and a Tower

Pen with brown and some grey ink, and washes of both, heightened with white bodycolour, 215 × 280mm. Fully mounted on an 18th-century mount.

Chatsworth 875

Engraved: by R. Earlom, *Liber Veritatis*, III, no.85, in 1777

Provenance: presumably William, 2nd Duke of Devonshire

Literature: Röthlisberger, 1968, no.58; M. Chiarini, *Selected Drawings*, Philadelphia, 1968, facs. pl. VII

Exhibitions: London, Arts Council, 1969 (43); Newcastle-upon-Tyne, 1969 (30, pl.5); Pittsburgh, etc., 1987–8 (118)

A vigorously executed work of 1630–5, close in character of composition and *chiaroscuro* to Paulus Bril in such a drawing as Chatsworth 698 (cat. no.154). As Röthlisberger pointed out, 'the incisive, minute penmanship is above all reminiscent of several of his first etchings, of around 1635 (Blum nos.1, 8, 9, 18). The uneven handling differs from plane to plane: bold strokes in the foreground, fine lines in the foliage, a lighter ink in the distance and the sky'. It is close in character also to the pastoral at Holkham (Röthlisberger, 1968, fig.340, then doubted by him as by Claude) which is signed, bottom left: *CLAVD.../16 [?2]*. The drawing has lost some of its sharpness by over-exposure in the sixth Duke's Sketch Gallery.

Both the round tower, and the stylea temple beside it, are found in Claude's early paintings e.g. the Seward Johnson *Coast Scene* and the Kimbell Art Museum *Rape of Europa* (exh. Washington, 1982, nos.17 and 15).

209 Claude Gellée, called Le Lorrain

(Chamagne 1604/05–1682 Rome)

Wooded Landscape with Diana and Callisto

Pen and brown ink with brown and grey washes, heightened with white bodycolour, over preliminaries in black chalk, 257 × 335mm.

Signed, lower right *CLAUDIO INV FEC*

Chatsworth 945

Engraved by R. Earlom, *Liber Veritatis*, III, no.90, in 1777

Provenance: William, 2nd Duke of Devonshire (L.718)

Literature: Röthlisberger, 1968, no.950 (as Diana and Callisto?);

208

M. Kitson, 'Claude Lorrain as a figure draughtsman,' in D. Dethloff (ed.), *Drawing: Masters & Methods: Raphael to Redon*, London, 1992, p.66, fig.2

Exhibitions: London, RA, 1949–50 (490); Manchester, 1961 (86); Washington, etc., 1969–70 and London, V & A, 1973–4 (118); Tokyo, 1975 (99); Richmond, etc., 1979–80 (75)

A drawing of *c*.1665, the subject was identified by M. Kitson. No painting is known to have been exactly based on this drawing. As Kitson points out, 'the treatment is only a little simpler and more informal, and the mood somewhat more intimate, than would be the case in a painting of the same date'.

210 Claude Gellée, called Claude Le Lorrain

(Chamagne 1604/05–1682 Rome)

Landscape with the Journey of Jacob

Pen and brown ink with brown wash, 256 × 387mm. Fully mounted on an early 18th-century mount.

Chatsworth 948

Engraved: Earlom, *Liber Veritatis*, III, no.96 (as Jacob's Departure) in 1777

Provenance: William, 2nd Duke of Devonshire (L.718)

Literature: Röthlisberger, 1968, no.1097

Exhibitions: London, RA, 1949 (472); Pittsburgh, etc., 1987–8 (120)

An *abbot Chevalier* (perhaps the Benedictine Damien-Ignace Chevalier of the Abbaye d'Evron, Mayenne) commissioned the painting, dated 1677 (Williamstown, Mass.), for which this is a preliminary drawing, based on

209

210

211

Liber Veritatis no.107, with the pastoral subject of the earlier work transformed into one from the Old Testament. In this transformation the castle at the left is replaced by a hill town similar to *Liber Veritatis* no.188.

211 Claude Gellée, called Le Lorrain

(Chamagne 1604/05–1682 Rome)

Landscape with Christ preaching the Sermon on the Mount

Pen and brown ink with grey wash, 292 × 444mm.

Chatsworth 939

Engraved by R. Earlom, *Liber Veritatis*, III (100)

Provenance: William, 2nd Duke of Devonshire (L.718)

Exhibitions: London, RA, 1949–50 (494); Washington, etc., 1969–70 and London, V & A, 1973–4 (117)

One of five elaborate composition drawings for the very large and complex painting (*Liber Veritatis* 138) executed in 1656 for François Bosquet, Bishop of Montpellier (New York, Frick Collection). In it the mount on which Christ is preaching is a much more dominant feature.

212 Gaspard Dughet, called Gaspard Poussin

(Rome 1615–1675 Rome)

Mountain Road winding through Woodland and Rocks

Black chalk with touches of white chalk on *carta azzurra*, 428 × 309mm, the lower right corner repaired. Mounted in full on an early 18th-century mount.

Chatsworth 951

Provenance: William, 2nd Duke of Devonshire (L.718, on the repaired corner)

Literature: J. Shearman, *The Drawings of Nicholas Poussin, IV (Part Four, The Landscape Drawings)*, London, 1963, no.G26; M. Chiarini, *Paragone*, 1965, no.187, fig.60 (as *Studio per San Martino ai Monti*); idem, 'Gaspard Dughet: Some Drawings Connected with Paintings,' *Burl. Mag.*, CXI (1969), p.750, n.5; Marie-Nicole Boisclair, *Gaspard Dughet, 1615–1675*, Paris, 1986, no.951, p.94, fig.130 (dating it 1648–9); Hilliard T. Goldfarb, *From Fontainebleau to the Louvre. French Drawing from the Seventeenth Century*, Cleveland Museum of Art, Ohio, 1989, pp.85–6 (under cat.no.39)

Exhibitions: Pittsburgh, etc., 1987–8 (121)

Classed at Chatsworth as 'Claude Lorrain' or 'style of Gaspard Poussin', this drawing is manifestly of the 1640s and by Gaspard himself, inspired by his familiarity with the Roman Campagna. Comparison may be made with drawings in the Kunstmuseum Düsseldorf (especially Christian Klemm, *Gaspard Dughet und die ideale Landschaft*, Düsseldorf, October-December 1981, cat.no.1, ill. p.8). In a taller form, and with differences particularly obvious in the foreground vegetation and in the trees on the right, it anticipates the landscape in one of Dughet's larger frescoes on the wall of the right aisle of SS. Silvestro e Martino ai Monti in Rome: *Elias Anointing Hazael, King of Syria, and Jehu, King of Israel* (I Kings 19:15–16). This subject, not named by Chiarini, is identified by the lettering of Pietro Parboni's engraving of 1810 after the fresco.

The payments to Gaspard for his work in the Carmelite church range from December 1647 to May 1651. The landscape of Chatsworth 951 was adapted by him to the proportions of the fresco, with some alterations to the foreground and other details of trees and tufa rocks. A drawing now in the Fogg Art Museum at Harvard University (1964.82) is drawn characteristically in pen and brown ink with brown wash, like others of his direct preparations for this first, very important public

212

213

commission (cf. Chiarini, *loc. cit.*, figs. 49 and 51). The sequence, not made quite clear by Chiarini, is first, the independent Chatsworth drawing with two staffage figures; second, the Fogg drawing, a specific preparation for the fresco in the basilica, the figures deliberately omitted; third, the *modello* at Hamburg; and fourth, the fresco with a narrative of figures probably introduced by Pietro Testa. This sequence points to a characteristic working habit, hitherto unremarked, in Dughet's use both of chalk drawings on blue paper and of pen and wash drawings on white paper.

213 Nicholas Raymond Lafage

(Lisle-en-Albigeois 1656–1690 Lyon)

The Toilet of Venus

Pen and brown ink, with grey and yellowish brown washes, over preliminaries in black chalk, 205 × 401mm, fan shaped, overall 275mm. Fully mounted on a 19th-century mount.

Signed in pen and brown ink, lower left, *Raimont Lafage Roma*

Chatsworth 702

Provenance: Peter Sylvester (L.2018); 'R.R.' (an inscription partly erased and unknown); presumably William, 2nd Duke of Devonshire

Literature: Nathan T. Whitman, *The Drawings of Raymond Lafage*, The Hague, 1963, p.66; J. Arvengas, *Raymond Lafage, Dessinateur*, Paris, 1965, p.35, fig.28; M. Kopplin, *Kompositionen in Halbrund: Fächerblätter aus vier Jahrhunderten*, Staatsgalerie Stuttgart/Museum Bellerive, Zürich, 1984, under cat. no.17, repr.

Exhibitions: Pittsburgh etc., 1987–8 (122); *Raymond Lafage 1656–1684: dessins et gravures, Centenaire du Museé Raymond Lafage*, Lisle sur Tarn, 1990 (14)

This design for a fan leaf, executed during Lafage's year in Rome 1679–80, reflects his interest in the Roman baroque from the Galleria Farnese decorations onwards. A fan design belonging to the Courtauld Institute repeats, less forcefully, certain motifs of this Chatsworth drawing and so must be a later production. P.-J. Mariette (*Cabinet de M. Crozat*, Paris, 1741, p.124) remarks, as part of lot 1043, 'huit dessins (de la Fage) dont cinq ont été faits pour servir de modèles à les Peintres d'Eventails'; another of similar size and technique belonging to the Louvre from the collection of Saint-Morys (seized as *émigré* property in 1793) was exhibited also in the Raymond Lafage exhibition, 1990 (11), *The Dream of Diana*.

This is the only drawing at Chatsworth to bear the mark of Sylvester, a physician and a Protestant who fled early to Holland, where he served in the army of Prince William of Orange. He died in 1718, having been an associate of Lord Somers. The second Duke, although his mark is not on this drawing, could have obtained it directly from Sylvester or from his heirs.

214

214 Charles de la Fosse

(Paris 1636–1716 Paris)

Detail of 'The Final Reconciliation of Marie de Médicis and Her Son Louis XIII,' after Rubens

Black and red chalks, heightened with white bodycolour, on buff paper, 310 × 215mm. Fully mounted on an early eighteenth-century mount.

On the *verso*, said to be inscribed *Rubens in ye Luxembourg Gallery*; on the face of the mount, in pencil, *P. P. Rubens*

Chatsworth 952

Provenance: presumably William, 2nd Duke of Devonshire

Exhibitions: Pittsburgh, etc., 1987–8 (123)

Painters in seventeenth-century Paris found it hard to respond to the wealth of pictorial suggestion offered by Rubens's cycle of political allegories decorating Marie de Médici's first gallery in her Palais de Luxembourg. Indeed the paintings installed under Rubens's own supervision in the 1620s were not published by engraving for eighty years. Nevertheless, the conversion by Roger de Piles, arch-*Rubéniste*, of Charles de la Fosse is well attested, although no graphic evidence of a precise link was identified before this drawing's exhibition at Pittsburgh in 1987–8. The enthusiasm of de la Fosse for Rubens is manifest in his study for the St Bruno engraved by Audran (Musée de Besançon, collections Gigoux; London, RA, 1958, no.184); and especially close to this drawing is his study *en trois crayons* for a *St John the Evangelist* to fill a pendentive of the cupola of Les Invalides, which was decorated in 1703–6 (Cleveland Museum of Art; exhibited in *French Master Drawings of the 17th and 18th Centuries*, Toronto, Art Gallery of Ontario, etc., 1972–3, 67, ill.).

The Chatsworth drawing is a prime document of the earliest sympathetic interest of a French painter in the Rubens cycle, preceding by at least a quarter of a century those copies of individual heads and figures which were made by the young Watteau (e.g. *Watteau*, Grand Palais, Paris, 1984, no.143; and private collection, Baltimore, which includes the head of the Queen in *The Final Reconciliation*). Margaret Stuffman ('Charles de la Fosse', in *Gazette des Beaux-Arts*, July/August, 1964, pp.15–16) discusses the effect of the publication in 1681 of Roger de Piles, *Dissertation*, on de la Fosse as a painter.

215 Nicolas Poussin

(Villers, nr Grand-Andely 1594–1665 Rome)

Apollo and Daphne

Pen and brown ink, 200 × 174mm.

Chatsworth 859

Provenance: Sir Peter Lely (L.2092); William, 2nd Duke of Devonshire (L.718)

Literature: Friedländer, Blunt, Wittkower, *The Drawings of Nicolas Poussin*, III, 1953, 17 (172)

Exhibitions: Manchester, 1961 (88); Washington, etc., 1969–70 and London, V & A, 1973–4 (119); Oxford, 1990–1 (41)

The subject is from Ovid (*Metamorphoses*, I, 533): Daphne, already transmogrifying into a laurel, runs from Apollo to her father, the river god Perseus. Friedländer and Blunt connect this drawing of *c.*1635 with a painting, now lost but described in some detail by Bellori (1672). The *Pan and Syrinx* of *c.*1637 (Dresden) seems to echo the design and to repeat some details. Chatsworth 859 is close in pen-work to Poussin's drawings for the Richelieu *Bacchanals* of 1636 (Oxford, 1990, no.38).

215

216

216 Nicolas Poussin

(Villers, nr Grand-Andely 1594–1665 Rome)

The Rape of the Sabines

Pen and brown ink with brown wash, 164 × 225mm.

Chatsworth 861

Provenance: William, 2nd Duke of Devonshire (L.718)

Literature: Friedländer, Blunt and Wittkower, *The Drawings of Nicolas Poussin*, II, 1949, p.9, no.114, pl.91; Wild, 1980, p.61 (under no.61)

Exhibitions: Paris, 1960 (149); Washington, etc., 1969–70 and London, V & A, 1973–4 (120); Oxford, 1990–1 (29)

Poussin painted this subject at least twice: once (New York, Metropolitan Museum), *c.*1634–5; secondly *c.*1637 for Cardinal Omodei. Chatsworth 861 is a study for the latter. Another very similar drawing for it is in the Uffizi (Friedländer, *op.cit.*, no.115), with variations, particularly on the right. The figures in the Louvre picture, as H. Brigstocke points out in the catalogue to Oxford 1990–1

(his fig.16), are 'orchestrated within a much more clearly defined architectural space and the subject is interpreted with tragic detachment as an antique ritual. The violence and horror of the subject and the transitory emotions of the participants are all contained in frozen gestures and fixed mask-like expressions ... However the spirit of the present drawing is far less controlled than the final picture. There is a baroque fury in the lateral movement of the figures, and a correspondingly wild and expressive energy in Poussin's rapid use of pen and brush.'

For a summary of opinions regarding the dating of the two versions, see P. Rosenberg, *La Peinture Française du XVII siècle dans les collections Américaines*, Paris/New York/Chicago, 1982, p.310 (under no.90).

217 Antoine Watteau

(Valenciennes 1684–1721 Nogent sur Mer)

A Shepherdess seated with her Swain

Red chalk, 208 × 354mm, the top arched. Fully mounted on an 18th-century mount.

Chatsworth 866

Provenance: either 2nd Duke of Devonshire (L.718), or 3rd Duke of Devonshire (L. Suppl.718)

Literature: Martin Eidelberg, 'P. A. Quillard, an assistant to Watteau', in *AQ*, 1970, XXXIII, no.1, p.54, fig.23 (as by Antoine Quillard); E.Croft-Murray, 'Watteau's Design for a Fan-Leaf', *Apollo*, XCIX, 1974, pp.176–81, fig.2; Paul Hulton, *Watteau Drawings in the British Museum*, London, 1980, under no.6; Monika Kopplin, *Kompositionen im Halbrund: Fächerblätter aus vier Jahrhunderten*, Staatsgalerie Stuttgart/Museum Bellerive, Zürich 1984, cat. no.22 (ill.)

Exhibitions: Tokyo, 1975, no.100; Pittsburgh etc., 1987–8 (124, as Watteau)

This *pastorale* designed for a fan leaf was recognised by David Carritt in 1966 among four other sheets of red chalk drawings then attributed at Chatsworth to a 'follower of Watteau' (Chatsworth 865–9 are by P. A. Quillard). Carritt's recognition of the hand of the young Watteau was promptly supported by K. T. Parker. In the style of drawing with red chalk it is close to *La Déclaration* (K. T. Parker

and J.Mathey, *Antoine Watteau: Catalogue Complet de Son Oeuvre Dessiné*, Paris, 1957, cat.no.103). The cartouche effect is still in the manner of Callot. As Monika Kopplin recalled, in Balzac's *Le cousin Pons* (1846) Sylvain Pons acquires a fan painted and signed by Watteau; and outside the realm of the novel, Spire Blondel recorded an auction in 1875, *Catalogue d'éventails anciens des cours Louis XIV et Louis XVI*, of April 1861 (cat.no.145): 'Antoine Watteau. Le concert champêtre, une des plus rares et des plus remarquables feuilles de ce maître. Gouache d'un magnifique dessin et d'une très-belle couleur'.

218 Jacques Callot

(Nancy 1592–1635 Nancy)

The Callot Album (Prints XXI) containing about 270 Etchings and 146 Drawings, related to Callot

Binding: early 19th-century red morocco, fully tooled in gilt in an early 18th-century style; roll-tooled gilt border, enclosing in the centre of the top, bottom and sides the Devonshire crest within the Garter surmounted by a ducal coronet; at the corners of the central rectangle leaf sprays issue from ducal coronets; at the corners of the binding a rectangular frame of 3 line gilt fillets enclosing roll-tooled gilt compartments with an infilling of flower and leaf tools, the ground of the central compartment with leaf sprays within arabesque compartments, the arms of the 6th Duke in gilt in the centre of the sides (rebacked, old spine preserved), large folio. The paper on which the drawings and prints are pasted has an 1826 Whatman watermark ('Turkey Mill').

Inscriptions: on the title-page, in pen and brown ink (in handwriting no earlier that the second quarter of the 19th century and probably of the third quarter; perhaps that of Sir James Lacaita or of George W. Reid) *The Works of Callot, Drawings & Etchings/Baur/ Van der Cabel/ and a few others*; and in pencil (added by Eugénie Strong, with her initials) *Stefano della Bella.3*

Provenance: Israël Henriet, Paris, rue de l'arbre sec; Israël Silvestre (at least the drawings for *Il Solimano*, from 1661); William Spencer, 6th Duke of Devonshire, from sometime after the Mariette sale in Paris, and before 1826

Literature: A. F. Blunt, in London, RA, 1949, pp.130–1; D. Ternois, in *Revue des Arts*, 1953 and *GBA*, no.43, 1954; Paris, 1962, pp.24–5

Exhibitions: London, RA, 1949–50 (565)

This plump and well-filled album, brought to A. F. Blunt's attention in 1948 by F. W. Thompson, then Librarian at Chatsworth, contains, besides a considerable number of prints, drawings for most of Callot's major series of landscape etchings, with three pen and wash drawings for the production in Florence of *Il Solimano* (Meaume 434–9), and thirteen for the *Grande Passion* (Meaume 12–18, etc.).

Blunt, in cataloguing this item for the *Landscape in French Art* exhibition in London at the Royal Academy in 1949, claimed that it included some drawings for the *Combat à la Barrière* (Meaume 492–503); but this is not so. His confusion may have originated in communication with Thompson, who had mistakenly connected a single sheet of studies penned on vellum for the *Guerra d'Amore*, proposing triumphal cars and the costumes of individual participants, which is indeed to be found in the Album, with designs for the *Combat à la Barrière*. On the other hand Blunt chose not to mention the *Bourgeoises dans différents attitudes*, of which series the Album contains no less than 19 original drawings in black chalk and 14 copies in pen attributable to Israël Henriet.

The Chatsworth volume is generally identified with one which belonged to the engraver Israël Silvestre, which is mentioned by André Félibien (*Entretiens*, Trévoux, 1725, III, pp.370, 380). Silvestre was the first real collector of Callot drawings. Félibien refers explicitly to the drawings for *Il Solimano*. He states that Silvestre acquired them from his predecessor in charge of the *Magasin des Antiques* of Louis XIV, Jean Vivot (d.1673) (cf. Edmond Bonnaffée, *Amateurs français du 17e siècle*, Paris, 1884, p.327). Félibien further mentions in Silvestre's volume 42 landscape drawings given by Callot to Silvestre, which can almost certainly be identified with nos.319–360 in the Chatsworth volume; and he adds that Callot had them prepared for lessons which he gave to Gaston, duc

d'Orléans, brother of Louis XIII, when he was in exile at Nancy in 1629–30. Félibien writes that Gaston de France repaired daily to Callot's lodging in the company of the Comte de Maulévrier to occupy himself for two hours at a stretch in exercises in drawing. No.320 in the Chatsworth Album is a heavy-handed copy, likely enough the work of Gaston following the demonstration piece, no.319.

According to Léopold Zahn (*Die Handzeichnungen des Jacques Callot*, Munich, 1923, p.85), cited by Blunt in 1949, the Silvestre volume also contained 12 drawings of the *Passion* (which appears to agree with Nos.407–19 in the Chatsworth Album, except that at Chatsworth there are 13 of *La Grande Passion* instead of 12), seven studies of women (there are in the Chatsworth Album nineteen originals in black chalk, nos.296–314) and 54 landscapes other than those already mentioned (the Chatsworth Album contains 45). But Zahn, who was evidently unaware of the Chatsworth Album, does not cite any source for this statement. Blunt supposed that some further history of Callot drawings was traceable through Florent le Comte who, in his *Cabinet des Singularitez*, first published in 1699 (pp.171–2), states that the plates had passed to Silvestre's son-in-law Nicolas Petit de Loigny, who had sold them to Fagnani, a well-known Italian dealer living in Paris until his death sometime between 1729 and 1735.

Blunt unwarrantably was in no doubt that from Fagnani the drawings mounted in the Chatsworth Album were acquired by William Cavendish, second Duke of Devonshire (1672–1729), being confident that it was the second Duke's insignia which appears on the binding of the book. He did not examine the text of Florent le Comte carefully enough, nor the Album's binding, nor the paper; and Ternois (*op.cit.*, 1962) followed his assertion that the ducal arms stamped in gold on the binding of the folio are those of the second Duke. In fact, as P. Day informs me, there is no example known at Chatsworth of armorials being stamped on a binding of an album made up for the second Duke, not even on the splendid binding of Claude's *Liber Veritatis* (on which see Kitson, 1978, p.137).

However, the second Duke's mark as a collector (L.719) is stamped on two magnificent drawings undoubtedly by Callot which were sold by the eleventh Duke at Christie's on 3 July 1984 (lots 47–8): *Bathers and Figures embarking on a Boat on a River by a City* (Chatsworth 947), and *Louis de Lorraine-Guise, Prince de Phalsbourg, in Armour on Horseback* (Chatsworth 696). He also acquired, presumably at Lord Somers's sale at Motteux's rooms in London in 1717, two drawings which had belonged to Padre Sebastiano Resta: a *Beggar with a Jug* ('d.76'), attributed by Resta to *Callotto*, but which is only a coarse copy in pen after one of the 25 etchings in the 1622–3 suite of *Beggars* (Lieure

484); and a fine original study, comparable to Album nos.369 and 382, but drawn in red chalk on white paper of a *Group of Willows* ('d.103'). The latter appears without attribution in the list of Resta/Somers drawings compiled by a secretary in London for Lord Somers. These are in the 1928 Chatsworth Inventory as nos.695 and 936 respectively. Moreover, the second Duke's mark is stamped on a very large pen drawing on vellum bearing the arms of Porcellets, the *View of Toul* (Chatsworth 697).

In the eighteenth century the engraving after this was the cause of controversy. The Paris dealer Gersaint, who wrote in 1744 the *Catalogue de Quentin l'Orangère*, believed the print to have been based on a drawing by Callot. Mariette regarded Silvestre, who in his early days followed Callot closely, as the designer, and Collignon as the engraver. Later Mariette suggested Israël Henriet, whose nephew and sole heir was Silvestre, as the engraver. That opinion was followed in 1962 by D. Ternois, but not by J. Byam Shaw, for whom the superb quality of this large and highly finished presentation drawing, penned on vellum as an especial compliment to the Bishop of Toul or the Comte de Porcellets, suggested that Gersaint's instinct was correct and that it was indeed drawn by Callot and not by any gifted imitator. The three figures seen from the back under the oak tree in the left foreground, including the draughtsman, and the subtleties of the middle-distance, including both the city and the flocks and carts, are particularly fine.

The Callot volume at Chatsworth, as we know it, was undoubtedly bound and mounted with prints and drawings for the sixth Duke. There is only one piece of evidence to imply that the second Duke owned more drawings by Callot or Callot's imitators than are cited in the preceding paragraph; a drawing in sanguine for the foreground group in the engraving of the *Siege of Breda*, of the backview of the marchese Amrogio Spinola mounted with his aides (cat. no.220 below); although this is not stamped with the second Duke's mark, it was never part of the sixth Duke's Album. However it is possible that some relevant album or portfolio belonging to the second Duke was sufficiently dilapidated by the 1820s for the sixth Duke to order the material to be mounted afresh in a new and luxuriously bound folio.

In that early nineteenth-century volume, G.W.Reid, employed on behalf of the seventh Duke in the mid-1870s, certainly catalogued the prints contained in it. The volume was in fact known to be at Chatsworth from the sixth Duke's day. Blunt was again misleading in stating that F.W.Thompson 'discovered' it in the Library there.

There is no evidence that anything which was mounted in the sixth Duke's Callot album had descended to him from his admired ancestor, the collector. Print Volumes xcv and xcvi in the Library at Chatsworth are in early eighteenth-century bindings, and so are likely to have been acquired by the second or third Duke for Devonshire House. These prints, mostly of the 1650s and 1660s, were catalogued by Lacaita as *Israel Silvestre – Livres de diverses veues, perspectives, paysages faits au naturel. Paris, chez Van Brugge, 1665, 2 vols.*, although at least one print is dated 1669; and they are lettered respectively *Silvestre Tome I* and *Silvestre Veues de Paris Tome II*.

Most of the etchings are printed, as Blunt wrote in his 1949 catalogue entry, directly on the pages, in fact two or three at a time: but a few were pasted in and there are also several large folded engravings tipped in. Van Brugge(n)'s name appears, as publisher, on some of the prints. So also do those of Israël Henriet and Silvestre. Blunt referred to this pair of volumes as a 'volume of engravings by Silvestre', adducing it as confirmation of it being the second Duke's taste that acquired also the Callot Album. Blunt further opined that the Silvestre volume 'must therefore be a volume specially prepared by Silvestre or perhaps by Fagnani to whom many of his (i.e. Callot's) plates passed (*cf.* P.-J.Mariette, *Abécédarió*, I, p.290)'. The second Duke's penchant for Callot is confirmed, but not thereby any closer connection of Silvestre with the contents of the Callot Album at Chatsworth.

We have on the other hand to reckon with lot 1185 at the auction of Mariette's drawings in Paris, catalogued in 1775 by F.Basan and bought by Tersan. Among seventy drawings by Callot in this small folio album was the suite of drawings for *La Grande Passion*. Thirteen of those subsequently found their way to the sixth Duke in England. The simplest and most likely answer to these problems is that the sixth Duke, not himself a connoisseur and collector in the mode of the second Duke, acquired a treasure of Callot's art and had the entire contents of the Album reorganized as a magnificent salute to the taste of his ancestor. It was absolutely his way to buy *en bloc*. At Chatsworth, for example, the small 'Volume XXII' (Prints), the only other there under Callot's name, entitled *Les Tableaux de Rome*, carries the ex-libris of Thomas Dampier. This shows it to have been part of the big purchase of rare books made for the sixth Duke in 1811 after the death of Bishop Dampier. It is likely that the content of his future large Callot Album came to him in a similar way.

218(b)

218(c)

218(a–c) Jacques Callot

(Nancy 1592–1635 Nancy)

Album XX: Models for the Livres/des Paysages de Callot/Paris chez I.Mariette/Mis en lumière par Israël, *after Callot; and for the* Livre de Paysages anonymes

Pen and brown ink with brown wash, with framing lines, 80/90 × 155mm, average.

Mostly etched by imitators of Callot in the same sense as the drawings (see below) and published by Israël Henriet in Paris without date. The prints are lettered *M.Callot invente* (*sic*) and dedicated to Monseigneur Louis de Crevant, Marquis d'Humières. The second edition, published by Langlois, was titled: *Livre de Paysages de Callot propre à la Noblesse et aux ingénieurs pour apprendre à dessiner à la plume avec liberté et en peu de temps.* For the third edition Mariette only changed the name of the publisher

Three Landscapes (mounted together)

(a) *Recto: Farm Buildings under the Trees* (T.1326)

COLOUR PLATE XVI

Verso: The Bridge at Malzéville on the Meurthe (the *verso* omitted by Ternois, 1962)

Orange brown wash on white paper, 118 × 257mm.

Chatsworth 391. For the verso, *cf.* Chatsworth Album 362

Exhibitions: Nancy, 1992 (420)

(b) *Gibbet at the Entry to a Wood* (T.1327)

Orange brown wash, 121 × 252mm.

Chatsworth 392

Exhibitions: Nancy, 1992 (421)

(c) *Recto: a turretted Château*

Verso: Landscape with a large Tree on the Left

Black chalk and brown wash (pale on recto, stronger on verso), 119 × 238mm.

M.1158: 'Suite de Paysages anonymes' Jean Mariette

Chatsworth 393

Exhibitions: Nancy, 1992 (435, as 'imitateur de Callot', but surely both sides are drawn by Callot himself)

219(a–c) Jacques Callot

(Nancy 1592–1635 Nancy)

Drawings for La Grande Passion

Brush and brown wash over black chalk, 96, 97 or 98 × 215mm.

Provenance: perhaps Israël Silvestre; in a collection in Paris in 1684 (Félibien, 1685, ed.1725, III, pp.376–7); P.-J.Mariette; his sale, Paris 1775 (part of lot 1185), catalogue by F.Basan, bt. Tersan; acquired by William Spencer, sixth Duke of Devonshire

Literature: Gersaint, 1744, p.60; Mariette, *c.*1750, II, ff.14 *verso* and 60 *verso*; Meaume, 1860, I, p.108 and II, pp.38–44, nos.12–18; D. Ternois, 'La Passion de Jacques Callot', *Revue de l'Art*, 1953, no.3; Ternois, 1962, p.98, cat. nos.577–89; Providence, Rhode Is., 1970, under cat. no.12

Exhibitions: London, RA, 1949, no.565; Washington, etc., 1969–70, nos.111–14; Nancy, 1992 (552–4, 556, 558–9, 563, 565, 567, 569–70)

Only seven etchings of a projected cycle of fourteen with scenes of the *Passion of Christ* were completed by Callot, his first major independent religious series (Meaume 12–18; Lieure, 281–7). Only in the eighteenth century did Nicholas Cochin the Elder engrave the remaining five scenes. Six of the prints are directly based on the thirteen preparatory drawings at Chatsworth. For the seventh print, the *Last Supper*, no preparatory drawing is known. Records of the Paris sale in 1775 of P.-J.Mariette's collection indicate that the series was complete when that part of the small folio was acquired by Tersan. Thus the missing drawing was for the *Last Supper*. In addition to the Devonshire series of thirteen drawings, three of which are exhibited here, there are the *Crowning with Thorns* in the Rosenwald Collection and *Christ carrying the Cross* (neither in Ternois, 1962). Numerous sketches, most in black chalk, for individual figures used in the compositions are in the Album Julienne in the Hermitage, St Petersburg, and in the Album Mariette in the Louvre (Ternois, 1962, nos 593–602).

The sketches and compositions appear to have been drawn in Florence. Callot's work on the plates was between 1619 and 1624. The paper used for most of the prints in this first state is a Lorraine paper with the 'double C' watermark (Lieure watermarks 29 and 30). So the printing would have been done after his return home to Nancy. The figures are etched, the architectural backgrounds engraved with the burin. The staging of the scenes was doubtless influenced by Parigi's work for the Grand Ducal Court of Tuscany.

Lot 1185 in the Mariette Sale of 1775 was catalogued by Basan (p.181) under Callot as: 'Un volume petit in-folio en maroquin rouge, contenant (1) 70 Dessins de compositions & Etudes de diverses Figures, dont la suite de la grande Passion, le Massacre des Innocents, le Portrait de

219(a)

Dervet, la Conversion de St.Paul, plusieurs Paysages; le tout à la plume & au bistre, & très-bien conservé'. This well-preserved selection of drawings by Callot was knocked down at 574 *livres*, and the small folio broken up into lots. Lempereur took 156 drawings which went to the Louvre, and Tersan took 14, according to Meaume (1860, I, p.108) at 73 *livres*. The sixth Duke acquired of this lot only 13 preparatory drawings for *La Grande Passion*. The only other Callot lot in Mariette's sale was the preceding, a work in oil colours on paper of *St Sebastian* ('on en connoit l'Estampe').

219(a) Jacques Callot

(Nancy 1592–1635 Nancy)

Christ washing the Disciples' Feet

Black chalk extensively washed in brown, 97 × 217mm.

Etched in reverse by Callot (M.12; L.281)

Chatsworth Album 407

Provenance: P.-J. Mariette; his sale, Paris, 1775, no.1185 (album); 14 sketches for La Grande Passion acquired by Tersan for 73 *livres*; William Spencer, 6th Duke of Devonshire

Literature: Ternois, 1962, no.574

Exhibitions: London, RA, 1949–50 (565)

There are pen copies of the Chatsworth drawing in the Louvre and the British Museum. The Royal Institution of Truro (Cornwall) has in the De Pass Collection a preliminary drawing in black chalk and brown wash, 88 × 100mm, the architecture particularly indented with

a stylus (Ternois 575). In it the three servants are missing, there are numerous differences in the apostles and the architecture is without wash. Twelve related figure studies are in the Hermitage (Ternois 593–604).

219(b) Jacques Callot

(Nancy 1592–1635 Nancy)

The Agony in the Garden

Black chalk extensively washed with brown ink, 97 × 216mm.

Chatsworth Album 408

Provenance: P.-J. Mariette; his sale, Paris, 1775, no.1185 (album); 14 sketches for *La Grande Passion* acquired by Tersan for 73 *livres*; William Spencer, 6th Duke of Devonshire

Literature: A. F. Blunt, *Art and Architecture in France 1500 to 1700*, London, 1953, p.128, pl.85A; Ternois 576

Exhibitions: London, RA, 1949–50 (565)

This shows Callot's feeling for natural scenery applied to a religious subject.

219(b)

219(c)

219(c) Jacques Callot

(Nancy 1592–1635 Nancy)

The Taking of Christ

Black chalk extensively washed with brown, 98 × 215mm.

Chatsworth Album 409

Provenance: P.-J. Mariette; his sale, Paris 1775, no.1185 (album); 14 sketches for *La Grande Passion* acquired by Tersan for 73 *livres*; William Spencer, 6th Duke of Devonshire

Literature: Ternois, 1962, no.577

Exhibitions: London, RA, 1949 (565); Washington etc., 1969–70 and London, V&A, 1973–4 (111A); Richmond etc., 1979–80 (72A); Nancy, 1992 (552, with partly incorrect provenance)

Exceedingly dramatic in its torchlight effect, this drawing was not etched, perhaps (as suggested by Ternois, *loc. cit.*) because Callot was daunted by the difficulty of maintaining this effect in a print.

220

220 Jacques Callot

(Nancy 1592–1635 Nancy)

Three Horsemen

Red chalk, 161 × 245 mm, evidently trimmed. Fully mounted.

Inscribed *Israel Silvestre ex. Parisiis*

Chatsworth 694

Provenance: presumably William, 2nd Duke of Devonshire (never a part of the 6th Duke's Album)

Exhibitions: Pittsburgh etc., 1987–8 (116, as Callot)

Recently classed at Chatsworth as 'manner of Callot', although its autograph standing should not be in doubt (*cf*. Ternois, 1962, no.874). The principal figures appear with others dismounted, in reverse and on a considerably reduced scale, in the foreground of Callot's etching on the lower left of six plates for the large *Siege of Breda* (Meaume, 1869, no.510; and Howard Daniel, *Callot's Etchings*, New York, 1974, pl.213). The plumes of the hats are notably exaggerated in the print, where the group appears at the lower right.

Callot in 1627 made a trip to the Netherlands to design the *Siege of Breda* for the Infanta Isabella Clara Eugenia. The figure with his back towards us is distinguished only by his commander's bâton as the marchese Ambrogio Spinola, the victor at the siege.

Select Bibliography

Initials

AB	*The Art Bulletin*
AQ	*The Art Quarterly*
AV	*Arte Veneta*
B	Adam von Bartsch, *Le peintre graveur*, 21 vols, Vienna, 1803–21
GBA	*Gazette des Beaux Arts*
HdG	C. Hofstede de Groot, *Die Handzeichnungen Rembrandts*, Haarlem, 1906
KdK	*Klassiker der Kunst*
L.	Frits Lugt, *Les Marques des Collections de dessins et d'estampes*, Amsterdam, 1921. *Supplément*, The Hague, 1956
MD	*Master Drawings*
OMD	*Old Master Drawings: a quarterly magazine for students and collectors*

Names

Ames-Lewis, 1981   Francis Ames-Lewis, *Drawing in Early Renaissance Italy*, New Haven and London, 1981

Andrews, 1985   K. Andrews, *Catalogue of Netherlandish Drawings in the National Gallery of Scotland*, 2 vols, Edinburgh, 1985

Bacou, 1965   Roseline Bacou, Maurice Sérullaz et al., *Le XVIe siècle européen. Dessins du Louvre*, Paris, 1965

Baglione, 1642   G. Baglione, *Le vite de' pittori, scultori e architetti dal Pontificato di Gregorio XIII del 1572 in fino a' tempi di Papa Urbino Ottavo nel 1642*, Rome, 1642

Bagni, 1985   Prisco Bagni, *Il Guercino e il suo falsario. I disegni di paesaggi*, Bologna, 1985

Bellori, 1672   Giovanni Pietro Bellori, *Le vite de' pittori, sculturi e architetti moderni*, Rome, 1672

Benesch, 1954–7   Otto Benesch, *The Drawings of Rembrandt*, 6 vols, London, 1954–7

Berenson, 1938   Bernard Berenson, *The Drawings of the Florentine Painters, classified, criticized and studied as documents in the history and appreciation of Tuscan art*, 2 vols, London, 1903 (2nd ed., Chicago, 1938)

Bierens de Haan, 1948   J. C. J. Bierens de Haan, *L'oeuvre gravé de Cornelis Cort*, The Hague, 1948

Blunt & Cooke, 1960   Anthony Blunt and Hereward L. Cooke, *The Roman drawings of the XVII and XVIII Centuries in the Collection of Her Majesty The Queen at Windsor Castle*, London, 1960

Blunt, 1980   Anthony Blunt, *Maestri Romani del sei e settecento: Domenichino, Sacchi, Lanfranco, Bernini, Pietro da Cortona, Testa, Mola . . ., Biblioteca dei disegni*, vol.25, Florence, 1980

Bode, 1883   W. Bode, *Studien zur Geschichte der holländischen Malerei*, Braunschweig, 1883

Bodmer, 1939   H. Bodmer, *Lodovico Carracci*, Burg. bei Magdeburg, 1939

Bohn, 1984   Babette Bohn, 'The Chalk Drawings of Lodovico Carracci', *MD*, XII, 4, 1984

Braun   Braun & Cie, Paris (photographer)

Brigstocke, 1978   H. Brigstocke, 'Some further thoughts on Pietro Testa', *Münchner Jahrbuch der bildenden Kunst*, vol.29, 1978

Buchner and Feuchtmayr, 1924   E. Buchner and K. Feuchtmayr (eds), *Beiträge zur Geschichte der Deutschen Kunst*, Augsburg, 1924

Burchard-d'Hulst, 1963   L. Burchard and R.-A. d'Hulst, *Rubens Drawings*, 2 vols, Brussels, 1963

Burl. Mag.   *The Burlington Magazine*, London, from 1912

Byam Shaw, 1976   James Byam Shaw, *Drawings by Old Masters at Christ Church*, 2 vols, Oxford, 1976

Byam Shaw, 1983   James Byam Shaw, *The Italian Drawings of the Frits Lugt Collection*, 3 vols, Paris, Institut Néerlandais, 1983

Carroll, 1976   E. Carroll, *The Drawings of Rosso Fiorentino*, 2 vols, London and New York, 1976

Clark, 1959   K. Clark, *Leonardo da Vinci*, Cambridge, 1952 (revised ed. 1959)

Clark & Pedretti, 1968   K. Clark, *The Drawings of Leonardo da Vinci in the Collection of Her Majesty the Queen at Windsor Castle*, 3 vols (2nd ed. revised with the assistance of Carlo Pedretti) London 1968

Cocke, 1972   Richard Cocke, *Pier Francesco Mola*, Oxford, 1972

Cocke, 1984   Richard Cocke, *Veronese's Drawings*, London, 1984

Cohen, 1980   Charles E. Cohen, *The Drawings of Giovanni Antonio da Pordenone*, Florence, 1980

Comm. Vinc.   *Commissione Vinciana. I Manoscritti e Disegni di Leonardo da Vinci pubblicati dalla Reale Commissione Vinciana*

Copertini, 1949   Giovanni Copertini, *Nuovo contribuito di studie ricerchi sul Parmigianino*, Parma, 1949

Coutts, 1986   Howard Coutts, 'Richard Cocke: Veronese's Drawings', *MD*, 23–4, 1986

Crosato, 1986   Luciana Larcher Crosato, 'I disegni di Paolo Veronese', *AV*, 1986 (review)

Crowe & Cavalcaselle   J. A. Crowe and G. B. Cavalcaselle, *Raphael: his life and works with particular reference to recently discovered records and exhaustive study of extant drawings and pictures*, 2 vols, London, 1882

Cust   L. Cust, *Anthony van Dyck: an historical Study of his Life and Works*, London, 1900

Degenhart & Schmitt, 1969   B. Degenhart and A. Schmitt, *Corpus der Italienischen Zeichnungen, 1300–1450, I : Sud- und Mittelitalien* 4 vols, Berlin, 1968

Delacre, 1932   M. Delacre, *Recherches sur le rôle du dessin dans l'iconographie de Van Dyck. Mémoires de l' Académie Royale de Belgique*, 2nd series, Brussels, 1932

Demonts, 1937, 1938   L. Demonts, *Musée du Louvre. Inventaire général des dessins des écoles du nord*, 2 vols, Paris, 1937–8

Denucé   M. J. Denucé, *De Antwerpsche "Konstkamers", Inventarissen van Kunstverzamelingen te Antwerpen in de 16e en 17e eeuwen*, The Hague, 1932

Dimier, 1900   L. Dimier, *Le Primatice*, Paris, 1900

Dürer Society   *The Dürer Society*, with contributions by C. Dodgson, G. Pauli and S. Montagu Pierce, 12 vols, London, 1898–1908 and 1911

Egger, 1911, 1932   Hermann Egger, *Römische Veduten. Handzeichnungen aus dem XV.–XVIII Jahrhundert*, 2 vols, Vienna and Leipzig, 1911 and 1932

Emiliani, 1986   Andrea Emiliani, *Federico Barocci*, 2 vols, Banca Popolare Pesarese, n.d. (1986)

Félibien, 1685 ed. 1725   A. Félibien, *Entretiens sur les vies et les ouvrages des plus excellents peintres*, Paris 1685, ed. Trévoux, 1725

Fischel, 1898   Oskar Fischel, *Raphaels Zeichnungen : Versuch einer Kritik der bisher veröffentlichen Blätter*, Strasburg, 1898

Fischel, 1935   Oskar Fischel, *Raphaels Zeichnungen*, Berlin, 1935

Fischel, 1942   Oskar Fischel, *Raphaels Zeichnungen*, VIII, Berlin, 1942

Fischel, 1948   Oskar Fischel, *Raphael ; translated from the German by Bernard Rackham*, 2 vols, London, 1948

Freedberg, 1950   Sidney J. Freedberg, *Parmigianino : his works in painting*, Cambridge (Mass.), 1950

Friedländer   M. J. Friedländer, *Die altniederländisch Malerei*, 14 vols, Berlin and Leiden, 1924–37

Frommel, 1967–8   Christoph Luitpold Frommel, *Baldassare Peruzzi als Maler und Zeichner (Beiheft zum Römischen Jahrbuch für Kunstgeschichte, ii)* Vienna and Munich, 1967–8

Ganz, 1939   Paul Ganz, *Die Handzeichnungen des Hans Holbeins d. J.*, Berlin, 1937

Gaye, 1840   Giovanni Gaye, *Carteggio inedito d'artisti dei secoli XIV, XV, XVI*, 3 vols, Florence, 1840

Gere, 1969   J. A. Gere, *Taddeo Zuccaro*, Oxford, 1969

Gere, 1971   J. A. Gere, *Il Manierismo a Roma*, Milan, 1971

Gere, 1981   J. A. Gere, 'Some early drawings by Pirro Ligorio', *MD*, IX.1, 1981

Gere & Pouncey, 1983   J. A. Gere and Philip Pouncey, *Italian Drawings in the Department of Prints and Drawings in the British Museum. Artists working in Rome c.1550 to c.1640*, London, 1983

Gersaint, 1744   E. F. Gersaint, *Catalogue raisonné des diverses curiosités du cabinet du feu M. Quentin de Lorangère*, Paris, 1744

Gerson and ter Kuile, 1960   H. Gerson and E. H. ter Kuile, *Art and Architecture in Belgium, 1600–1800*, Harmondsworth, 1960

Glück, *Essays*   G. Glück, *Rubens, Van Dyck und ihr Kreis*, Vienna, 1933

Glück-Haberditzl   G. Glück and F. M. Haberditzl, *Die Handzeichnungen von P. P. Rubens*, Berlin, 1928

Goldner, 1988   G. R. Goldner, with the collaboration of L. Hendrix and G. Williams, *European Drawings. I. Catalogue of the Collections*, J. Paul Getty Museum, Malibu, 1988

de Grazia, 1991   Diane de Grazia, *Bertoia, Mirola and the Farnese Court*, Nuova Alpha Editoriale, 1991

Hadeln, 1925   Detlev, Baron von Hadeln, *Venezianische Zeichnungen der Hochrenaissance*, Berlin, 1925

Harris, 1967   Ann Sutherland Harris, 'Notes on the Chronology and Death of Pietro Testa', *Paragone*, November, 1967

Harris, 1989   Ann Sutherland Harris, 'Old Master Drawings from Chatsworth', *MD*, XXVII, no.1, 1989

Hartmann, 1970   K. Hartmann, *Pietro Testa : The Chronology of his Work and Evolution of his Style*, Ph.D. dissertation, London University, 1970

Hartt, 1958   Frederick Hartt, *Giulio Romano*, 2 vols, New Haven, 1958

Haverkamp-Begemann, 1964   E. Haverkamp-Begemann, Review of L. Münz, 1961 (see below), in *MD*, II, 1964

Heawood   E. Heawood, *Watermarks. Mainly of the Seventeenth and Eighteenth Centuries*, Hilversum, 1950

Held, 1959   J. S. Held, *Rubens. Selected Drawings*, 2 vols, London, 1959

Held, 1980   J. S. Held, *The Oil-Sketches of Peter Paul Rubens : a critical Catalogue*, 2 vols, Princeton, 1980

Held, 1986   J. S. Held, *Rubens. Selected Drawings*, 2 vols, Oxford (2nd ed.), 1986

Hind, 1915   A. M. Hind, 'Van Dyck : his original Etchings and his Iconography', *Print Collector's Quarterly*, V, April, 1915

Hind, 1932–33   A. M. Hind, 'A Landscape Drawing attributed to Van Dyck', *British Museum Quarterly*, VII, no.3, 1932–33

Hollstein   F. W. H. Hollstein, *Dutch and Flemish Etchings, Engravings and Woodcuts*, c.1450–1700, Amsterdam, 1947 (in progress) ; or *ibid.*, *German Engravings, Etchings and Woodcuts*, c.1400–1700, Amsterdam, 1954– (in progress)

Höper, 1988   Corinna Höper, *Bartolommeo Passarotti (1529–1592)*, II doctoral dissertation, Worms, 1988

Jaffé, 1966   Michael Jaffé, *Van Dyck's Antwerp Sketchbook*, 2 vols, London, 1966

Jaffé, 1977   Michael Jaffé, *Rubens and Italy*, Oxford, 1977

Joannides, 1983   Paul Joannides, *The Drawings of Raphael, with a complete catalogue*, Oxford, 1983

Johnston, 1970   Catherine Johnston, *Il seicento e il settecento a Bologna*, Milan, 1970

Johnston, 1974   Catherine Johnston, *The Drawings of Guido Reni*, unpublished Ph.D. dissertation, London University, 1974

Kitson, 1978   Michael Kitson, *Claude Lorrain : Liber Veritatis*, London, 1978

Knab, Mitsch, Oberhuber, 1983   Eckhart Knab, Erwin Mitsch, Konrad Oberhuber, unter Mitarbeit von Sylvia Ferrino-Pagden, *Raphael : die Zeichnungen*, Stuttgart, 1983 (*Veröffentlichungen der Albertina, Wien, Nr.19*)

Krönig, 1936   W. Krönig, *Der italienische Einfluss in der flämischen Malerei im ersten Drittel des 16. Jahrhunderts*, Würzburg, 1936

Kurz, 1937   Otto Kurz, 'Giorgio Vasari's "Libro de' Disegni"', *OMD*, XII, 45, 1937

Kurz, 1955   Otto Kurz, *Bolognese Drawings of the XVII and XVIII centuries in the collection of Her Majesty the Queen at Windsor Castle*, London, 1955

Kuznetsov, 1974   Y. Kuznetsov, *Risunki Rubensa*, Moscow, 1974

Lauts, 1962   Jan Lauts, *Carpaccio: Paintings and Drawings*, London, 1962

Le Blanc   Charles le Blanc, *Manuel de l'amateur d'estampes*, 4 vols, Paris, 1854–8

Lieure   J. Lieure, *Jacques Callot. Catalogue raisonné de son oeuvre gravé*, 2 vols, San Francisco, 1982

Lieure, 1969   J. Lieure, *Jacques Callot*, 5 vols, Paris, 1924–9 (reprint N. York, 1969)

Lippmann   F. Lippmann, with W. Bode, Sidney Colvin, F. Seymour Haden and J. P. Heseltine, *Original Drawings by Rembrandt Reproduced in Phototype*, ed. C. Hofstede de Groot, London, Paris and The Hague, 1889–1911

Longhi, 1951   Roberto Longhi, P. Barocchi, *Il Rosso Fiorentino*, Roma, Gismondi, 1950, *Paragone*, 2, no.13 (January 1951) review Reprinted in Roberto Longhi, *Cinquecento classico Cinquecento manieristico 1957–70. Edizione della opere complete di Roberto Longhi*, 8, no.2, Florence, 1976

Lugt, 1920   Frits Lugt, *Mit Rembrandt in Amsterdam*, Berlin, 1920

Lugt, 1943   Frits Lugt, 'Rubens and Stimmer', *AQ*, VI, 1943

Lugt, 1949   Frits Lugt, *Musée du Louvre. Inventaire général des dessins des écoles du Nord. Ecole Flamande*, 2 vols, Paris, 1949

Mahon & Turner, 1989   Denis Mahon and Nicholas Turner, *The Drawings of Guercino in the Collection of Her Majesty The Queen at Windsor Castle*, Cambridge, 1989

Mahoney, 1977   Michael Mahoney, *The Drawings of Salvator Rosa*, 2 vols, New York, 1977

Malvasia, 1678   C. C. Malvasia, *Felsina Pittrice. Vite de pittori bolognesi*, Bologna 1678 (2nd ed., with additional notes by Malvasia and G. P. Zanotti, Bologna, 1841)

Mariette, 1741   Pierre-Jean Mariette, *Description sommaire des dessins des grands maîtres . . .*, Paris, 1741

Martin, 1965   J. R. Martin, *The Farnese Gallery*, Princeton, 1965

Mauquoy-Hendricx, 1956   M. Mauquoy-Hendricx, *L'Iconographie d'Antoine van Dyck. Catalogue Raisonné*, Brussels, 1956

Mayer, 1923   A. L. Mayer, *Anthonis van Dyck*, Munich, 1923

Meaume, 1860   E. Meaume, *Recherches sur la vie et les ouvrages de Jacques Callot*, 2 vols, Paris, 1860

Meaume, 1869   E. Meaume, *Catalogue de l'oeuvre de Callot*, Paris, 1869

Merz, 1991   Jörg Martin Merz, *Pietro da Cortona: der Aufstieg zum führenden Maler im barocken Rom*, Tübingen, 1991

Möhle, 1966   H. Möhle, *Die Zeichnungen Adam Elsheimers*, Berlin, 1966

Morelli, 1892   Giovanni Morelli, *Italian Painters. The Borghese and Doria Pamphilj Galleries in Rome*, London, 1892

Morelli, 1893   Giovanni Morelli, *Italian Painters. The Galleries of Munich and Dresden*, trans. C. J. Ffoulkes, London, 1893

Müller-Hofstede, 1977   Justus Müller-Hofstede, *Peter Paul Rubens 1577–1640*, Cologne (exhibition catalogue), 1977

Münz, 1961   Ludwig Münz, *Bruegel. The Drawings*, London, 1961

Oberhuber-Fischel, 1972   *Raphaels Zeichnungen, begründet von Oskar Fischel fortgeführt von Konrad Oberhuber*, Part IX: *Entwürfe zu Werken Raffaels und seiner Schule im Vatican 1511/12 bis 1529*, Berlin, 1972

Olsen, 1955   H. Olsen, 'Federico Barocci: a critical study in Italian cinquecento painting', *Figura*, VI, 1955

Olsen, 1962   H. Olsen, *Federico Barocci*, Copenhagen, 1962

von der Osten, 1961   G. von der Osten, 'Studien zu Jan Gossaert', *De artibus opuscula XL. Essays in Honour of Erwin Panofsky*, New York, 1961

Palluchini, 1969   Rodolfo Palluchini, *Tiziano*, Florence, 1969

Panofsky, 1969   Erwin Panofsky, *Problems in Titian, mostly iconographic*, London, 1969

Parker, 1956   K. T. Parker, *Catalogue of the Collection of Drawings in the Ashmolean Museum, II, Italian Schools*, Oxford, 1956

Parma Armani, Genoa, 1986   Elena Parma Armani, *Perin del Vaga. L'anello mancante*, 1986

Passavant, 1836   J. D. Passavant, *Tour of a German Artist in England*, 2 vols, London 1836

Passavant, 1839   J. D. Psssavant, *Rafael von Urbino und sein Vater Giovanni Santi*, 2 vols, Leipzig, 1839. References are to the catalogue in vol. II of the Paris edition of 1860

Pepper, 1984   D. Stephen Pepper, *Guido Reni: a complete catalogue of his works with an introductory text*, Oxford, 1984

Popham, 1926   A. E. Popham, *Drawings of the early Flemish School*, New York, 1926

Popham & Wilde   A. E. Popham and Johannes Wilde, *The Italian Drawings of the XV and XVI Centuries in the Collection of His Majesty the King at Windsor Castle*, London, 1949

Popham & Pouncey, 1950   A. E. Popham and Philip Pouncey, *Italian Drawings in the Department of Prints and Drawings in the British Museum. The Fourteenth and Fifteenth Centuries*, London, 1950

Popham, 1936   A. E. Popham, 'Sebastiano Resta and his Collections', *OMD*, XI, 41, 1936

Popham, 1952   A. E. Popham, *The Drawings of Parmigianino*, London, 1952

Popham, 1957   A. E. Popham, *Correggio's Drawings*, London, 1957

Popham, 1971   A. E. Popham, *Catalogue of the Drawings of Parmigianino*, 3 vols, New Haven and London, 1971

Posner, 1971   Donald Posner, *Annibale Carracci. A study in the reform of Italian Painting around 1590*, 2 vols, 1971

Pouncey & Gere, 1962   Philip Pouncey and J. A. Gere, *Italian Drawings in the Department of Prints and Drawings in the British Museum, Raphael and his Circle*, London, 1962

Quintavalle, 1971   Augusta Ghidiglia Quintavalle, *Parmigianino Disegni*, Florence, 1971

Ragghianti & Regoli, 1975   Carlo L. Ragghianti and Gigetta Delli Regoli, *Firenze, Dalli 1470–1480: Disegni dal Modello*, Pisa, 1975

Reveley, 1820   Henry Reveley, *Notices illustrative of the Drawings and Sketches of some of the most distinguished Masters*, London, 1820

Richardson, 1722   *An Account of some of the Statues, Bas-reliefs, Drawings and Pictures in Italy, etc., with remarks by Mr Richardson Sen. and Jun.*, London, 1722

Richardson, 1980   Francis L. Richardson, *Andrea Schiavone*, Oxford, 1980

Roli, 1969   Renato Roli, *I disegni italiani del seicento: scuole Emiliana, Toscana, Romana, Marchigiana, e Umbra*, Treviso, 1969

Röthlisberger, 1968   Marcel Röthlisberger, *Claude Lorrain: The Drawings*, 2 vols, Berkeley and Los Angeles, 1968

Royalton-Kisch, 1992   M. Royalton-Kisch, 'Rembrandt's Landscape Drawings', in *Drawing: Masters and Methods. Raphael to Redon*, ed. D. Dethloff, London, 1992

Rudolph, 1978   Stella Rudolph, 'The Toribio Illustrations and some considerations on engravings after Carlo Maratti', *Antologie di Belle Arti*, II, 7–8, 1978

Ruland, 1876   (Carl Ruland), *The Works of Raphael Santi da Urbino as represented in the Raphael Collection in the Royal Library at Windsor Castle, Formed by H.R.H. The Prince Consort, 1853–1861, and Completed by Her Majesty Queen Victoria*, privately printed, 1876

Schaar, 1967   Anne Sutherland Harris and Eckhard Schaar, *Die Handzeichnungen von A. Sacchi und Carlo Maratti*, Düsseldorf, 1967

Schilling, 1950   E. Schilling, 'Eine Niklaus Manuel Deutsch-Zeichnung von Rubens retuschiert', *Zeitschrift für schweizerische Archäologie und Kunstgeschichte*, XI, 1950

Schmarsow, 1914   A. Schmarsow, *Federico Barocci Zeichnungen: eine Kritische Studie, Abhandlungen der philologisch-historischen Klasse der König. Sächsischen Gesellschaft der Wissenschaften*, XXX, Nr. 1, 1914

Shearman, 1972   John Shearman, *Raphael's Cartoons in the Collection of Her Majesty the Queen, and the Tapestries for the Sistine Chapel*, London, 1972

Spear, 1982   Richard E. Spear, *Domenichino*, New Haven and London, 1982

Stix & Spitzmüller   A. Stix and A. Spitzmüller, *Beschreibender Katalog der Handzeichnungen in der Graphischen Sammlung Albertina*, 6 vols, Vienna, 1926–41

Strong, 1902   S. Arthur Strong, *Drawings by Old Masters in the Collection of the Duke of Devonshire at Chatsworth*, London, 1902

Strong, 1905   (the late) S. Arthur Strong, *Critical Studies and Fragments*, London, 1905

von Térey   G. von Térey, *Die handzeichnungen des Hans Baldung, genannt Grien*, 3 vols, Strassburg, 1894–6

Ternois, 1962   D. Ternois, *Jacques Callot, catalogue complet de son oeuvre dessiné*, Paris, 1962

Thöne, 1940   F. Thöne, 'Zu Rubens als Zeichner', *Berliner Museen*, LXI, 1940

Tietzes, 1944   Hans and Erica Tietze-Conrat, *The Drawings of the Venetian Painters*, 2 vols, New York, 1944

Titi, 1674   F. Titi, *Ammaestramento utile, e curioso di pittura, scoltura et architettura nelle chiese di Roma (1674)*, Rome, 1721, 1763

Vasari, 1568   Giorgio Vasari, *Le vite de' più eccellente pittori, scultori, ed architettori*, 2nd edn, Florence, 1568 (ed. G. Milanesi, Florence, 1878–85)

Vasari Society   *The Vasari Society for the Reproduction of Drawings by Old Masters*, I–IX, London, 1905–15; 2nd series, I–XVI, 1920–35

Venturi   Adolfo Venturi, *Storia dell' Arte italia*, 11 vols, Milan, 1926–38

Vergara, 1982   L. Vergara, *Rubens and the Poetics of Landscape*, New Haven, 1982

Vey, 1962   H. Vey, *Die Zeichnungen Anton van Dycks*, 2 vols, Brussels, 1962

Vitzthum, 1971   Walter Vitzthum, *Il barocco a Roma*, Milan, 1971; or *Il barocco a Napoli e nell'Italia meridionale*, Milan, 1971

Vlieghe, 1972   H. Vlieghe, *Saints. Corpus Rubenianum Ludwig Burchard*, VII, 2 vols, London 1972–3

Waagen, 1854   Gustav F. Waagen, *Treasures of Art in Great Britain*, 3 vols, London, 1854

Weizsäcker, 1936   H. Weizsäcker, *Adam Elsheimer, Der Maler von Frankfurt*, 1936

Wethey, 1987   Harold E. Wethey, *Titian and his Drawings with reference to Giorgione and some close contemporaries*, Princeton, 1987

White, 1984   Christopher White, *Rembrandt*, London, 1984

Wild, 1980   Doris Wild, *Nicolas Poussin*, Zürich, 1980

Winkler   F. Winkler, *Die Zeichnungen Albrecht Dürers*, 4 vols, Berlin, 1936–9

Winner, 1961   M. Winner, 'Zeichnungen des älteren Jan Brueghel', *Jahrbuch der Berliner Museen*, III, 1961, pp. 190–241

Winner, 1972   M. Winner, 'Neubestimmtes und Unbestimmtes im zeichnerischen Werk von Jan Brueghel d. Ä.', *Jahrbuch der Berliner Museen*, XIV, 1972

Winner, 1985   M. Winner, 'Vedute in Flemish Landscape Drawings of the 16th Century', in *Netherlandish Mannerism. Papers given at . . . Stockholm*, Stockholm, 1985

Wittkower, 1952   R. Wittkower, *The Drawings of the Carracci in the Collection of Her Majesty the Queen at Windsor Castle*, London, 1952

Exhibitions

Arranged alphabetically by town and by date.

Aarhus, 1973   Aarhus Kunstmuseum, *Mestertegninger fra Chatsworth*, 1973

Amsterdam, 1935   Amsterdam, Rijksmuseum, *Rembrandt-tentoonstelling*, catalogue by F. Schmidt-Degener and D. C. Roëll, 1935

Amsterdam, 1969   Amsterdam, Rijksmuseum, *Rembrandt 1669–1969*, drawings catalogue by L. C. J. Frerichs and P. Schatborn, 1969

Amsterdam, 1991   Amsterdam, Rembrandthuis, *Around Rembrandt and Titian*, 1991

Amsterdam, 1992–3   Amsterdam, Rembrandthuis, *Episcopius: Jan de Bisschop (1628–1671), Lawyer and Draughtsman*, 1992–3

Antwerp, 1899   Antwerp, Museum voor Schone Kunsten, *Exposition Van Dyck*, 1899

Antwerp, 1949   Antwerp, Koninklijk Museum voor schone Kunsten, *Van Dyck Tentoonstelling*, 1949

Antwerp, 1956   Antwerp, Stedelijke Feestzaal en Provinciaal Veiligheidsmuseum, *Scaldis*, 1956

Antwerp/Rotterdam, 1960   Antwerp, Koninklijk Museum voor schone Kunsten; Museum Boymans-van Benningen, *Antoon van Dyck*, Tekeningen en olieverfschetsen, 1960

Arezzo, 1981/2   Arezzo, Casa Vasari, *Giorgio Vasari*, 1981

Avignon, 1992   Avignon, Grande Chapelle du Palais des Papes, *Catherine de Sienne*, 1992

Berlin, 1975   Berlin, SMPK Kupferstichkabinett, *Pieter Bruegel d. Ä. als Zeichner*, catalogue by Hans Mielke, 1975

Berlin, 1980   Berlin, Staatliche Museen Preussischer Kulturbesitz, *Bilder vom Menschen in der Kunst des Abendlandes*, 1980

Berlin/Amsterdam, 1991   Berlin, SMPK Altes Museum; Rijksmuseum, Amsterdam, *Rembrandt, the Master and his Workshop. Drawings and Etchings*, catalogue of drawings by P. Schatborn, 1991

Bologna, 1956   Bologna, Palazzo dell'Archiginnasio, *Mostra dei Carracci, catalogo critico dei disegni a cura di Denis Mahon*, 1956 (2nd ed., 1963)

Bologna, 1968   Bologna, Palazzo dell'Archiginnasio, *Il Guercino, catalogo critico dei disegni a cura di Denis Mahon*, 1968

Bologna, 1969   Bologna, *Niccolò dell'Abate, catalogo a cura di Sylvie Béguin*, 1969

Bologna, 1975   Bologna, Museo Civico, *Mostra di Federico Barocci a cura di A. Emiliani, con un repertorio dei disegni di Giovanni Gaeta Bertelà*, 1975

Bologna, 1991   Bologna, Museo Civico, *Mostra del Guercino, catalogo dei disegni a cura di Denis Mahon e Nicholas Turner*, 1991

Brussels, 1938–9   Brussels, Palais des Beaux-Arts, *Dessins de Pierre Paul Rubens*, 1938–9

Brussels, 1963   Brussels, Musées Royaux des Beaux-Arts, *Le siècle de Bruegel*, 1963

Cambridge, 1988   Cambridge, Fitzwilliam Museum, *Bandinelli*, catalogue by Roger Ward, 1988

Chicago, 1969   Chicago, Art Institute; Institute of Fine Arts, Minneapolis, *Rembrandt after 300 Years*, catalogue by J. Richard Judson, E. Haverkamp-Begemann and Anne-Marie Logan, 1969

Cleveland/Yale, 1978   Cleveland Museum of Art; Yale University Art Gallery, *The Graphic Art of Federico Barocci: selected Drawings and Prints*, catalogue by Edmund P. Pillsbury and Louise J. Richards, 1978

Eastbourne, 1979   Eastbourne and Sheffield, *Anthony van Dyck: Drawings and Sketches from Chatsworth House*, 1978–9

Florence/Paris, 1976   Florence, Istituto Universiario Olandese; Paris, Institut Néerlandais, *Omaggio a Tiziano*, catalogue by Bert W. Meijer, 1976

Florence, 1980   Florence, Palazzo Strozzi, *Firenze e la Toscana dei Medici nell'Europa del Cinquecento: il Primato del Disegno, a cura di L. Berti*, 1980

Florence, 1992   Florence, Uffizi, *Il Disegno Fiorentino del Tempo di Lorenzo il Magnifico*, ed. by Anna Maria Petrioli Tofani, 1992

Frankfurt, 1966–7   Frankfurt, Städelsches Kunstinstitut, *Adam Elsheimer*, 1966–7

Frankfurt, 1988–9   Frankfurt, Schirn Kunsthalle, *Guido Reni and Europe*, 1988–9

Genoa, 1955   Genoa, Palazzo dell'Accademia, *100 opere di Van Dyck*, 1955

Helsinki/Brussels, 1952–3   Helsinki, Ateneum, Académie des Beaux-Arts de Finlande; Musée des Beaux-Arts, Brussels, *P. P. Rubens. Esquisses, Dessins, Gravures*, 1952–3

Jerusalem, 1977   Jerusalem, The Israel Museum, *Old Master Drawings, a loan from the collection of the Duke of Devonshire*, 1977: catalogue entries based on those of Washington, etc., 1962–3 and 1969–70.

Koblenz/Bonn, 1992   Koblenz, Mittelrhein-Museum; Rheinisches Landesmuseum, Bonn, *Vom Zauber des Rheins ergriffen . . .*, catalogue by Klaus Honnef, Klaus Weschenfelder and Irene Haberland, 1992

Leeds, 1868   Leeds, *National Exhibition of Works of Art*, 1868

London, New Gallery, 1894–5   London, New Gallery, Regent Street, *Exhibition of Venetian Art*, 1894–5

London, RA, 1927   London, Royal Academy, *Exhibition of Flemish and Belgian Art, 1300–1900*, 1927

London, RA, 1929   London, Royal Academy, *Exhibition of Dutch Art. 1450–1900*, catalogue by H. Schneider and A. M. Hind, 1929

London, RA, 1930   London, Royal Academy, *Italian Drawings*, catalogue by A. E. Popham, 1930

London, RA, 1938   London, Royal Academy, *17th Century Art in Europe*, 1938

London, Arts Council, 1949   The Arts Council of Great Britain, *Old Master Drawings from Chatsworth*, catalogue entries by A. E. Popham, 1949

London, RA, 1949–50   London, Royal Academy (Arts Council), *An Exhibition of Landscape in French Art 1550–1900*, 1949–50

London, Wildenstein, 1950   London, Wildenstein and Co., *Peter Paul Rubens*, 1950

London, RA, 1950–51   London, Royal Academy, *Catalogue of the Exhibition of Works by Holbein and other Masters of the 16th and 17th Centuries*, catalogue by E. K. Waterhouse et al., 1950–51

London, RA, 1952   London, Royal Academy, *Leonardo da Vinci: quincentenary Exhibition (drawings)*, catalogue by A. E. Popham, 1952

London, RA, 1953   London, Royal Academy, *Drawings by Old Masters*, catalogue by K. T. Parker and J. Byam Shaw, 1953

London, RA, 1953–4   London, Royal Academy, *Flemish Art 1300–1700*, 1953–4

London, Wildenstein, 1955   London, Wildenstein, Bond Street, *Artists in Seventeenth Century Rome*, catalogue by Denis Mahon and Denys Sutton, 1955

London, RA, 1958   London, Royal Academy, *The Age of Louis XIV*, 1958

London, RA, 1960   London, Royal Academy, *Italian Art and Britain*, the drawings catalogued by A. E. Popham, 1960

London, Hayward, 1968   London (Arts Council), Hayward Gallery, *The Art of Claude Lorrain*, catalogue by Michael Kitson, 1968

London, RA, 1969   London, Royal Academy, *Old Master Drawings from Chatsworth*, 1969: catalogue reprinted from Washington, 1962–3 (see below) omitting five drawings

London, V & A, 1973–4   London, Victoria and Albert Museum, *Old Master Drawings from Chatsworth*, 1973–4: catalogue reprinted from Washington, 1969–70 (see below)

London, NG, 1975   London, National Gallery, *The Rival of Nature. Renaissance Painting in its Context*, edited by Michael Levey and the staff of the Gallery, 1975

London, BM, 1977   London, British Museum, *Rubens. Drawings and Sketches*, catalogue by John Rowlands, 1977

London, V & A, 1981   London, Victoria & Albert Museum, *Splendour of the Gonzaga*, edited by David Chambers and Jane Martineau, 1981

London, BM, 1983–4   London, British Museum, *Drawings by Raphael from the Royal Library, the Ashmolean, the British Museum, Chatsworth and other English collections*, catalogue by J. A. Gere and Nicholas Turner, 1983–4

London, RA, 1983–4   London, Royal Academy, *The Genius of Venice*, edited by Jane Martineau and Charles Hope, 1983–4

London, BM, 1991   London, British Museum, *Drawings by Guercino from British Collections*, catalogue by Nicholas Turner and Carol Plazzotta, 1991

London, Courtauld Institute of Art, 1992   London, Courtauld Institute of Art, *Drawing in Bologna 1500–1600*, catalogued by Elizabeth Llewellyn and Cristiana Romalli

Los Angeles, 1961   Los Angeles, County Museum of Art, *Pieter Bruegel the Elder. Prints and Drawings*, 1961

Lugano/Rome, 1989–90   Lugano, Museo cantonale d'Arte Lugano/Rome, Musei Capitolini, *Pier Francesco Mola*, catalogue by Nicholas Turner, 1989

Mainz, 1986–7   Mainz, Landesmuseum, *Wenzel Hollar: Reisebilder vom Rhein*, catalogue by Ralph Melville, Horst Reber and Norbert Suhr, 1986–7

Manchester, 1961   Manchester City Art Gallery, *Old Master Drawings from Chatsworth*, 1961

Manchester, 1963   Manchester, City Art Gallery, *Wenceslaus Hollar 1607–1677, Drawings, Paintings and Etchings*, catalogue by F. G. Grossmann, 1963

Manchester, 1965   Manchester, City Art Gallery, *Between Renaissance and Baroque. European Art 1520–1600*, catalogue by F. G. Grossmann, 1965

Mantua/Vienna, 1989–90   Mantua, Palazzo del Tè; Vienna, Kunsthistorisches Museum, *Giulio Romano*, catalogo a cura di Manfredo Tafiri, Howard Burns, Sylvia Ferino Pagden, Kurt W. Forster, Christopher L. Frommel, Konrad Oberhuber, 1989

Milan, 1939   Milan, *Mostra di Leonardo*, 1939

Nancy, 1992   Nancy, Musée historique Lorrain, *Jacques Callot, 1592–1635*, catalogue edited by B. Heckel, with contributions by D. Ternois and others, 1992

Newcastle, 1961   Newcastle upon Tyne, Hatton Gallery, *The Carracci Drawings and Paintings*, catalogue by Ralph Holland, 1961

Newcastle, 1969   Newcastle upon Tyne, *The Art of Claude Lorrain*, a smaller version of the London, Hayward, 1969 exhibition

New York, 1987   New York, Pierpont Morgan Library, *Raphael and his Circle*, catalogue by J. A. Gere, 1987

New York, 1991   New York, Pierpont Morgan Library; Kimbell Art Museum, Fort Worth, *The Drawings of Anthony van Dyck*, catalogue by Christopher Brown, 1991

Notre Dame, 1983   Notre Dame, Saite Museum, *Religious Narrative in Rome*, 1983

Nottingham, 1957   Nottingham University, Department of Fine Art, *Paintings and Drawings from Chatsworth*, 1957

Nottingham, 1960   Nottingham University, Department of Fine Art, *Paintings and Drawings by Van Dyck*, 1960

Nottingham/London, 1983   Nottingham University/London, Victoria & Albert Museum, *Drawing in the Italian Renaissance Workshop*, catalogue by Francis Ames-Lewis and Joanna Wright, 1983

Nuremberg, 1971   Nuremberg, Germanisches Nationalmuseum, *Albrecht Dürer 1471–1971*, ed. P. Strieder, 1971

Oxford, 1990   Oxford, Ashmolean Museum, *A Loan Exhibition of Drawings by Nicolas Poussin*, catalogue by H. Brigstocke, 1990–91

Paris, 1935   Paris, Petit Palais, *Exposition de l'art italien de Cimabue à Tiepolo*, 1935

Paris/Brussels, 1949 Paris, Bibliothèque Nationale; Musée Royal, Brussels, *Dessins de Van Eyck à Rubens*, 1949

Paris, 1960 Paris, Musée du Louvre, *Exposition Nicolas Poussin*, catalogue by A. Blunt, 1960

Paris, Marais, 1978 Paris, Centre culturel du Marais, *Albrecht Dürer 1471–1528. Gravures, dessins*, 1978

Philadelphia, 1971 Philadelphia Museum of Art, *Giovanni Benedetto Castiglione, Master Draughtsman of the Italian Baroque*, catalogue by Ann Percy, 1971

Philadelphia/Cambridge, 1988–9 Philadelphia Museum of Art/ Harvard University Art Museum, *Pietro Testa. Prints and Drawings*, catalogue by Elizabeth Cropper, 1988–9

Pittsburgh, etc., 1987–8 The Frick Art Museum, Pittsburgh; The Cleveland Museum of Art; Kimbell Art Museum, Fort Worth; Los Angeles County Museum of Art; The Center for Fine Arts, Miami, *Old Master Drawings from Chatsworth. A loan exhibition from the Devonshire Collections*. Introduction and catalogue entries by Michael Jaffé, 1987–8

Pordenone, 1984 Pordenone, S. Francesco a Pordenone, *Il Pordenone, catalogo a cura di Caterina Furlan*, 1984

Providence, 1971 Providence, Rhode Is. School of Design, *Caricature and its Role in graphic Satire*, Department of Art, Brown University, 1971

Providence, 1973 Providence, Rhode Is. School of Design, *Drawings and Prints of the First Maniera 1515–35*, Department of Art, Brown University, 1973

Richmond, etc., 1979–80 Virginia Museum of Fine Arts, Richmond; Kimbell Art Museum, Fort Worth; The Toledo Museum of Art; San Antonio Museum Association; New Orleans Museum of Art; California Palace of the Legion of Honour, San Francisco, *Treasures from Chatsworth, The Devonshire Inheritance, 1979–80*, introduction by Anthony Blunt. The exhibition was also shown at the Royal Academy in 1980.

Rome, 1973 Arpino/Rome, Palazzo Venezia, *Il Cavaliere d'Arpino, catalogo a cura di Herwath Röttgen*, 1973

Rotterdam, 1936 Rotterdam, Museum Boymans, *Jeroen Bosch – Noord-Nederlandse Primitieven*, 1936

Rotterdam, 1939 Rotterdam, Museum Boymans, *Tekeningen van Peter Paulus Rubens*, 1939

Rotterdam, 1948–9 Rotterdam, Museum Boymans-van Beuningen, *Tekeningen van Jan van Eyck tot Rubens*, 1948–9

Rotterdam, 1969 Rotterdam, Museum Boymans-van Beuningen, *Erasmus en zijn tijd*, 2 vols, 1969

Sheffield, 1966 Sheffield, Graves Art Gallery, *Master Drawings from Chatsworth*, introduction and entries by T. S. Wragg, 1966

Siena, 1990 Siena, Pinacoteca Nazionale di San Agostino, *Domenico Beccafumi e il suo tempo, a cura di Paola Barocchi e i suoi collaboratori*, 1990

Stockholm, 1956 Stockholm, Nationalmuseum, *Rembrandt*, catalogue by Carl Nordenfalck, 1956

Tokyo, 1975 Tokyo, National Museum of Western Art, *Old Master Drawings from Chatsworth*, catalogue entries based on those of Washington, etc., 1962–3 and 1969–70

Venice, 1976 Venice, Fondazione Giorgio Cini, *Disegni di Tiziano e della sua cerchia, a cura di Konrad Oberhuber*, 1976

Venice, 1986 Venice, Palazzo Ducale, *Venezia e la Difesa del Levante da Lepanto a Candia 1570–1670*, 1986

Viadana, 1971 Viadana, *Disegni di Gerolamo Bedoli, a cura di Mario di Giampaolo*, 1971

Vienna, 1981 Vienna, Graphische Sammlung Albertina, *Guido Reni Zeichnungen, Katalog v. Ausstellung Veronika Birke*, 1981

Washington, etc., 1962–3 Washington, National Gallery of Art; The Pierpont Morgan Library, New York; Museum of Fine Arts, Boston; Cleveland Museum of Art; National Gallery of Canada, Ottawa; Art Institute of Chicago; and California Palace of the Legion of Honour, San Francisco, *Old Master Drawings from Chatsworth*, introduction by T. S. Wragg, catalogue entries by A. E. Popham, 1962–3

Washington, etc., 1969–70 Washington, National Gallery of Art; Philadelphia Museum of Art; The Pierpont Morgan Library, New York; The Art Gallery of Toronto; Art Institute of Chicago; Los Angeles County Museum of Art; M. H. de Young Memorial Museum, San Francisco; William Rockhill Nelson Gallery of Art, Kansas City; and Museum of Art, Rhode Island School of Design, *Old Master Drawings from Chatsworth*, foreword by T. S. Wragg, introduction and catalogue entries by J. Byam Shaw, 1969–70

Washington, 1982 Washington, National Gallery of Art, *Claude Lorrain*, catalogue by H. Diane Russell, 1982

Washington, NGA, 1983–4 Washington, National Gallery of Art, *Master Drawings from the Woodner Collection*, catalogue by George R. Goldner, 1983–4

Washington/Parma, 1984 Washington, National Gallery of Art/ Parma, Galleria Nazionale, *Correggio and his Legacy: sixteenth century Emilian drawings*, catalogue by Diane de Grazia, 1984

Washington, 1986 Washington, National Gallery of Art; the Pierpont Morgan Library, New York, *The Age of Bruegel: Netherlandish Drawings in the Sixteenth Century*, catalogue by John Oliver Hand, J. Richard Judson, and others, 1986

Washington, 1988–9 Washington, National Gallery of Art, *The Art of Paolo Veronese 1528–88*, catalogue by W. R. Rearick, 1988–9

Washington, 1990 Washington, National Gallery of Art, *Rembrandt's Landscapes. Drawings and Prints*, catalogue by Cynthia P. Schneider, 1990

Concordance I

Chatsworth numbers and the present catalogue.

Chatsworth number	Catalogue number	Chatsworth number	Catalogue number	Chatsworth number	Catalogue number	Chatsworth number	Catalogue number	Chatsworth number	Catalogue number
5	16	278	149	544	77	738	19	964	161
14	131	280	42	552	133	739	27	964A	183
16	113	281	171	553	7	751	140	984	186
24	13	291	92	555	96	753A	67	986A–B	165
32	12	306	134	565	130	759	125	995	166
38	70	308	63	571	93	763	50	1002A	167
39	135	323	62	582	94	766	51	1003	163
41	107	333	32	584	95	790A–B	103	1007A	184
46	82	334	2	586	49	806	102	1008	187
51	118	335	3	591	53	808	18	1009	162
67	119	353	189	599	11	816A–B	30	1016	175
86	72	362	46	610	64	819A–D	80	1018	174
88B	194	364	15	611	52	830	201	1022	179
90	71	368	20	613	127	834	195	1023	178
110	73	374	159	617	100	836	203	1030	181
117	74	376	145	621	44	837	204	1033	180
124	65	386	22	623	138	838	185	1043	176
127	81	390	10	626	136	841	158	1046	177
143	110	391	90	629	88	846	156	1050A–B	141
147	85	393	104	634	105	851C	202	1053	57
157	143	397	160	642A	68	858	45	1063	55
160	17	399	115	642C	199	859	215	1065	168
163	142	402	126	646	91	861	216	1076	101
168	144	407	28	648	25	866	217	1095A–B	188
175	106	410	39	654	54	875	208	1101	191
176	147	420	34	661A	33	885A–B	69	1107	190
177	146	421	41	664	197	890	9	1147	192
181	139	435	35	666	170	894	56	1172	8
182	114	436	36	672	155	900	128		
183	5	443	37	676	157	904	117		
189	43	451	29	684	164	906A–B	116		
190	4	467	38	690	206	908	151		
194	152	480	124	691	207	909	97		
195	153	485	123	694	220	918A	14		
198	83	490	122	698	154	923A–B	31		
201	84	492	21	702	213	931	200		
202	150	496	26	703A–B	137	933	198		
206	66	497	40	705	86	934	193		
218	48	502	60	707	109	935	169		
220	47	506	59	710	132	939	211		
228	98	507	6	712	129	945	209		
229	23	508	58	714	111	948	210		
236	112	515	76	716A	1	951	212		
255	24	518	75	717	79	952	214		
276	89	524	61	728	120	958	172		
277	148	533	78	737A–B	121	961A–C	87		

Hollar drawings:
H.4, 10, 16;
S.189, 219, 240

Callot:
From 6th Duke's
Album, 391–3
and 407–9

Loose, unnumbered
drawings:
99, 173, 182, 196

Framed drawing:
108

Concordance II

Numbers in M. Jaffé, *The Devonshire Collection of Italian Drawings: A Complete Catalogue*, London (Phaidon Press), 1993, which were finalised too late to include in the British Museum's catalogue entries.

Catalogue number	Jaffé number	Catalogue number	Jaffé number	Catalogue number	Jaffé number	Catalogue number	Jaffé number
1	147	40	521	79	880	118	319
2	434	41	524	80	882	119	321
3	673	42	84	81	408	120	305
4	435	43	859	82	407	121	336
5	433	44	864	83	31	122	617
6	439	45	862	84	30	123	619
7	442	46	526	85	32	124	622
8	548	47	162	86	34	125	904
9	1	48	164	87	40	126	908
10	156	49	169	88	247	127	418
11	157	50	648	89	810	128	57
12	4	51	651	90	123	129	58
13	5	52	173	91	251	130	344
14	119	53	176	92	252	131	62
15	122	54	180	93	256	132	71
16	81	55	182	94	250	133	725
17	82	56	26	95	261	134	835
18	643	57	27	96	268	135	836
19	743	58	532	97	270	136	423
20	645	59	535	98	895	137	103
21	19	60	531	99	659	138	353
22	855	61	537	100	815	139	354
23	760	62	542	101	672	140	841
24	775	63	788	102	681	141	360
25	776	64	184	103	711	142	366
26	454	65	543	104	599	143	374
27	782	66	544	105	279	144	359
28	458	67	794	106	283	145	101
29	460	68	193	107	89	146	107
30	473A–B	69	29	108	92	147	110
31	471A–B	70	202	109	49	148	843
32	467	71	206	110	294	149	846
33	479	72	220	111	51	150	393
34	480	73	211	112	823	151	391
35	485	74	231	113	831	152	398
36	488	75	558	114	214	153	400
37	499	76	566	115	901		
38	506	77	569	116	611		
39	515	78	575	117	318		

Index of Artists